I AM NOT
AFRAID OF
LOOKING INTO
THE RIFLES

I AM
AFRAID
LOOKING IN
THE RIFLES

Women of the Resistance
in World War One

RICK STROUD

SIMON &
SCHUSTER

London · New York · Sydney · Toronto · New Delhi

ɔimon & Schuster UK Ltd, 2024

First published in © Rick Stroud, 2024

ᴋ Stroud to be identified as the author
ᴋ has been asserted in accordance with
Th opyright, Designs and Patents Act, 1988.

1 3 5 7 9 10 8 6 4 2

Simon & Schuster UK Ltd
1st Floor
222 Gray's Inn Road
London WC1X 8HB

Simon & Schuster: Celebrating 100 Years of Publishing in 2024

www.simonandschuster.co.uk
www.simonandschuster.com.au
www.simonandschuster.co.in

Simon & Schuster Australia, Sydney
Simon & Schuster India, New Delhi

A CIP catalogue record for this book
is available from the British Library

Hardback ISBN: 978-1-3985-0706-7
eBook ISBN: 978-1-3985-0707-4

Typeset in Sabon by M Rules
Printed and Bound in the UK using 100% Renewable
Electricity at CPI Group (UK) Ltd

I AM NOT AFRAID OF LOOKING INTO THE RIFLES

Women of the Resistance in World War One

RICK STROUD

SIMON &
SCHUSTER

London · New York · Sydney · Toronto · New Delhi

Simon & Schuster UK Ltd
1st Floor
222 Gray's Inn Road
London WC1X 8HB

Simon & Schuster: Celebrating 100 Years of Publishing in 2024

www.simonandschuster.co.uk
www.simonandschuster.com.au
www.simonandschuster.co.in

Simon & Schuster Australia, Sydney
Simon & Schuster India, New Delhi

A CIP catalogue record for this book is available from the British Library

Hardback ISBN: 978-1-3985-0706-7
eBook ISBN: 978-1-3985-0707-4

Typeset in Sabon by M Rules
Printed and Bound in the UK using 100% Renewable Electricity at CPI Group (UK) Ltd

MIX
Paper | Supporting responsible forestry
FSC® C171272
www.fsc.org

For Clover

'I am going to show you Germans that a Belgian woman knows how to die'

GABRIELLE PETIT

Contents

1916

1917

1918

FOREWORD

This is not a history of the First World War. It is the story of the women of the resistance in Belgium and occupied northern France during that conflict. There are too many of them to tell all their stories, so I have used eight main characters as a lens through which to describe the work of all the others. In 1914, before the Germans invaded, they were ordinary people: some were poor, some were rich, some were low-born and others were from the top echelons of society. At the beginning of the war they were drawn together against an invader who had stormed in on false pretences and enslaved their country. One of the first underground networks was formed on an ad hoc basis by women trying to repatriate Allied soldiers marooned behind enemy lines. The work was dangerous and the penalties severe – life imprisonment or death. As the war went on the Allies recruited Belgian civilians as spies. One of their main activities was to monitor the movements of German troops by train. Their work was not glamorous, it was often boring and always essential. By 1918 the invading force that had marched in with such arrogance was too exhausted to go on; lacking manpower, resources and money, it threw in the towel and left the Belgians in peace. The people I have written about show what the individual can do when faced with apparently overwhelming odds. In so doing they set a very high moral standard for us all to live up to.

PROLOGUE

On the evening of 31 March 1916 a 23-year-old woman stood in her cell in the prison of Saint-Lazare in occupied Brussels as a German military translator read an official letter from Berlin. Next to him stood the officer who had brought the letter to the prison. It informed her that the application to commute her death sentence had been refused and that she was to be executed at dawn the following morning. The translator stood in silence while the young woman absorbed the news. Then the officer told her to make arrangements for the disposal of her possessions and money. She was then allowed out of her cell to take her final exercise in a small caged outdoor area; as she passed through the door she wrote on the jamb: 'They consent to shoot me tomorrow. Farewell to all my unknown and much-tried friends.'

At five the next morning, 1 April, the prison chaplain came to hear her confession. As she was led from her cell, Belgian warders lined the corridor, a sign of respect in defiance of the German occupying forces. One of the guards reported that the young woman walked through the dark prison corridors 'like a soldier'. Wearing a long blue coat, she stepped into the pre-dawn gloom of the outside world where a motorised carriage awaited her. Next to it stood the prison chaplain with a rosary and a prayer book in his hands. As they set off, he asked whether, when the time came, she would like a blindfold. 'I am not afraid of looking into the rifles,' she replied calmly. 'I have been expecting this for a long time.'

Dawn broke as the car was driven through the sleeping suburbs of the city. The young woman began to recite the rosary: 'Hail Mary full of grace, pray for us sinners ...' After twenty minutes they reached the entrance to the execution ground, a grim building with a massive stone tower looming over its centre. Four soldiers swung open a red and white security barrier. The woman finished her rosary: 'Pray for us sinners, now and at the hour of our death.' Then she kissed the crucifix hanging from the beads.

The carriage drove into the grounds and the road became a bumpy, unmade track. After a few hundred yards it stopped. The door was opened and the woman stepped out. Waiting for her were 250 armed and uniformed men. Next to them was a bank of earth in front of which a heavy post had been hammered in. In front of the stake stood twelve men, their rifles ready, their faces anonymous under their helmets. Their commander was a young officer. A bugle sounded. The woman stood still.

A voice boomed: 'By the order of the Third War Council ...' The assembled party listened as the woman's crimes were listed. Finally, the sentence: '... has been condemned to death for espionage'.

She handed her rosary and prayer book to the chaplain, her coat bright against the morning gloom.

The officer drew his sabre and commanded the soldiers to fix bayonets. The woman was led to the execution stake. A soldier tied her hands, then passed a rope round her waist, fastening it behind the post. As he tried to blindfold her she twisted her head away. The clergyman whispered to her: 'Let nothing disturb your thoughts of heaven.' She paused, nodded and allowed her eyes to be bandaged.

'Firing party – present,' ordered the young officer in command.

The men brought their rifles to their shoulders. The officer raised his sabre.

'Firing party – load.'

Each man chambered the one round that was in his magazine. The metallic clinking of the bolts sliding backwards and forwards echoed around the yard. The woman stood alone, her back straight.

'Firing party – aim.'

Each member of the squad squinted down the barrel of his rifle, breathed in, bringing the sights up to the woman's heart, then held his breath and his aim, his right index finger tensed on the trigger.

With one move the officer swung the sabre tip in an arc to the ground.

'Fire.'

Shots echoed. The young woman died instantly. Shattered by bullets, her upper body slumping forward, held back by the rope, her head dangling lifelessly.

Smoke from the rifles drifted across the scene. A doctor stepped forwards, towards what was now a mass of crumpled blue. He examined the corpse and declared that the prisoner's execution had been determined 'by a bullet to the heart'.

One of the Allies' most important spies was dead.

1914

CHAPTER ONE

DEATH COMES TO SARAJEVO

On Sunday, 28 June 1914, Archduke Franz Ferdinand and his wife, Sophie, Duchess of Hohenberg, descended from a train in Sarajevo and were shown to an open-top car. Sophie, being of lower status, was not usually allowed to accompany her husband on ceremonial visits. This time, however, the archduke had been invited to inspect the troops in his capacity as inspector general of the Austro-Hungarian armed forces and, since it was a military rather than a royal engagement, protocol permitted his beloved wife to sit beside him. They set off, their vehicle in the middle of a six-car convoy, heading for the town hall, where Franz Ferdinand was to give a speech. A band played, the weather was sunny and crowds lined the streets cheering the royal couple. Among the throng were Gavrilo Princip and five other men, all conspirators with orders to kill the archduke. The first assassin lost his nerve, another felt sorry for the duchess and went home. A third threw a hand grenade which bounced off the royal car, rolled under the car behind and exploded. The car was wrecked and the passengers seriously injured. The drivers of the surviving cars accelerated away from the chaos. The remaining conspirators ran for it.

Later that day, Franz Ferdinand gave instructions that he was to be taken to the hospital to visit the passengers injured in the attack. On the way his driver got lost and turned down a side road. Ahead of him was a delicatessen outside of which, by complete coincidence, stood Gavrilo Princip. In his pocket he carried a Browning pistol loaded with six .380 calibre rimless bullets. The driver, realising his mistake, stopped, put his car into reverse and stalled it. Gavrilo stepped forward, pulled out the pistol and fired at point-blank range, hitting the archduke in the throat. Policemen wearing white gloves and carrying ceremonial swords clattered towards the gunman as he fired again, aiming for the archduke but hitting the duchess in the abdomen. Before he could let off a third shot Princip was knocked to the ground and arrested. A few hours later the archduke – heir presumptive to the throne of Austria-Hungary – and his wife were dead. The assassination was the catalyst that, within four weeks, would plunge Europe into war.

Unaware of the events in Sarajevo, the 44-year-old nurse Edith Cavell was staying with her arthritic mother in Norwich, in the county of Norfolk. She was on a short holiday from her work as the matron of an important teaching hospital in Belgium. Her father had been the vicar of Swardeston, a Norfolk parish, and his rectory was where she had spent her childhood. Every day at 8am her father led them in prayer to a God that demanded sacrifice, devotion and service to the poor. Every Sunday was spent in more prayer and listening to one of her father's long and dull sermons. That Sunday, as Franz Ferdinand and his wife lay dying, Edith accompanied her mother to church and took communion. As she prepared to take the sacrament she listened to the words that had been the bedrock of her life. 'Godliness is great riches, if a man be content with that he hath for we brought nothing into the world neither may we carry anything out ... we are not worth so much as to gather up the crumbs under thy table ... this is my blood of the New Testament which is shed for you and for many in the remission of sins ...'

The service over, she held her mother's arm as they walked slowly into the hot Norfolk sunshine. One familiar phrase stuck in her mind: 'Who goeth a warfare at any time of his own cost?'

The following day Edith could read little of the assassination in the local paper, the *Eastern Daily Press*, which carried stories about

Mrs Pankhurst being taken to Holloway prison and the bowls tournament at the Swardeston Dog Show.

Then, a month later, on Monday, 27 July, the newspaper's leading article carried the headline 'The Brink of War' and told readers that 'It seems as though the continental war ... may be precipitated.' But it concluded that, while it was a perilous time, 'all that can be said is that war has not yet broken out'.

In Devon, the 39-year-old Princess Marie de Croÿ was also on holiday, with some aristocratic English friends. The princess lived in a chateau in the small village of Bellignies, on the Franco-Belgian border. A telegram arrived which read: 'If you are going home, go at once.' Her hostess tried to reassure her that there was no problem and that Prime Minister Lloyd George would act to prevent any war, soon everything would be back to normal. Nevertheless, the princess, a small and determined woman with a passion for photography, ordered her bags to be packed and caught the next train to London. By the next day she was in Valenciennes in the Hauts-de-France region, where she was met by her brother Reginald with his motor car and chauffeur. On the 15-mile drive to their chateau at Bellignies her brother told her that villagers in the reserve had already received orders to report to their regiments. That evening after dinner the family sat talking about the future, wondering what they should do. Her younger brother Leopold had arrived from a holiday in Russia and said that he and several friends were going to volunteer the next day. The princess announced that she was going to offer the chateau to the Red Cross as an ambulance station or a field hospital. The holder of a diploma in nursing, she knew that she could quickly convert the house into a medical establishment of some sort. She persuaded Reginald to help her. Listening to all this was her frail grandmother. The family worried that the outbreak of war might kill the old lady. The following morning Leopold left to join up.

By 31 July the front page of the *Eastern Daily Press* announced: 'OMINOUS NEWS FROM BERLIN'. The next day, Saturday, 1

August, Edith received a telegram from the teaching hospital in Belgium. It wondered how she was going to get back. Train and telephone links between Belgium and Germany had been cut. The *Eastern Daily Press* headline for that day read: 'DAY OF GLOOM'. In England most of the ferry links to the continent had been cancelled. Edith realised that she had to return to the school immediately or wait until the war ended. On Sunday, 2 August, Edith was on a train as it pulled out of Norwich station heading for Dover, where she hoped to catch a late ferry to Ostend.

She watched as the county of her childhood slid by the windows. It was a landscape that she had drawn and painted since she was very young. She had once described her upbringing as 'fresh and beautiful'. Along with drawing and painting she had enjoyed learning languages and the company of her brother and sisters in what had been a happy family.

Now she wondered whether she would ever again see the flat Norfolk landscape dotted with churches and villages made up of clusters of small orange-brick houses faced in black and white knapped flint. She remembered something she had written to her brother years before, when she was twenty-eight and working as a governess in Belgium. She told him that her work was temporary, saying that 'someday, somehow, I am going to do something useful ... [for people who are] ... so helpless so hurt and unhappy'.

As Edith Cavell made her way back to Brussels, a young woman living in the same city, Gabrielle Petit, wrote to her fiancé, the cavalry sergeant Maurice Gobert, who she knew would soon be sent to the front. She began:

> My very dear boyfriend, I am so very afraid that you will have
> to depart suddenly. I love you so much! ... Say my little Maurice
> if ever danger arrived, I would try to enlist in your regiment's
> Red Cross unit. It is your good and sublime behaviour towards
> others that makes me love you so passionately. Sometimes I
> dream that I sit next to you. I have a heart attack and I die.

Then I would ask God – since I am becoming pious again – to take you as well, and all those I love. Aren't I bad to talk like this? I can't help it, it's stronger than me.

Gobert was a young man who had risen fast through the ranks and was studying to become an officer. He was the same age as the 21-year-old Gabrielle and had met her earlier in the year, when she was working as a waitress in a café near the Gare du Nord in Brussels. He was attracted to her air of authority, which marked her out from her fellow workers. He thought she was too good for waitressing and urged her to leave the job.

Over the next few weeks they got to know each other and found that they came from the same area. He thought she was an intelligent, educated girl and persuaded her to quit the café and become his girlfriend. He was only vaguely aware that she came from a broken home. Her mother had died when in her early thirties and her father was a ne'er-do-well spendthrift who had abandoned his family. Then her mother died and Gabrielle was placed in an orphanage. After this her education had taken place in an institution run by nuns where she was very lonely and ignored by her father and family, her eyes often red from weeping in the night.

After leaving the nuns at fifteen she had worked as a governess but gave it up because she was treated like a skivvy. She then worked in a fashion store where she claimed to be happy. However, her employer thought she was slovenly and complained that she never changed or mended her underclothes. She moved on and had various other jobs, including working as an assistant in a pastry shop. Before she was twenty she had an affair with a divorced man which lasted for more than a year. Her moods changed rapidly and sometimes she became depressed and bitter about the way she had been treated by her relatives. In 1912 she tried to commit suicide by drinking oxalic acid. Her one real friend during this time was a woman called Marie Collet, with whom she lived for a while. Marie was sixty years old, with white wavy hair and a kind face. She lived with her husband above a baker's shop and Gabrielle moved into the little garret on the top floor of the building. The old couple provided her with what was described as a 'hive of happiness, where everything breathed valiance and honesty ... from that moment onwards [Gabrielle] had a father and a mother'. It was Marie Collet who rescued Gabrielle when she took the oxalic acid.

Soon Gabrielle followed Maurice Gobert's advice and left the café. She had her photograph taken, looking happy and smart, wearing a simple long black skirt and a white blouse, her head erect, her hand on her hip, and staring with a confident challenge at the camera. She was pleased with the result and sent the picture to a friend writing, 'As for me you can see from this card, I look pretty much the same as always.' She and Maurice became engaged. She finished her letter to him by saying, 'I am so afraid that my baby, the fiancé I respect and love with all my soul, will be taken from me ...'

She signed it:

Your loving and faithful little fiancée
GABY.
1st August 1914.

The same day as Gabrielle was writing to Maurice, the Germans declared war on Russia and began to implement their plans to invade Russia's ally, France. Belgium and Luxembourg, both neutral states, were caught between Germany and France. The City of Luxembourg was the site of one of the most important railway junctions in Europe. The station in the capital held a huge marshalling yard through which German troops could pass, heading for both the eastern and the western fronts. Tens of thousands of German troops poured into the tiny, landlocked country and quickly reached the capital. Among the many citizens watching the arrival of the unwelcome army were a well-to-do couple, Camille Rischard and his wife Lise. A rumour began to circulate that the president of the Council of Ministers had blocked the road in front of the invaders and presented them with a document guaranteeing his country's neutrality. He had been ignored and the Germans marched on, vastly outnumbering

Luxembourg's own troops – a contingent of four hundred men, most of whom were part-time.

Eventually Camille and his wife returned to their large, comfortable villa on the exclusive boulevard Royale. Once at home they climbed the wide steps, flanked by stone balustrades, that led to their front door, which was opened for them by a servant. Mme Rischard's father, an industrial chemist, had made a fortune in the iron ore business. Her husband was a doctor and the medical adviser to the Luxembourg Railway Company. Lise had a son by a previous marriage who was studying in Paris and she was worried about what might happen to him.

Darkness fell on the villa, the shutters were closed and the curtains drawn. The couple heard that their country was now under German rule. The next day the French and Belgian ambassadors were expelled. In Berlin plans were under way to make the City of Luxembourg the Kaiser's headquarters.

Five days later, on a sweltering Sunday afternoon, 2 August, Count Julien Davignon waited in his large comfortable office for the arrival of the German ambassador to Belgium, Karl Konrad von Below-Saleske. The atmosphere in the office was quiet, the sounds of the street barely audible through the large plate-glass windows and the heavy curtains that hung in front of them. Davignon was known to be imperturbable; people liked him and found him charmingly optimistic. He expected the count to bring news that Germany was going to respect Belgian neutrality. The door opened and the count staggered in, a tall, distinguished German aristocrat, elegant with a waxed black moustache. His face was white, one hand clutching his chest. He grabbed a table to keep his balance.

'What is the matter? Are you ill?' asked Davignon.

The ambassador was breathing heavily, and stuttered, 'I came up the stairs too quickly.' He tried to catch his breath. 'It's nothing.'

He pulled an envelope from his pocket and held it out to the foreign minister.

'I have a most confidential communication to make to you on behalf of my government.'

Davignon tore open the envelope and spent several minutes trying to read the communication. It was in German, a language he had only a limited understanding of.

The words swam in front of his eyes. The Germans claimed to have reliable information that France was about to invade Belgium to gain passage through to Germany itself. They were demanding to be allowed to cross Belgium to deal with this supposed French threat. He read on, struggling to understand the message, slowly realising that the communication warned that should Belgium refuse the demand, or attempt to resist the German army in any way, Germany would be compelled to consider Belgium an enemy.

It was clear that the Germans intended to avoid crossing their own border into France, which was heavily defended against them. Instead they would cross Luxembourg into Belgium and then move on to France through the much less heavily defended Belgian border. If this plan worked, victory could be swift.

The communication finished by putting him on notice that Belgium had until seven the following morning to reply, just twelve hours away.

The letter fell from his hands. 'No, surely! No! It's not possible.'

The two men stood in silence, staring at one another. Davignon leaned down and picked the letter up from the polished parquet floor. Then von Below-Saleske began to repeat the terms of the ultimatum. Davignon lost his temper, declaring that the idea of a French assault was a lie, that it was Germany who was about to launch an attack. The Germans, Davignon protested, were violating international law and breaking their own promises to respect Belgian neutrality. He ended by saying that he would present the letter to the Belgian cabinet for immediate consideration.

Von Below-Saleske left the room and descended the wide marble staircase. A porter opened the door and he stepped out into the baking-hot air and crossed the courtyard to where his car was waiting.

For the next five hours, the government and the Belgian king argued about how they should respond to the ultimatum. At about half past eight Davignon's secretary, Count Albert de Bassompierre, slipped away and headed for the Place Royale. He crossed the enormous square lined with waiting horse-drawn cabs and the newly installed trolley bus system, heading for a restaurant. As he ate he looked around at his fellow diners and wondered at their innocence about what was unfolding in the ministry. He knew that by morning the carefree mood would be shattered. He felt crushed by what he knew and wondered if he was in the grip of a nightmare that he might suddenly wake up from. By 7am the Belgian answer arrived at the German legation: blank refusal to accept the terms.

In the small French village of Saint-Waast-la-Vallée, near the Belgian border and not far from Bellignies, the 24-year-old teacher Louise Thuliez was on holiday from her work and staying with her family. The day was hot and the village deserted. From the square tower of the church, the bells began to ring. Cottage doors opened and women slowly emerged into the glare of the sun, fear on their faces. In the fields, men working on the harvest straightened in alarm, dropped their tools and headed for home. Louise knew what the pealing bells were saying – they were ringing the tocsin, the alarm that war was about to break out. The next day the first men to be mobilised said goodbye to their wives and families, who waved them off as the train pulled out of the station.

Later that day the American ambassador to Belgium, Brand Whitlock, sat in his office with the secretary to the German legation. The man suddenly leaned forward and covered his face with his hands, sobbing. Then he looked up at Whitlock and said, 'Oh those poor Belgians! Why don't they get out of the way? I know what it will be. I know the German army. It will be like laying a baby on the track before a locomotive.' He waved his arms in front of him, repeating, 'I know the German army … It will cross Belgium like a steamroller, like a steamroller!'

Meanwhile, the steamroller itself waited to cross the border. Six hundred thousand well-equipped, expertly trained and disciplined soldiers. Some had been told by their officers, 'Let nothing stop you!

Belgium has dared to declare war upon us; the more terrible you are, the sooner you will go forward. The sooner you will achieve victory! Spare only the railway stations – they will be more useful to us than the cathedrals!'

By now Edith Cavell had arrived back at the teaching hospital in Brussels. She was welcomed home by her comrades, Sister Wilkins and Sister White, who had spent seven years helping her turn what had been a ramshackle group of adjoining houses into an immaculately run hospital. As the women embraced, a scruffy dog ran towards her, barking with joy and jumping up. This was Jack, her devoted companion whom she had adopted as a stray.

In 1907, Edith, at the age of forty-two, had been hired by a surgeon, Antoine Depage, the founder of the hospital. Seven years later Depage described it as 'setting the benchmark for nursing standards in Belgium'. Her career as a nurse had started at the lowest level in Fountain Fever Hospital in London, where she had nursed patients with diphtheria, typhoid and smallpox. She had gone from there to the London Hospital, where she had come under the influence and strict rule of Matron Eva Lückes, who insisted that 'You have chosen a profession in which there is simply no limit to the good you can do ... truthfulness, obedience and punctuality are indispensable', adding that 'a want of self-control is selfish, showing you do not put your patients first'.

Edith had instilled in her nurses the same commitment to a profession that she said was of the 'widest social form, the purest philanthropy, the truest humanity'. Nurses, she told them, were the handmaids of 'that science which not only assuages and heals the suffering of today but reaches on through her widening circles to the dawn of perfect manhood when disease shall be unknown'.

For nearly ten years Matron Edith Cavell had led her nurses on a crusade of humanity and caring based on discipline. She had no idea that she was also leading them to war.

CHAPTER TWO

The Germans Invade

On 4 August 1914, at eight o'clock in the morning, two Belgian border guards stood on the road that led into the small village of Gemmenich. Ahead they could see a small company of twenty-five mounted soldiers, trotting towards them out of the sun, coming from the direction of Germany. The cavalrymen carried lances from which fluttered small pennants. Unseen in a house, a third border guard, the sergeant in charge, watched his men block the road, holding up their hands, squinting against the bright light and shouting, 'Halt! Belgian border.'

The cavalry officer at the head of the mounted soldiers shouted back, 'I am perfectly aware of that ... the French have crossed the border and we're going to continue on our way.'

He kicked his horse into a trot and the group carried on their way down into the village. Dust from the horses' hooves billowed round them.

From his hidden observation post the sergeant phoned his headquarters. 'A platoon of cavalry crossed the frontier and is descending into Gemmenich.'

The message travelled along the telephone wires from Liège to Brussels and from there to the embassies in London and Paris.

While the news of the invasion spread across Europe and from there to the rest of the world the villagers of Gemmenich listened while the cavalry officer read a proclamation from the commander-in-chief of the German army. Astride his horse, his voice carrying across the quiet square, he read that he and his comrades had been forced to cross the frontier because the French had violated Belgian neutrality. He assured them that they came in friendship and meant no harm. He warned them, though, that the destruction of bridges, tunnels and railways would be regarded as hostile acts.

As he read, an endless column of grey-blue soldiers appeared over the hill, heading without pause for the village.

The officer finished reading. 'It depends on your discretion and wisely conceived patriotism to save your country from the horrors of war.'

Cavalry and villagers stood for a moment in silence. The soldiers kicked their horses into a trot and then a canter, heading for Visé, ten minutes to the west, an important railway junction. The border guards fled as the first elements of the infantry began to flood through the village.

In Westrozebeke, a village near the Belgian border with France, the Cnockaert family had been celebrating the return of their eldest son, Omer, from military service. The party over, Mrs Cnockaert was ironing when her husband burst into the room.

'The Germans have invaded Belgium ... King Albert has ordered general mobilisation. The boys will have to make to their depots by the first train. It is terrible. Our troops are massing on Liège and Namur.'

His wife stopped ironing and turned to her 22-year-old daughter, Marthe, telling her to go out and bring the boys in. Then she turned to her husband and told him not to worry, assuring him that the French army would soon arrive to deal with 'these Boches'.

Outside, Marthe, who was a trained nurse, set off to find her brothers, running past houses garlanded with flowers, left over from the harvest festival.

At Visé, two of the border guards lay dead in the road, killed by the first German soldiers to reach the village. They were the first to die in the war that was erupting all around them. The Germans discovered that the railway bridge had been blown up in the night. It was midday. Half an hour later the cashier at the railway station returned from eating his lunch at home. He was immediately arrested and shot. By the evening of the first day of the invasion many villages in the path of the invaders were burning and scores of innocent Belgian citizens had been tortured or killed.

Sergeant Gobert and his comrades in the 1st Carabiniers received the order to move towards the enemy and marched out of their smart new barracks heading for a position about 20 miles to the south. The sergeant wondered whether Gabrielle would try to follow him. In the heat and the dust they marched in dark-green uniforms that had hardly changed since they were designed in 1853. Their great-coats bore brass buttons and were cutaway as if for the hunting field. On their heads they sported old-fashioned Tyrolean top hats. Some units travelled by bicycle, some were mounted, most were on foot. Powerful dog teams pulled limbers carrying Maxim machine guns. The army could muster only 120 of these weapons. Neither the 1st Carabiniers nor any of their 200,000 comrades making up the nation's fighting force were equipped with heavy artillery.

In Brussels the telephones and telegraph had stopped working. The streets were crowded with people talking about the war and wondering if it would soon be over. Above their heads hung flags in yellow, red and black, the Belgian colours. Newspapers were appearing almost hourly and selling in their hundreds on every street corner. Strangers fell into intense conversations about what was going to happen.

In England men and women spent the night of 4 August wondering what the next day would bring. Sigismund Payne Best spent it in the Café Royal in Piccadilly, London, sitting with his friends drinking 'endless cups of coffee'. At midnight a news seller came in with the first editions. The newspapers bore the headline: 'WAR DECLARED'.

Early the next morning Best, wearing a monocle firmly screwed into his eye socket, went straight to the recruiting office in New Scotland Yard. He was rejected on the spot – poor eyesight. Best left the recruiting office a disappointed man but was determined to try again.

On 5 August, the commander of a new establishment, the Intelligence Corps, roamed the corridors of the War Office looking for recruits who could be sent with the British Army if it was ordered to France. He had already earmarked some men and was looking for officers who could speak French and German. Men with a knowledge of foreign languages and who were familiar with the continent were what he needed. He decided to scour the civilian world for recruits. Soon, university lecturers, public schoolmasters, artists, actors, musicians, industrialists, men from commerce and 'professional adventurers' would be startled to receive offers of commissions in an organisation they had never heard of.

On 5 August cars driven by Belgian army officers toured the streets of Brussels with loud-hailers attached to the roofs. They were calling for volunteers to join the army immediately. In the night, German shops and businesses had had their windows smashed. It was rumoured that Liège was burning. German nationals were ordered to leave the city and the police went from house to house checking for those people who had now become enemy aliens.

In her hospital Edith Cavell told her staff that she was full of enthusiasm for the war and full of confidence in the Allies. Nevertheless, she had several probationer nurses who were German. She told them they ought to leave before they were arrested. There was a special train arriving to take passengers into Holland – it would be the last until the war ended. The German nurses packed their few possessions into suitcases, restricted to one each. Then, led by Edith, they headed for the Gare du Nord. Edith waited with them all night. When at last the train arrived she hugged each one in farewell. Standing by her as the train pulled out was her personal maid, Marie, a German who had no one to go to. Back in the hospital she told the English nurses, including Sister Wilkins and Sister White, that they should go back to England where they would be safer. The women refused and demanded to stay by her side. Cavell was touched by their loyalty, especially that of a young nurse called Grace whom she found to be 'very quiet and brave'.

People appeared offering rooms and beds, or to help rolling bandages, anything, even motor cars to transport the wounded when they arrived. Edith had no idea how she was going to feed the casualties. Many of the existing patients discharged themselves, fearing what might happen to them when the German army appeared. Finally, the hospital was put under the protection of the Red Cross, which made it a neutral place, theoretically safe from the fighting.

Expecting that her own hospital would soon be full with patients Edith looked for temporary quarters that she could use until the conflict was over. She found a small, empty factory and quickly enrolled local help. Volunteers whitewashed the walls, creosoted the floors and turned the cellar into a storeroom. Soon the makeshift medical station was lined with narrow beds, each 'with white linen sheets and blankets neatly tucked in'. Everywhere there were small tables covered with clean towels and jugs of water, ready for use. Thanks to the volunteer help, the whole operation had cost just thirty francs.

The queen of Belgium offered the Royal Palace to be used as a Red Cross hospital. It became the 'Ambulance du Palais'. The great staterooms with their marble and crystal fittings were divided into wards and lined with beds. A sluice room, an X-ray room and a linen room were created, and a mortuary was set up in the grounds.

From 6 August the German army began the siege of Liège. Heavy artillery battered at the forts which had been built to defend the town. The surrounding villages were set on fire and the inhabitants forced from their homes. In the village of Fécher, German troops began to smash open the doors of houses, dragging out the owners and force-marching them to a new, half-built church, driving them along with their rifle butts. The air was filled with the moans of the injured and the screams of frightened people. Two old men who were paralysed had to be carried. A woman held her dead child in her arms. Nearly a thousand people were crammed in, without food, water or sanitation.

Four hundred of the men had their hands tied behind their backs, the rough cords cutting into their wrists. Then they were marched through the burning countryside, heading for Liège itself, about 6 miles to the west. By nightfall the stumbling column reached an unmanned fort called the Chartreuse on the outskirts of the city. Here they spent the night, again without food and water or any provision for sanitation. The next morning they were marched ahead of the German army across the bridges into the city, acting as a human shield and preventing the bridges from being blown up. Many of the captives were forced to stand there for the next five days. Inside the city the remnants of one column were paraded before the dismayed inhabitants. It had been a week since they had been seized, many were half-dressed and barefoot.

In the nearby town of Verviers, a group of sixty-nine men were marched into a field, their hands tied behind their backs, then lined up and shot.

On 9 August the British Expeditionary Force, known as the BEF, began to embark for France, led by officers who, days before, had been asked to settle their mess bills and get their swords sharpened. The crowds cheered and bands played as 80,000 professional soldiers marched onto the boats. They were going against more than a million German conscripted men. The Tommies carried Lee-Enfield rifles which they had been trained to fire at the rate of fifteen rounds a minute and could hit a man-sized target at 300 yards. They expected a quick victory and would, they hoped, be home by Christmas.

The mayor of Boulogne issued a poster which read: 'My Dear Citizens ... this very day there arrive in our town the valiant British troops, who come to co-operate with our brave soldiers to repel the abominable aggression of Germany ... The citizens are requested on this occasion to decorate the fronts of their houses with the colours of the two countries.'

By 14 August Edith had heard about the big battle raging at Liège. The wounded began to arrive in numbers. She had seen the young men going off to fight and now they were returning, beaten, demoralised, some mutilated and crippled for life. Edith knew that, as well as splints, analgesics and antiseptics, the men would need to be nourished with food, warmth and love.

German soldiers at all levels became convinced that Belgian civilians were fighting against them. The German army was full of rumours of atrocities, of German soldiers whose ears, noses, genitals or other parts of their bodies had been cut off. One officer complained: 'Disgraceful! An honest bullet in an honest battle – yes, then one has shed one's blood for the fatherland. But to be shot from ambush, from the window of a house, the gun barrel hidden behind flowerpots – no, that is not a nice soldierly death.'

In the newly fallen town of Namur posters appeared on the walls warning that civilian resistance would be met with the most severe punishments. That evening German soldiers panicked when they heard rifle shots coming from the outskirts of the city and opened fire on the inhabitants. Thirty civilians were shot and over a hundred houses burned before the order came to stop.

The next day, just after dawn, four hundred hostages were taken and herded into the riding school. A German officer addressed them in bad French, bellowing that as his soldiers had been fired on he was going to treat them as resisters in other towns had been treated – they would be shot. He added that any Belgian who had cut off the ears, noses or fingers of his men would also be shot. Luckily for the shivering, terrified men listening to his speech he did not carry out his threat.

On 19 August the inhabitants of Louvain woke to deserted streets and squares. Silence reigned where only the day before there had been the uproar of a retreating army as the Belgian military withdrew, heading west, away from the advancing Germans. After a while German aircraft flew across the sky. Then the sound of hooves echoed from the walls as dusty cavalrymen trotted into the streets, followed by tired, filthy soldiers, some with bandaged wounds, then came vehicles and lorries pulling guns. By midday the streets were choked with uniformed Germans. Cars pulled up in the wide, open square in front of the town hall, a strange spiky Gothic building, with dreamlike towers and domes, that dated from the sixteenth century. Soldiers ran up the steps and broke open the doors. Officials were dragged out, including the mayor, several magistrates and civil servants, their hands tied. Then it was the turn of members of the university to be dragged away. Staff officers entered the building, requisitioning it as their HQ. White posters appeared all over the town proclaiming the new order and instructing the civilian population to stay inside, keep their doors open and leave lights in their windows at night. By the end of the day 15,000 invaders had made Louvain their home.

After a tense week shooting broke out on the edge of the town. A group of German soldiers reacted, thinking they were under attack, and fired back. Men fell dead and the shooting stopped. The soldiers did not realise that the dead had been killed by their own side. Howls of rage went up. Civilians were dragged out of their homes and shot, old men and women and children were among the murdered. By mid-morning the garrison was in the grip of a revenge mania. Soldiers moved from house to house, using petrol and phosphorus to set fire to the buildings. Women were raped in the streets and men tortured.

Flames burst through the windows of the university library; black smoke billowed into the sky as nearly a quarter of a million books were incinerated. Medieval manuscripts, priceless documents were turned to ashes in the colossal heat. The mayor of the town and the rector of the university were shoved against a wall and shot. The chaos of lust and anger went on for three days. Officers and men dragged valuables from the houses and shops. Wine, money, silver, gold, anything of value was stolen and piled onto lorries.

From the new headquarters in the town hall a senior officer stared through the window at what his countrymen were doing, thinking, 'That will teach these people not to resist us.' For no reason, five shells were fired into the town, exploding with roaring crashes among the burning buildings, sending sparks and white-hot wooden splinters high into the air.

On 28 August the violence came to an end, the soldiers spent and exhausted. The swollen bodies of 248 men, women and children of all ages lay in the streets or were thrown into ditches. Some 1,500 citizens were loaded onto railway cattle trucks and hauled off to Germany. The rest of the townsfolk, nearly 24,000 people, were forced into the smouldering, ruined streets, gagging at the stench of rotting flesh, covering their mouths and noses with soaking, filthy rags. Then they were marched out of the town into the surrounding fields where they were abandoned.

The world had no proper words to describe what had happened in Louvain over the three days of carnage. The *Daily Mail* in London called it 'The Holocaust of Louvain'.

Edith Cavell wrote: 'After the period of high enthusiasm came the days of anxiety.' She knew that the Germans were rampaging across Belgium. Rumours of rape, looting and annihilation were everywhere. She said that the words 'we wait for England' were on everyone's lips, with the hope that the British Army would appear and stop the devastation. Cannon fire could be heard in Brussels itself. At night the horizon glowed red, stained by the flames of burning towns and villages.

Edith spent her evenings taking hot coffee and food to the men of the *garde civique* – untrained civilians crouching in the trenches they had dug round the city. She knew that even someone like her, who was not a soldier, could see that the men would be flattened by the military juggernaut heading towards them. She again tried to persuade her two English nurses to return home but they refused.

On the evening of 19 August, Edith and her nurses watched events from the roof of the hospital. In the east, under the crimson sky, clouds of thick black smoke rolled towards the city. The noise of the guns was now so loud that the concussion from the firing broke windows. Her dog Jack stayed close to her side, frightened by the noise, flinching and snarling at each detonation. Edith rubbed his ears to calm him. One of the nurses wept uncontrollably. Edith sat with her and told her not to give way to her feelings but to remember that she was a nurse and that her duty was to her patients.

At midnight they heard the mournful wail of bugles blowing to order the *garde civique* to lay down their arms and leave their posts. The population closed their doors and windows and hid behind their shutters, waiting for whatever was coming with the dawn.

The sun rose and the city was silent. Midday passed, then, at two o'clock, the heavy figure of the nursing school janitor burst in, shouting, '*Les Boches sont là.*' By late afternoon German troops were marching through Brussels. Brand Whitlock was among the spectators and he described the arrival of the soldiers as

> a mighty grey, grim, horde, a thing of steel, that came thundering on with shrill fifes and throbbing drums ... nervous horses and lumbering guns and wild songs ... They came in endless grey columns heading for the southwest, France and Paris. Dazed, sullen, silent citizens lined the streets watching the sweating men go by. It took two days for the parade to pass. The marching troops made an impassable barrier. From time to time a halt was called and food was distributed from carts. Exhausted soldiers sat on the pavements and fell asleep. Others took their boots off to reveal bleeding feet. Some of the soldiers did not know where they were, some thought they were already in Paris, others picked up Belgian children to hug them, give them chocolate or let them sit on the tired horses.

Edith and her nurses watched the spectacle feeling a combination of hatred for the enemy soldiers who were devastating Belgium and at the same time sorrow for those same men who were fighting far from home.

Eventually staff cars drove across the Grand-Place to the town hall. Armed men entered the building and the Belgian flag was taken down. In its place fluttered the flag of imperial Germany. German soldiers stood guarding the doors.

In the evening Edith gathered her nurses and told them that however much they hated the enemy they must remember that each one was a man, someone's father, husband or son. Their work, she reminded them, was for humanity and they must not take sides. A wounded man was a wounded man, whatever his nationality. Each must be treated with the same care and compassion. Nursing, Cavell said, knows no frontiers.

CHAPTER THREE

THE BRITISH ARMY ARRIVES

Soon after the fall of the city, Victor Jourdain, the owner of the newspaper *Le Patriot*, sat in his office. The paper had been closed down by the invading authorities and outside the building stood an armed German sentry. With Jourdain was a younger man, Eugène van Doren, a relation by marriage. On Jourdain's desk lay copies of three newly established journals – *La Belgique*, the *Bruxellois* and the *Quotidien*, each a German-funded propaganda paper. Van Doren held a sheet of paper in his hand. On it were the words '*Mort au Boches*', printed by hand on a primitive 'jelly duplicator'. The two men decided to produce a clandestine paper, properly printed and distributed. They called it *La Libre Belgique* in defiance of the German *La Belgique*.

The first soldiers of the BEF to meet the Germans were the men of a reconnaissance patrol, mounted on bicycles. On 21 August, near the village of Obourg, they ran into a German unit. Shots were fired and the first British soldier to die in the conflict lay in the dust, tangled in his bicycle.

On the same day, at Bellignies, standing in her garden, Princess Marie de Croÿ could hear the noise of distant gunfire drifting over the fields where the harvest stood ready to be gathered. In the afternoon a company of weary British soldiers led by a tired lieutenant marched through the gates. The princess walked out to greet him. He told her that his men had not eaten for twenty-four hours. He asked if there might be some boiling water. Soon the princess and her staff were cutting bread, spreading the slices with butter and jam and handing them to the soldiers who queued patiently. The officer, swaying with fatigue, stood by, murmuring gently to each man, 'No wolfing.' The princess tried to make him sit down but he refused, insisting that if he sat down he would never be able to stand up again. In any case he had to organise the detachments to guard roads and bridges and, if necessary, blow them up. Soon the men were ordered to their feet and formed up into a column. With quiet orders they were marched off the lawn, through the gates and out into the dusk, towards the sound of the guns.

The next day, early in the morning, the princess's maid burst into her bedroom. There were more British soldiers on the lawn, she said. The princess looked out of the window. Lying on the dewy grass were officers who had spread maps on the damp ground and were peering through binoculars, staring down the hill in the direction of Mons. The princess dressed in a hurry and went outside. One of the men politely told her that they were members of General French's staff and asked if she had any maps of the region. She replied that she had maps in the house that she used for touring trips in her motor car. These were distributed and then the men left, heading for Mons across the border in Belgium, just over 21 miles away. The noise of gunfire was getting louder. Soon the villagers turned out to watch columns of mounted troops streaming through, heading for the battle. The local people were amazed at the shiny harnesses and immaculate turnout of the horses.

By now the first elements of the British Army were on the outskirts of the mining town of Mons. On the way they had been showered with flowers, fruit, bread and cigarettes. The church bells were ringing and the soldiers advanced into a dream landscape, passing miners and their wives dressed in their best Sunday clothes getting ready for mass. All around were black slag heaps pointing up like witches' hats, railway sidings, bridges, everything black and grimy.

They halted in front of a stinking, slime-covered canal, 60 miles long and 70 yards wide – this was now the front line. Ahead they could hear the booming of unseen cannons.

In the darkness of the night of 20 August, a young director of one of the local mines, Herman Capiau, had made contact with the advance guard of the British cavalry. He had been educated in England and was fluent in both English and German. He knew the area very well and offered to lead the advancing cavalry along the north bank of the canal that joined Mons and the town of Condé. He scrambled ahead, leading them along roads hidden by tall hedges and along old disused sunken tracks that gave them some protection from shell, machine-gun and rifle fire.

He saw them on their way and went back to his colliery. He realised that the battlefield would soon deteriorate into chaos. He knew that before long there would be wounded men and wondered how they would be cared for. His colliery had several large disused buildings that he thought might make a temporary hospital. In the following hours the young engineer made contact with British medical officers, organised a makeshift field kitchen and set about converting the large sheds into a crude operating theatre with beds for the wounded. It was, he thought, better than nothing.

In the infantry Harry Beaumont and his company came round the corner of a slag heap and dug in. Three days later, at dawn, the German field guns began to fire; shells howled overhead, bursting everywhere and sending screaming villagers running to the shelter of their houses. At nine o'clock in the morning Beaumont and his company had their first sight of the enemy, thousands and thousands of men marching in massed formation, banners flying as though they were on a public display. When the enemy was 1,000 yards away, the infantry opened up with rifle fire so rapid the advancing troops thought they were being machine-gunned. The enemy line faltered and pulled back, leaving their dead all over the field. Later in the morning they advanced again, this time in open formation. Before long it was the British and French who were withdrawing.

In the afternoon sun Harry Beaumont was crossing a stubble field when German machine guns opened up. He felt a hammer blow near his groin and fell to the ground. The firing stopped; he struggled to sit up and saw that all around him lay dead and wounded comrades. In agony he pulled himself towards a manure heap, collapsing behind it; three other wounded men were already there. Later, they crawled towards the wall of a shattered barn. A shell landed, the wall collapsed and Harry passed out. When he woke up it was dark and he was alone.

On the same day Colonel Dudley Boger had been wounded in the side and the spur on his riding boot had gone into his foot. He had started the day with a thousand men; there were now only two hundred left standing. Boger lay still as German soldiers passed through his position. One of them leaned down and pulled his revolver from its holster and tore the binoculars from round his neck. While this was happening, other soldiers took rifles and equipment from those lying near him and then moved on. When night fell Boger began to crawl off the battlefield, looking for help.

The temporary field hospital set up in the mining shed in Mons by Herman Capiau was now full of wounded soldiers.

At Bellignies the princess and her volunteers finished setting up hospital beds in all the rooms. In the kitchen a huge amount of soup and stew stood ready to be heated on the range. People came to the house with news that there were wounded soldiers lying along the roads and in farmhouses. The princess sent her chauffeur to try to collect them. Cars and horses began to arrive carrying exhausted men. Volunteers poured milk from jugs placed on long trestle tables by the doors. They held the glasses to the men's parched lips before lifting them down and helping them into the house. Two troopers led a horse carrying a wounded officer. He tried to drink the milk which turned red with blood and bits of bone flowing from his mouth where a bullet had destroyed his palate. The man groaned as they filled his mouth with a cotton wool dressing, then he staggered upright and was half led and half carried to a bed in the house. More and more men arrived. Another officer with a bullet in his shoulder was treated by a doctor who cut off the sleeve of the man's jacket, and dressed the wound. The bullet needed a surgeon and he could not remove it. When he had finished, the doctor told the princess that a special train would take the wounded to Amiens.

'But who is going to give orders for the train?' asked the princess.

'You are,' said the doctor, who walked away leaving the princess 'feeling like a character out of Alice', albeit in a bloodstained Wonderland.

More and more men streamed by the house, coming back up the hill heading away from the battle. The princess walked through the gates of the chateau and stood in the hot afternoon sun watching the troops file past, thousands of them, an army of retreating men.

She stopped an officer and villagers crowded round, anxious to know what was going on.

'Are the Germans coming?' she asked.

'Can anyone understand English?' he replied, looking at the villagers who had gathered to watch the retreat.

'No.'

The man became agitated, lowering his voice. 'Do *not* tell them that the enemy is close behind, we *must* keep the roads free. They will be here in a few hours. Send away the wounded as quickly as possible and leave yourself. We will have to blow you up.'

Then he turned away and disappeared into the slow trudging columns of dusty, disorganised and exhausted soldiers.

The princess's brother appeared with the car to help evacuate the wounded. He spent all night ferrying the men a few miles south to Bavay, where there was a British ambulance station. By dawn, all the wounded were gone except for four men who were too badly injured to move. The roads round the village had become impassable, choked with men, guns, military vehicles and refugees fleeing in front of the German steamroller bearing down on them. Along the 250-mile front, any form of transport was pressed into use – wagons, broken carts of every description, old carriages, rusty barrows, bicycles – pulled by oxen, donkeys, ponies, horses and human beings, all jostling against each other, jamming up with the troops. The wounded lay on carts open to the sun with no medical help, shouting in agony as they were thrown about, blood staining their filthy bandages.

In the chateau the princess tried to get her grandmother to leave but the old lady refused. As dawn broke she told her chauffeur to take the car and drive it south to find any element of the Belgian army that would take it. Soon the powerful and expensive vehicle was nosing its way into the throng.

Two days later Louise Thuliez watched as Scottish and Irish troops retreating from Mons passed through her village, Saint-Waast-la-Vallée. It was a sad sight made worse by the sound of the bagpipes that accompanied the beaten men. In the night, trains full of casualties passed through the local station.

By 25 August a silence had descended on the village of Bellignies. In the early morning the princess and others were walking round the deserted village when they heard the jink of a harness and the sound of horses trotting on the road. Two cavalrymen appeared, dressed in field grey and carrying long lances. This was the first time the princess and her friends had seen the enemy and they were disgusted in a way she could not describe. Two hostile German soldiers on French soil, parading through the quiet village that was her home. One of the women with her whispered, 'What does it matter? We will not be conquered until we are all dead.'

The cavalry trotted by; more neighbours came to the gates of the chateau to watch as now an endless stream of disciplined German troops marched past their homes. The numbers made the progress of the British Expeditionary Force a few days before seem like a trickle. A fat officer stopped his horse and demanded to know the way to Saint-Waast; the soldiers passing by looked sullen and angry. The princess and her party walked back to the house where there were still a few wounded British soldiers lying in the improvised hospital. Behind them on the drive, a long grey military motor car appeared. A German officer jumped out and barked in French, 'In an hour you will receive an army staff which you must lodge.'

The women hurried into the house, worried that many of the wounded soldiers still had their rifles. They knew the Germans would not hesitate to shoot any enemy soldier carrying arms. The princess found a sergeant and explained the danger. Minutes later the rifles were clattering down the sides of a deep well, disappearing into the dark, splashing into the thick mud at the bottom.

Later that day German troops pushed open the high double doors leading into the stable yard. They were hot, tired and bad-tempered, demanding water and trying to fill their cans from the taps that had water for cleaning the carriages. They were told that this was not clean and shown the only tap with fresh water. The business of filling water cans went very slowly, the sergeant in charge shouting and kicking his men, telling them to get back on the road.

In her drawing room, now lined with beds holding wounded men, the princess watched as more long grey cars turned into the drive. Each had a steel blade welded to the bonnet and the princess thought they looked like Viking ships. The cars drove to the front of the house, soldiers ran to open the car doors and two officers got out, marching straight up the steps where they met the princess standing in the hall. Immaculate in their uniforms, they clicked their heels and saluted her. The first, a stout bearded man, introduced his greying tall, thin companion as 'General von Kluck'; the general then said, 'And this is the empress's son, the Duke of Schleswig-Holstein.' Outside, the drive swarmed with officers who trooped into the house followed by orderlies with bags and cases.

The princess showed the general and the duke to a suite of two interconnected rooms. A few minutes later the duke reappeared and sent for his doctor, a pompous man in a tight-fitting blue uniform. The duke demanded to see 'the prisoners', by which he meant the wounded men. Minutes later they were in the drawing room, pulling bandages off the wounded. One man with an injured leg was made to stand; the pain was so great that he fainted. The princess rushed forward to stop the proceedings and began to protest. The duke said that he was merely trying to make sure that they were genuine wounded and not men who would leap up in the night to slit their throats. He demanded they surrender their weapons but was told they had none. For three hours the house was filled with the noise of stamping feet and shouted orders as the temporary field headquarters was set up. Night fell and things settled into an uneasy silence.

A few miles away in Saint-Waast, Louise Thuliez was working with a neighbour, her close friend and companion Henriette Moriamé, dealing with the wounded. The 24-year-old Henriette was physically strong, very devout, and had ideas of joining a religious order. She wore her hair up in a bun and had a silver crucifix on a chain round her neck.

At first the two women had used the local town hall, the *mairie*, as a hospital, but now most of the patients had gone, leaving just six men who were carried across the village on stretchers to makeshift wards in Henriette's house. By noon the job was done and Saint-Waast too fell silent, waiting for the arrival of the troops that had earlier marched through Bellignies.

The first to arrive were the Death's Head Hussars, riding slowly, scanning the hedgerows and houses for signs of an ambush, revolvers in hand. When they reached the end of the village and realised there were no hidden enemy soldiers their mood changed. They began to shout and laugh, breaking into houses, whooping out loud as they smashed windows and threw chairs, tables, clothing, bottles, cutlery and anything else they could find onto the road.

By the middle of the afternoon the soldiers had dragged a piano into the street; some had pulled on women's clothes over their uniforms, while some carried white parasols, and all were drunk, singing and dancing. Others smashed the windows of the few shops and loaded the contents onto carts, supervised by their approving and equally sozzled officers.

Henriette and Louise had piled the muddy and bloodstained clothes of the wounded soldiers onto the grass outside the house trying to dry them. Passing soldiers saw them, dismounted and broke into the house. Inside, they searched the ground floor before slowly mounting the stairs. A terrified Henriette appeared. One of the men shouted, 'A woman.' They put their pistols away, ran up the remaining stairs and burst into a bedroom where they found a wounded man. They ripped his bandages off and began to shout at him, demanding to know where he had been in the previous day's battle, the number of regiments and the route they had taken.

Outside, Louise Thuliez was seized by another officer. Pulling out his pistol he demanded to know how many wounded men they had.

'Tell the truth or you will be shot.'

She was terrified. 'Six,' she replied.

At the top of the village the Germans berated the mayor, demanding that he provide bread for them. When he said this was impossible, he was frogmarched through the village to the bakery and ordered to get baking. In another part of the village a customs officer was burned alive.

By now troops were pouring through the village, men, wagons, vehicles, horses, an endless stream. Cavalry clattered by, heading west for Valenciennes and in pursuit of the British. Scattered among the advancing troops were terrified civilian hostages with ropes round their necks, stumbling, dragged and choking in the dust, trying to avoid being trampled by the horses.

In Bellignies an unarmed Frenchman with his arms tied behind his back and a rope round his neck was dragged up the drive. He was soon surrounded by soldiers who began violently pulling off his clothes, searching him. The princess ran out and stood beside the man, trying to protect him. The duke came storming out of the house.

'Into the house, madame, this is no place for you.'

'I beg your pardon, monseigneur, this is a Red Cross hospital and I am its head. No one shall be maltreated here.'

The duke stared at her, furious, then ordered his men to stop hitting the prisoner. The soldiers released their grip and began to search the man's satchel.

The princess returned to the house and watched from a window as the man was interrogated. They had found some papers and were staring intently at him, pointing at the documents then waving them around and shouting in his face. Eventually he was dragged off, the rope still round his neck.

As the princess tried to deal with the chaos that had engulfed her house, an aide stopped her and said there would be twenty-two for dinner. Servants were called and the table laid for that number. The duke arrived, angry and puffed up, demanding to know why she had not set a place for herself and her brother. He sputtered that if she did not join them, 'you will have to take the consequences. If you wish to be treated like enemies, I will begin by sending your brother as a prisoner of war to Germany.'

Later, the duke's nephew, Prince Georg of Saxe-Meiningen, intervened and begged the princess and her brother to attend the dinner. Reluctantly the princess ordered two more places to be laid. She found herself sitting between the duke and General von Kluck.

At one point the general asserted, 'In a week we will be in Paris and in six weeks peace will be declared.'

One of his officers said, 'According to the English, the war will not begin for six months and may last from three to five years.'

'With the present means of destruction the war can't last six months,' replied von Kluck.

The duke nodded. 'Our army is far greater than the enemy is prepared for.'

At which point the general turned to all the officers and said, 'Please do not discuss the war.'

It became clear to the princess that the Germans were as much in the dark about the battle as everyone else.

In the back hall of the house soldiers had set up long tables with telephones and typewriters. Clerks and orderlies hunched over them as intelligence flowed into the room. Large boards held maps on which were marked the latest positions of the troops.

Outside the house, groups of soldiers sat round fires and stirred pots in which bubbled stolen chickens and rabbits. The men's rifles stood nearby, stacked in little pyramids. Soldiers moved about in the growing gloom, fetching straw to sleep on and buckets of water to wash with. All through the night cars arrived carrying officers with news for the general. Overhead the occasional drone of an aeroplane could be heard; bright flashes lit the horizon and there was the continual low rumble of heavy artillery.

In the early morning at Bellignies, while it was still dark, another car arrived. Exhausted orderlies stamped about the house waking their officers, who assembled in the hall, pulling on their uniforms, their eyes bleary from lack of sleep. The general announced to his staff that the British were in full retreat. They had left behind huge amounts of stores, including oats for the horses; it was possible, he said, that the retreat was turning into a rout. He ordered that his headquarters be moved at once in the direction of Bavay, about 3 miles away.

Men ran in all directions carrying the tables and communications equipment; lorries jolted across the lawns, their tyres spinning and slipping on the wet grass. From the stables came more shouting as the horses were harnessed and the first troopers trotted out onto the road. Staff officers ran to waiting grey cars, which pulled off over the same lawns, mud spraying over the soldiers carrying cases and equipment. Soon the last vehicle had left. Another strange silence descended. The sun began to rise, revealing ruined lawns, burnt-out fires, damp straw, sodden paper and human excrement. The princess moved around the house visiting the makeshift wards, checking on her patients.

Through the morning volunteers worked to clear the mess. The solitary gardener tried to fill the great ruts that vehicles had carved in the lawns. The rumble of artillery increased, giving warning that a terrible battle was raging.

In her study the princess listened to the complaints of the curate from the next village. He was outraged that the troops had stabled their horses in his church and used the altar clothes and holy garments for the horses to lie on. Worse, they had destroyed parish records, tearing them into small pieces and throwing them from the church doors.

As the people worked, more staff cars began to arrive. From one of them stepped General von Bauer and the Grand Duke of Mecklenburg-Strelitz. The princess watched, her heart sinking, as nearly forty more men got out of the cars and moved towards the house. She guessed that there were about ten officers and knew they would all demand clean beds and cooked meals.

A young officer approached her with great politeness and saluted, introducing himself as the grand duke's aide-de-camp. She informed him of what the curate had told her and added that similar predations had taken place in other villages. Shops had had their contents emptied into the street; oil, jam, butter, flour, vinegar had been tipped into people's beds. The cellars of a local chateau had been looted and the building was surrounded by empty bottles and jewellery cases. A notice had been nailed to the dining-room table from a German soldier saying that he had once been a servant in this chateau where he was now the master. When he heard what had happened, the grand duke was furious and sent staff officers to investigate and put a stop to it.

At the end of August Edith Cavell wrote to her mother telling her that there had been terrible loss of life and irreparable destruction of buildings. She added that, 'although one cannot imagine how near are the terrible dogs of war', nevertheless 'we go on quietly with our usual work and hope for the best'.

It was frustrating for Edith that, having prepared for the arrival of large numbers of wounded, all she and her staff were receiving were some lightly injured Germans. In spite of this, her nurses were exhausted and many spent their off-duty time lying weeping on their beds.

CHAPTER FOUR

DEFEAT

On 2 September the Princess de Croÿ watched in dismay as yet another convoy of German military vehicles swung through the gates of her estate. In the lead were the now familiar big open-top staff cars flanked by motorcycle outriders. Then came an endless stream of lorries, motorbikes and vehicles of every size and shape. From the first vehicle descended General Viktor Kühne, commander of the 25th Division of the German 4th Army. From the following cars the usual bevy of staff officers clambered out and orderlies clustered round, opening the doors, saluting, unloading the personal luggage and piling it in the drive ready to be taken into the house. All the other vehicles drove straight over the tortured lawns, parking wherever they could in more or less straight lines. The princess felt weary as the afternoon air echoed with the noise of shouted orders, tailboards slamming down, scraping wood as they unloaded heavy boxes, trestle tables, filing cabinets, plus paper, pencils, typewriters and signals equipment and all the other paraphernalia necessary for a mobile command centre. This was a bigger invasion of the chateau than before and the princess was relieved when she saw that some of the huge wooden crates had stencilled signs indicating they contained provisions. Soon the chateau was full of men running cables from room to room, setting up desks and telephones, and pinning maps to boards. Outside, more men heaved the cables across the lawns towards others who clambered up the telegraph poles, ready to connect the headquarters to the outside world. Soon, the telephones were ringing and clerks were hammering away at the typewriters from which emerged orders, briefings, assessments and an endless flow of information to be sent to all the elements of the division of which Kühne was in command. Information and orders began to come in from as far away as Berlin. As always, in the distance could be heard the solemn booming of the guns that were battering the garrison fortress of Maubeuge, which the local population had hoped was where the relentless advance would be stopped.

The people of Bellignies did not know it but the fortress was in flames. High-velocity shells smashed into it, adding to the chaos and destruction; black smoke drifted across the surrounding fields and the 49,000 men stationed there made plans to evacuate. Civilian refugees poured out of it, heading west where they hoped to find the protection of the Allied armies.

At the chateau the soldiers quickly settled into a routine. Work began for the staff officers at five o'clock in the morning, when the princess and her small staff of domestics struggled to keep up with the invaders' endless demands for breakfast with tea, coffee or hot chocolate. Each evening twelve senior officers sat down to dinner in the princess's dining room, where she and her brother Reginald, but not her grandmother, were expected to join them.

Wounded soldiers from the siege began to arrive at Bellignies. One was a man who had been shot in the jaw. His face was black and had swollen like a balloon, leaving only tight slits where his eyes and mouth had been. The princess and her helpers had never seen injuries like this. As they worked, they could hear a young lieutenant sitting on the stairs and sobbing at the news that his brother had been killed in the fighting.

News arrived that the fortress at Maubeuge had fallen, taking with it the hopes of an end to the fighting. On 8 September the soldiers began to move on, packing up their equipment and leaving the usual chaos of broken furniture, wastepaper, twisted cables, human filth and torn-up lawns. The sudden silence that filled the house was broken by the noise of Reginald playing Schumann on the piano.

The inhabitants of the nearby villages were not so lucky. Soldiers had broken into their houses, rounding up their pigs and cattle, slaughtering them ready for the field kitchens that sprouted in every lane and field. The villagers tried to restore order to their wrecked lives, wondering if the enemy would pay the reparations they had promised. One farmer found a note nailed to his table which said: 'Get your English friends to pay you.'

In the Belgian village of Westrozebeke rumours of what was happening reached Marthe Cnockaert and her family. The ominous pounding of heavy gunfire never stopped. At night the muzzle flashes of the big guns lit the sky, flickering along the horizon. The booming of battle was getting nearer and nearer with the passing of each day, an unseen monster with a life of its own.

The villagers waited in mounting fear. News came that Liège had fallen, and every day they expected to wake up to find men with spiked helmets and blue-grey uniforms parading in the village streets.

The news grew worse, and then the first refugee appeared, a woman leading a donkey cart piled with possessions. She had two children with her and looked stunned, almost unable to speak. She came to a halt outside Marthe's house and asked if there was any spare food for the children, offering to pay for it by working. Marthe led the little party into the house and on into the kitchen. As she and her children ate, the woman told them that she had been on the road for three days. Her husband had gone off to join his regiment after which they had heard nothing from him. She warned them that the Germans had advanced on her village, destroying it with shellfire. Now she was heading for Ypres but had no money left to buy food. Then she went on her way. The street through the village was now blocked by old carts, sweating animals and dust-covered men and women, all with the same look in their eyes. Many had children stumbling behind them.

For the next few days Westrozebeke became a huge transit camp. Every barn and outhouse was packed with families trying to get out of the way of the advancing invaders. Animals wandered about eating hedges and grass unchecked. Old people began to die on the carts where they lay and were buried without ceremony. Dead horses were cut up for food; bewildered children wandered about, lost in the chaos.

Then, after several days, three French soldiers appeared. Marthe thought they looked like wild animals, unshaven, filthy; staring from shell-shocked eyes, they spoke in an incoherent babble; their uniforms were torn and streaked with mud and blood, their shoes falling apart, their weapons lost. Night came; it rained and exhausted people slumped in the mud, too tired to find shelter of which in any case there was none.

Then the first shell landed. A rushing noise and roar that ended with a huge detonation in the village street, followed by silence. A mushroom cloud of black smoke rose into the air; bricks, mud, timber and bits of human flesh crashed down. Wounded people writhed in the mud, the dead lay in strange contorted positions, body parts were strewn everywhere and blood spattered everything. After the silence, the slow wailing cries of the wounded filled the air.

It wasn't long before the villagers themselves began to join the endless column of refugees. The village wagon maker went in style. After a shell had hit his workshop he pulled out his largest barrow and piled his best furniture onto it. He was soon to be married so he and his fiancée dressed in their wedding clothes. He wore a top hat, a long tail coat and shiny patent buttoned shoes. Next to him walked his future wife wearing a long white dress edged in lace. He said, 'No plundering swine is going to pig it in Germany with my best furniture.' And off the pair went wheeling the barrow and soon were lost in the shuffling crowd.

Blue-coated French cavalry arrived, led by an officer who warned Marthe: 'I advise you to go, mademoiselle, the machine-gunners will be here soon. We won't hold the Boches off for long.' As he spoke the cavalrymen swarmed over the house, smashing windows and bashing holes in the walls. Furniture was piled in front of the windows facing in the direction of the enemy. From an upstairs window Marthe watched hypnotised as troops appeared in the fields, moving closer and closer. Then a machine gun opened up from the house, its noise shattering and loud. Grey blobs appeared in the fields, returning fire. Bullets began to smack into the walls, some ricocheting into the street.

Marthe's mother screamed for her to come into the cellar. The grey blobs in the field now became the distinct shapes of men. More machine guns opened up, their noise a constant roar. Enemy soldiers fell in the dust, caught by the bullets, reminding Marthe of autumn leaves blown in the wind. Some lay where they fell, others crawled, trying to drag their wounded bodies out of danger. Shells shrieked overhead and crashed into the streets. Horses and farm animals plunged about in terror. The noise of the guns was joined by the sound of crashing masonry and the roar of flaming buildings. Thick black smoke billowed through the village. Marthe headed for the cellar. On the stairs lay a wounded French soldier, his intestines in his hands, pleading for water. Marthe tried to make him comfortable, propping him against a wall where she knew he would die. Shells crashed, voices shouted orders, men, women and animals shrieked in pain and the machine guns hammered like pneumatic drills. A shell hit the roof of the house, sending slates and brickwork crashing into the street.

In the cellar her father shouted, 'Courage! The French will beat them back.' The advancing infantry were now a solid mass of grey. Suddenly the machine guns stopped. Above, Marthe and her family could hear the crash of boots, shouted commands and then silence. After a while Marthe went up; the French defenders had vanished, the house had been wrecked. Groups of weary German soldiers, their rifles slung across their backs, were moving into the village. Wounded soldiers lay everywhere, blood spattered the walls. It was two o'clock in the afternoon.

A heavy boot kicked open the kitchen door to reveal a young, sweating German officer with a revolver in his hand. Behind him were armed men with fixed bayonets.

He wiped the sweat off his face and demanded to know if there was anyone in the house apart from Marthe.

'My father and mother and a friend are sheltering in the cellar.'

Some of the soldiers slouched into the house; others sat on the ground outside, lighting cigarettes. The officer saw the holes that had been bashed through the walls. He rounded on Marthe: 'This house has been loopholed. Is your father a civilian sniper? The penalty for that is death.'

He turned to one of his men. 'Bring them up, corporal.'

'My father is an old man. He is not a sniper. The loopholes were made by the soldiers who were fighting you. They were firing through them.'

'Fourteen of my men are casualties, the firing came from here. Don't lie to me. If the men who were shooting have run away, your father can suffer on his own.'

At this moment her father was dragged up from the cellar, his pipe still in his mouth. Marthe's mother nearly collapsed, while their friend and neighbour Lucelle Deldonck stared at the officer in defiance, her white hair dangling over her furious face.

The young man began to shout at the family, telling them that their house had been a 'nest of snipers' and would be burned down.

'And you, old man, will roast inside it. Corporal, get on with it.'

Marthe's father was dragged back to the cellar and thrown down the steps.

'You women can go, you have five minutes to gather your things.'

Soldiers began to pour oil over the furniture. Outside the house, the road was blocked with wounded men, doctors and orderlies, drunken soldiers, dead villagers and bewildered men and women. They could hear the noise of breaking glass, houses on fire, more shouted orders and the cries of terrified children. Smoke drifted everywhere and the failing light was reddened by the flames from the burning buildings.

In the chaos of that night Marthe's father managed to escape from the cellar before the flames brought the house crashing down. Before dawn fifty men and women, including Marthe, were rounded up.

The men were separated from the women and marched off into the darkness. The women were locked in a cellar where they remained for the next fourteen days. It was cold and dark; a few were allowed out once a day to find food and water; the cellar was never cleaned and there were no sanitary arrangements. Meanwhile, Lucelle had disappeared and Marthe worried that she had been shot.

The steamroller of the German army had flattened Belgium and was moving on into France, heading for Paris and victory. One of the first foreign correspondents to arrive in Belgium was the American Will Irwin, writing for *Collier's* magazine. He wrote about the devastation that the fighting had caused. He wrote that everywhere lay the rubbish the armies had left behind, broken vehicles, destroyed equipment, thousands of abandoned backpacks, torn uniforms and mile upon mile of old bloodstained bandages, all lying in the train of filth that marked the passage of the soldiers. Everything had been coated in a sort of white dust. Most of all he talked about the smell. It was the smell of half a million unwashed men, mingled with the odour of horse dung, faeces, blood and, above all, the stench of the dead – men and animals, shattered, torn apart, too many to bury, bloating and putrefying in the sun.

In Paris, six hundred red taxis with bright-yellow wheels began to gather in the great avenues in front of Les Invalides, the long and magnificent building created by Louis XIV as a home for infirm and disabled soldiers and under the great gold dome of which now lay the body of Napoleon. The vehicles had been requisitioned to carry men to the banks of the river Marne, where it was planned to stop the German advance. The taxis waited in long queues while 3,000 soldiers clambered aboard, five to a vehicle. Other reinforcements left by truck as artillery rolled out of the city on trains.

In the battle that followed the German army faltered. Their commander, General Moltke, had a nervous breakdown and, by 16 September, both sides were digging the first trenches that would soon stretch from Switzerland to the North Sea. Moltke wrote to his wife saying, 'Things have not gone well. The fighting east of Paris has not gone in our favour and we shall have to pay for the damage we have done.' It was rumoured that he had told the Kaiser, 'Your Majesty, we have lost the war.' From the Kaiser's campaign headquarters in Luxembourg the order went out to halt the advance.

At Bellignies Prince Georg of Saxe-Meiningen reappeared without warning. He had been wounded in the battle of the Marne River and said that all the staff officers who had stayed in the house had also been wounded, three of them had been killed.

The princess and her brother Reginald took to visiting the hospital at nearby Bavay, which was full of British wounded and which had become an unofficial conference centre for the town authorities. On one visit she saw a man who had spent several hours stationed at their home during the beginning of the retreat. His name was Captain Preston and he had been wounded in the leg. He whispered to Reginald that he was nearly mended and that he soon planned to escape. Reginald immediately offered a refuge at Bellignies if he could get there.

A few nights later Preston waited for the German guard to make his hourly check on the ward. When the man had gone, Preston got up, rolled his coat into a tube and laid it under his blankets. Then he put his cap on the pillow, hoping that in the gloom it would look as though he were still in the bed. Wearing only socks on his feet he crept out of the ward and along a corridor to a window, gently opened it and climbed out into the garden, each move made excruciating by the pain that shot up and down his damaged leg. The grounds of the hospital were bounded by the ramparts of the ancient town. He crept round the walls, looking for a way to get out. Eventually he found a chicken run and heaved himself up, crawling slowly along the top of the wide, rough wall and peering into the dark trying to spot the soldiers who guarded the entrance to the town. He could go only a few inches at a time and it took him an hour to get on the road to Bellignies, which was about 3 miles away. Hobbling along, he reached the chateau and managed to wake the gardener, who lived in a small cottage on the edge of the estate.

In her bedroom the sleeping princess woke to the sound of gravel rattling against her window. Looking out she saw the gardener, who gestured for her to come down and follow him. Making no noise, she woke her brother and together they went out of the house. The panic-stricken man gestured that she should follow him. They fumbled their way across the lawns to the lodge. Inside, in the light of a single oil lamp, sat Preston, drinking from a bowl of coffee given to him by the gardener's wife. The young officer's hands were shaking and his face was grey with fatigue and pain.

The Germans would soon discover that he had disappeared and then they would stop at nothing to find him. The hospital at Bellignies would be searched, as would all the other makeshift hospitals that had sprung up in the area. Nearby was a ramshackle chateau, lived in only by its owner and surrounded by thick forest. The princess and her brother thought that somewhere in the woods would be a place for Preston to hide until the situation calmed down. Preston was hauled to his feet and, supported by the gardener and Reginald, he set off to walk to the chateau.

It was nearly dawn when they arrived. Preston and the princess hid in the woods while Reginald went to find the owner. The man agreed to help and showed them to an old quarry, overgrown and hidden. They made a shelter out of branches and leaves where Preston collapsed, barely able to acknowledge the reassurances that for the time being he was safe. They left saying that in a few days he would be brought to Bellignies. Then he fell into a deep, exhausted sleep.

The princess and her brother thought that at Bellignies they had the ideal hiding place for Preston. At one end of the chateau was a huge round tower which had been built in the Middle Ages. Its walls were 3 yards thick and inside there was a disused staircase that had long ago been sealed up. Reginald had discovered it before the war and had uncovered the old wooden door that led to it. There were two wounded British soldiers still resident who knew how to use tools. With their help Reginald disguised the door by fitting a dummy store cupboard behind it, complete with shelves and medicine bottles. The ground floor of the tower had been used as a hospital ward and still contained beds. The cupboard looked as though it was part of the ward. If the Germans appeared, Preston could easily slip through it and hide in the old staircase. After some days they collected him from the quarry and ensconced him in the chateau. Now he was safe, but marooned and wondering if he would ever get home. He had no idea what had happened to his regiment.

Life under the occupation had begun.

CHAPTER FIVE

OCCUPATION

In towns and villages all over Belgium and occupied northern France, including Bellignies, white notices appeared like blown snow on the walls of public buildings and private houses. They told the population what would happen to them if they committed acts of 'hostility'. Punishment for such actions was death. Not only for civilians firing on soldiers but also for 'anyone approaching within 200 metres of a balloon or aeroplane post'. The same applied to the owners of houses where arms were discovered. If a hidden Belgian soldier was found, the people who'd concealed him would be sent into 'perpetual hard labour in Germany'. If a village committed an act of hostility it would be burned and if the act occurred on a road joining two villages they would both be burned. The notices warned that 'For all acts of hostility the following principles will be applied: all punishments will be executed without mercy, the whole community will be regarded as responsible, hostages will be taken in large numbers.'

In Brussels Edith Cavell wrote to her mother reassuring her that everything was quiet and safe and complaining that she had 'practically no work'. There were no trains running, the telegraph had been cut, there was very little coal available and, though there were many wounded soldiers in the town, very few of them were Belgian or British. Like many other towns all over Belgium, Brussels was flooded with refugees fleeing from the invading Germans.

Cavell received a visit from the military governor who reminded her that any British soldiers she treated must be reported to the authorities. The hospital wards and even the nurses' rooms were regularly searched. Payment for requisitioned property or food was cancelled, even kitchen utensils were taken to make ammunition. In the fashionable park, the Bois de la Cambre, German officers now exercised their horses and the area was forbidden to civilians. Everything was heavily censored.

At Saint-Waast the six men in the care of Henriette Moriamé and Louise Thuliez were recovering and the problem of feeding them was getting worse. At the end of October the Germans posted more notices, this time declaring that any French or Allied soldiers who had been hiding must give themselves up. Thuliez and Moriamé had no idea what to do. If they continued to hide the soldiers, they would incriminate the village and risk the harshest reprisals. They decided to visit Bellignies and talk to Prince Reginald and his sister, the Princess de Croÿ, neither of whom they knew.

They arrived to find the princess and her brother walking on the lawn. They hovered round the gates, too shy to go in. Reginald spotted them and invited them into the garden where they explained their predicament. The prince and his sister knew they had to help. He took the women in a rickety cart to the vast Mormal Forest, 10,000 acres of deciduous trees including oak, ash, hornbeam and beech, home to wild boar and deer. It was an untamed place where it was easy to get lost and which the armies of both sides had found a formidable obstacle. Reginald knew it well; he had played there as a boy and employed the woodsmen who lived there.

The cart creaked down a rutted track, the two women holding onto the sides. Eventually they came to a clearing in which stood a small, primitive house where a forest labourer lived. The man had been hiding a British soldier and was willing to provide a refuge for more.

Back in Saint-Waast they collected old civilian clothes to dress their fugitives and by midnight the six men were safely in their new refuge.

The next day Thuliez and Moriamé visited the mayor, to tell him that something terrible had happened. The soldiers they had been hiding had vanished and they had no idea where they had gone. The mayor was a patriot and at first pretended not to believe them.

'So you declare that these men have gone away? You swear you do not know where they are.'

'Monsieur le maire, on our oath, we have no idea.'

For a moment there was silence between the three of them. Then: 'Very well.'

And the mayor stalked off, wondering what other problems the invaders were bringing to his quiet village.

Even in the forest the men were in danger. Thuliez and Moriamé knew that soon they must get the men out, take them into Belgium and across the border into neutral Holland. They had no idea how to do this. They knew nothing about the state of the war and had no clue as to the position of the front line.

Reginald learned that there were other men in the forest and, on the pretext of visiting his sick employees, he again took the two women, Thuliez and Moriamé, into the woods to meet another gamekeeper who knew where the group was. The gamekeeper led them deep into the forest, the undergrowth high and impenetrable on either side. He turned onto a track that was almost invisible, walking slowly and quietly. The two women followed, their clothes snagging on branches and brambles. They stopped and the gamekeeper reached out and felt into a bush where there was a line of twine which he gently tugged. They heard, somewhere in the near distance, the noise of a tiny bell; it might have been on a dog or cat's collar. There was a movement; a khaki figure could just be seen, concealed by the bushes. Quietly, and in heavily French-accented English, Thuliez said, 'We're friends.' The figure moved, emerged onto the path: a British Tommy with a rifle over his shoulder and a mud-stained uniform. They spoke for a few minutes, neither side really understanding the other. Then the Tommy said he would go and ask his officer if the party could advance. He left saying, 'Stay here please.'

When he returned he beckoned for them to follow him, pushing through a thicket where another string sounded another bell. They emerged into a clearing. Standing staring at them were groups of soldiers, some French with red uniform trousers; some of the British soldiers had sergeant's stripes on their arms. All of them wore uniforms that were muddy and torn. Some of the men had bandages on their hands or round their heads, many had bad teeth. At the end of the clearing was a hut in the doorway of which stood a young man, an officer, in a clean uniform as if he had just stepped off the parade ground. He said that his name was Lieutenant Bushell and that he and the men had all been left behind after the battle of Mons. Louise thought there must have been about forty men in the camp. Bushell explained that they had spent the time trying to sabotage a nearby railway line. This had failed. Now the Germans were in the forest and had started a systematic search. Louise told him about the group of six men she had left with the woodsman, showing him on the map where the place was, a hamlet about 6 miles away called Obies. She suggested that he might move his camp there, especially if the food situation got too critical, or the Germans too close. Then the women left, following the gamekeeper back into the forest, watched by the suspicious eyes of the camp inhabitants.

Thuliez and Moriamé told the princess and her brother about the camp. They began to look for other fugitive soldiers and the pair now visited Bellignies on an almost daily basis, bringing news of the men they discovered. In her diary the princess referred to them as 'the Girl Guides'. When Captain Preston heard about the camp he immediately wrote a letter to Bushell and asked the princess to deliver it.

She set off in a broken-down cart pulled by a scruffy donkey who wore the remains of a harness held together with bits of string. Hidden in the princess's dress was Preston's letter, and hidden in the cart were two hundred rounds of rifle ammunition as well as a map and other documents. The journey took several anxious hours. At one point she was stopped by a German patrol. The soldiers began to poke at the cart, lifting bits of sacking, silent and menacing. The princess asked, in German, the way to 'the Kommandantur', the administrative head-quarters. Her polite question seemed to please the patrol. They gave her good instructions and as soon as the soldiers had gone she continued, driving the cart further into the forest. Unlike her brother, the princess did not know the intricacies of the tracks. After several hours she arrived at a village where she thought there was a schoolmistress who knew the whereabouts of the men. She found the woman, a tall frightened girl. The princess asked her for help and the young woman blurted out, 'I cannot. I promised my father not to go out any more. He told me he would not risk my being shot.'

The princess replied, 'Go and ask your father to give you back your word. When you have shown me the way you need never go again.'

The young woman hesitated then said, 'I will break my word to my father and go with you now – and tell him afterwards.'

The princess could have kissed her in relief and they set off on foot carrying baskets and bags with provisions. They pushed through the forest and to their horror were stopped by a party of German officers who were pheasant-shooting. The men were having a good day away from the war and, thinking the women were simple peasants, waved them on their way.

The women were intercepted by a British soldier on guard some distance from the camp. When the princess entered the compound she too was surprised by Bushell's immaculate turnout. He described his adventures after the battle of Mons, how he had been cut off from his regiment and had lain on a railway embankment for three nights as the German army went by. Eventually he had crept to a cottage and then had wandered into the forest where slowly other men had joined him.

The princess gave him Preston's letter and asked if she could do anything to help.

'Get us arms,' he replied, 'and ammunition, so we can defend ourselves.' He also told her that a young woman with spectacles had visited them and he was worried that she had been a spy. The princess wondered whether he was talking about Louise Thuliez.

Later he showed her a large dugout that they were building; its entrance was invisible and it was large enough for fifty men to hide in. The dugout was about half a mile from the main camp and on the way they passed a soldier tied to a tree. Bushell explained that several of the men had made friends with the villagers and were visiting them at night, risking the lives of everybody. The man tied up was especially delinquent and at first they had considered shooting him. Instead his punishment was to be tied to the tree for twenty-four hours without food. Bushell hoped this would discourage the others.

A few days after this a young woman appeared at Bellignies with a note for 'Capt. Preston'. She too was worried about a bespectacled woman snooping around and said that her father, the gamekeeper, was convinced she was a spy and wondered whether to shoot her. The princess knew this must be Louise and tried to convince the woman that Louise was a friend.

Meanwhile, elsewhere in northern France, a 26-year-old governess called Marie Birckel arrived at her home in Variscourt, just north of the cathedral town of Reims. Marie was petite, with wavy hair, brown eyes and a penetrating gaze. She had been forced by the invasion to give up her job and return home to her mother. Although the village was still in French hands the local people had very little idea of what was going on. As the days passed Marie and her neighbours watched the French soldiers vanish, heading away from the advancing enemy on any transport they could get hold of – motorised trucks, horses, bicycles – or on foot. Marie knew that the sound of distant gunfire indicated that her pretty little village would soon be overwhelmed. When the French soldiers had gone, two stragglers knocked on Marie Birckel's door. They had been left behind and were now marooned in a sort of no-man's-land. They asked her for help in getting back to their own lines. She went to her neighbours and collected old clothes to dress the two men as civilians. She sent them on their way, looking like two disconsolate agricultural workers. She had no idea whether they survived.

On 11 September the village was caught in the middle of an

artillery barrage between the French and the Germans. The villagers hid in cellars. The barrage continued through the afternoon and stopped as the sun was setting. Marie emerged into the fading light to be confronted by a German officer demanding food and drink. Before the invasion Marie's mother had worked for the mayor as a secretary and now the two women were forced by the Germans into liaising between the village authorities and the invaders. In the *mairie*, the small town hall that was the administrative centre of the village, and with the help of the mayor himself, the pair surreptitiously collected bundles of documents that they thought might be of interest to the Germans and burned them.

Marie Birckel and her neighbours knew the French army was not far away and prayed for the day they would once again see the familiar red trousers worn by the soldiers. Marie tried to memorise everything she saw that might be of interest to the French army when it returned, including the positions of the growing number of ammunition dumps, supply depots and airfields. The villagers were forced to live in the church. Dysentery was rife. In October, Marie's mother fell ill and died.

Being so close to the front line the village was regularly bombarded. By the end of November the proximity of the war made life intolerable. Half the village left, heading away from the violence. A few days later the remaining villagers were ordered to leave. They took with them what few possessions they could carry, joining the long, sad lines of refugees looking to escape the German steamroller. Marie wandered the country; winter had now set in and the weather was freezing. She understood what it was like to be a hunted animal looking for refuge.

Another woman on the run was a 34-year-old aristocrat, Louise de Bettignies, whose family could trace their lineage back to the court of Charlemagne. She had spent two years studying science at Oxford, and spoke English, French, Italian and German. She had spent much of her adult life as a governess to upper-class families in Poland and Italy. She was very feminine, small, slightly built, with large blue eyes and a head of beautiful dark-brown hair. She was fit and loved riding, swimming, golf and walking. She had poise and a commanding presence. Before the invasion she had wanted to become a Carmelite nun.

She and her sister had been caught in the city of Lille when it came under siege by the advancing Germans. The two women had helped feed the men fighting to defend the city, carrying tureens of soup, even under fire.

At 10am on 9 October the last train pulled out of the heavily damaged station at Lille heading for Paris. Two days later the garrison capitulated and German cavalry entered the city. For a while Louise worked as a courier for the 'Family Post', an ad hoc organisation trying to help refugees keep in touch with each other. Then she left, escaping through the woods, trying to get to Paris where she planned to volunteer to help fight the Germans.

Eventually she made her way to Folkestone where, like every other refugee, she was interrogated by the British. The questioning took place in a large room with a long table behind which sat military personnel, plus a few civil servants and Belgian secretaries.

It was a surprise to the interrogators to learn that Louise had escaped from occupied France. At first she spoke in French, then seeing that most of her interrogators could not understand her she began to talk in English. Then she revealed that she also spoke German and had talked to German soldiers, who had unwittingly supplied her with intelligence.

She was then asked where she was going and she answered that she was hoping to get back to France, to Saint-Omer, where her mother lived. At this point she was taken into another, much smaller room, where she met officers from British Intelligence. They told her that Saint-Omer was the location of their General Headquarters (GHQ). They proposed to take her there and introduce her to their commander-in-chief, Field Marshal French. Then they hoped she would agree to return to occupied France, to work as an undercover agent.

One of the officers who interviewed her remarked that if she was not a spy 'she ought to be'. She spent several days worrying about the proposal. She talked to French intelligence officers and her spiritual adviser, who told her that she could as easily carry out God's work on the field of battle as in a nunnery. She agreed to become an agent.

Soon she was back in Folkestone, where she received basic training in field work and was given the codename 'Alice Dubois'. Her orders were to organise a train-watching network around Lille in as large an area as she could manage.

As she set off for the Belgian border she was told, 'If you get caught we won't be able to help you. If you do have the misfortune to be caught, it will probably be your own fault. Good luck!'

Louise began the huge task of creating her network. She soon realised that she could not do it alone; she needed a second-in-command whom she could trust implicitly and who could act for her. She was introduced to a young woman called Marie Léonie Vanhoutte. Léonie was training as a nurse and, although Louise did not know it, had already helped smuggle her brother into Holland. Louise instinctively trusted the woman and without hesitation tried to recruit her, saying, 'You will be my lieutenant, you will be known as "Charlotte".' Then she said, 'If you feel any misgivings, leave it alone; but if you have the necessary courage, don't hesitate.'

Léonie took a day to think about what was being asked of her. She told a friend, 'Alice is so small ... but such strength in such a small slender body.' She talked to her father and confessed that she had 'felt Louise's influence at once', and was ready to follow her anywhere, 'for I knew instinctively she was a girl capable of great things', adding, 'She was just charming.' Later she confessed to admiring Louise's black, tailor-made costume trimmed with silk braid. She said that Louise always wore the coat open and that she 'looked wonderful'.

Another recruit who became a close ally was a man whose codename was 'Albert'. He said about Louise: 'One just had to follow her. It was impossible to refuse.' A woman who kept a safe house nicknamed her 'Vite Vite' – 'Quick Quick'.

CHAPTER SIX

THE FIRST FUGITIVES

By the end of October the young mining engineer Herman Capiau had succeeded in establishing a hospital in the three disused buildings at his colliery outside the village of Wasmes, near Mons. The sheds housed about forty men, mainly officers and NCOs. All the soldiers were badly wounded and most could not walk. Capiau had recruited two doctors to help him, plus a nurse and a band of volunteers. Because his English was so good, Capiau spent a lot of his time translating between the staff and the patients. At that point the Germans had no idea that the hospital existed, or that there were others in the area.

On 1 November 1914 Capiau sneaked through occupied Brussels accompanied by two scruffy-looking men. One appeared to have a crooked spine, the other was bearded, wore a black hat and was limping badly. The two men were escaping soldiers, one of whom was the badly wounded Colonel Boger, the other a sergeant called Meachin. Capiau was trying to find a safe place where they could shelter on their way to the Dutch border. He had made several unsuccessful attempts to find a safe place for the two men. His friend Marie Depage, wife of the doctor who had invited Edith Cavell to set up the teaching hospital, suggested that he try the matron. Now, armed with a letter from Marie, he and the two fugitives trudged the cobbled streets towards Edith's hospital in the rue de la Culture. Edith agreed to take the two men in and gave them beds. Boger's badly wounded foot was operated on and after a fortnight the men had recovered enough to think about the journey to Holland. Capiau had now become an important part of the small and amateur resistance operation.

Edith wrote to her mother describing the conditions in Brussels, which she said were like living in the Middle Ages. She wrote that there were no trains, no motor cars and even no bicycles. The post did not work, nor did the telephone, and the streets were dark. Food was short, especially bread, and news from the outside world was almost non-existent. People were beginning to starve and were selling their possessions. She was surprised at how quickly they had all got used to living in a world that had changed totally in only four months.

In the Mormal Forest, work on the dugout went on. On 3 November, at noon, the men who had been digging in the morning returned to the camp to have their midday meal in the woodman's hut, which was connected to the dig by a wire leading to an alarm bell. The men eating heard the noise of vehicles approaching the edge of the forest, followed by the sound of men clambering out, the clatter of rifles and shouted orders. The alarm bell rang and everyone ran for it, abandoning their food, knocking some of it to the ground as they went. When the Germans arrived they found the area deserted but it was clear that it had been occupied. By nightfall most of the fugitive soldiers had rendezvoused with Lieutenant Bushell. Some had disappeared. The Germans were searching the forest and Bushell knew they had to move on. He set off to find the camp at Obies that Louise Thuliez had described, where her six fugitives were hiding.

Moving in the night the group came upon a village with an inn. Bushell asked where they could find 'a fair young lady with spectacles' – a description of Louise Thuliez. The innkeeper's daughter was only ten but she was suspicious and asked to see their shirt collars to make sure that they were not the field grey of the German uniforms. Then she demanded to see the heels on their boots. British boots were shod with a distinctive iron horseshoe shape around the heel. Eventually satisfied that the men were British, she took them through the night to where the other men were hiding.

Two nights later, on 5 November, Louise Thuliez visited the men. Bushell insisted that he was going to stay where he was with his men, at least until the danger from the Germans forced them to move on. Louise did not like this plan and did not feel up to the challenge of looking after so many men. She set off through the night to travel the 6 miles to Bellignies to ask the prince and princess what they should do. They talked to Captain Preston, who said that he must speak to Bushell.

The next night they set off with Preston, heading for Obies. When they arrived the two officers were overjoyed to meet each other, brother officers. They agreed that the camp should be moved further into the forest and that Louise must have entire charge of the men, that she must be their 'captain'. They told her that, in the interests of security, she was to be the intermediary between the men and the locals so that as few people as possible would know where they were. Louise told Bushell that the plan was a bad one and that it would be better for the men to go to Bellignies. Bushell listened intently to her argument but refused to move the men.

For a while the men lived in a little camp of five huts in a 5-yard clearing. It was a quiet, silent life. Louise found an old charcoal stove to heat the soup that arrived every evening. The men passed the time smoking, tending the stove, and talking in whispers.

Meanwhile, the Germans intensified their search, dividing the wood into squares and searching a new square each day. Four men had already been captured. Louise became more and more anxious about secrecy, moving around near the camp, straightening grass and covering boot prints. With the winter the branches that had been used to screen everything had lost their leaves. At one point a German patrol passed within a hundred yards of the hideout.

Louise became desperate and argued with Bushell, demanding that they break camp, obliterate everything and move to Bellignies.

Bushell still did not want to do this. His men were armed, he said, and could fight it out. Louise shouted at him, reminding him that Preston was his superior officer and had ordered that they must, 'in case of alarm, strike the camp and go to Bellignies'. Bushell knew she was right, he could not disobey a direct order, and at last he agreed to move.

On the night of the march to Bellignies they spent the afternoon clearing all signs of occupation from the camp, putting what was left of their food into haversacks, wrapping clothes and socks round their boots to muffle the noise of marching and wearing as many clothes as they could get on. Finally, they slung their rifles across their backs and at eleven o'clock they moved off into the darkness and the torrential rain.

They moved in two groups, one led by Henriette Moriamé who was in the lead, and a second led by Louise with Bushell. They crept by three occupied villages and travelled along a main road which was used by German vehicles and patrols.

At midnight the wind got up, blowing away the clouds and revealing a bright moon which made it too dangerous to go on. They moved off the path and hid in the undergrowth until the moon disappeared.

At just after two in the morning the two groups arrived at Bellignies. They waited in a tool shed while Louise went to the house to tell the princess that the weary band had arrived. The princess took charge and, by the time Thuliez and Moriamé fell into bed, the men had been hidden in the attic of the gardener's house, which was concealed among overgrown shrubs and had never been searched by the Germans.

The gardener's wife, Juliette, immediately set about making soup and coffee for the fugitives. Bushell was in a state of nervous collapse and was led across the garden to the chateau, where he was put to bed in Preston's room, hidden in the tower.

A few days later, by 12 November, German patrols arrived. The princess knew that it was a matter of time before the men were discovered. Preston considered it his duty to order the men to give themselves up as prisoners of war. Anything else would endanger the local people who had helped hide and feed them.

Louise and Henriette were heartbroken at the thought that the men they had risked so much for were about to be taken into captivity. They toured the area looking for a way for the fugitives to break out. Without proper walking shoes or training, the two women covered nearly a hundred miles in their search and returned crestfallen and in agreement that the process of hiding the soldiers had become impossible.

Preston had a long talk with a member of the local chamber of commerce. They agreed that the men should be surrendered through the Red Cross and that everything should be done to hide the fact that they had been helped by local people. That evening Preston and the princess went to the gardener's house and there, the room lit by candles, they held a conference with the two sergeants in the group, leaving it to them to break it to the rest of the men that they must surrender.

When they heard the plan the men said it was their duty to fight on, but Preston pointed out that this was the only way to save their lives and the lives of everyone else who had helped them. The princess added: 'Think of the country people who have been risking their lives for you. Think of us all, for if you are caught we shall all be shot and the village burned to the ground. If we take you to the Red Cross no one need know where you come from and you will be treated as prisoners of war.' At last the men agreed, but insisted that the two officers should remain in the chateau. Bushell was still very weak and the stress of commanding the men in the forest had left him in a bad mental state.

The next problem was that many of the men had lost parts of their uniform. In the retreat many soldiers had thrown away their greatcoats. The Germans had ordered that these be given up but many were still hidden in cottages around the area. Louise thought she could make breeches out of them and for a whole day she, Henriette, the princess's maid and the housekeeper of the local clergyman cut and sewed until there were enough bits of uniform that under long coats would look quite respectable.

Finally, the men were given some money and paper and pencils to write letters home. The women wept as they watched the men prepare to set off into captivity. When all was done the men marched through the night, using quiet lanes and hedges for cover. They were led by Thuliez and Moriamé into the town of Bavay, where they were put to bed in the hospital. The next day the Germans were told that some soldiers had given themselves up after spending four months hiding in the forest. After a lot of argument from the Germans the story was accepted and the men disappeared into Germany.

By the end of the month conditions in Brussels had deteriorated further. Edith Cavell wrote again to her mother, saying that some of the nurses had been ill with a kind of colic, possibly caused by the black bread that was all they could buy and which was heavy and difficult to digest. Money was short everywhere and families that had been well-to-do only six months before were now reduced to living in the cheapest way possible. Unemployment was rife and men were prepared to work for a quarter of what they had earned before the invasion; some were even prepared to work for nothing, just bread and butter. Children roamed the streets begging for food, while in the hospital any spare or leftover food was left out on trays for them.

In December 1914 a new governor general of occupied Belgium arrived in Brussels, General Moritz von Bissing. Brand Whitlock described him as 'a man whose name is destined to stand forth in the world as a symbol of one of the darkest, cruellest and most sinister pages of its miserable history'. Von Bissing was seventy years old. A tall, thin man with oiled black hair and a cavalry moustache, he carried a sabre and wore silver spurs on his riding boots. His first act was to fine the Belgian people 480 million marks. He also issued an edict that all British, French and Russian nationals had to register at the École Militaire.

He was soon lampooned in the underground paper, *La Libre*

Belgique, the satirical publication that the publishers called a 'Bulletin of patriotic propaganda'. Its tone was irreverential, and it contained articles from other newspapers and censored news. The publishers said that the paper 'will live in spite of persecution and official censure because there is something stronger than might, stronger than Culture, something stronger than the Germans – the truth! And Belgium is the land of truth and liberty.' On the masthead the paper announced that the price per copy was variable, anything from zero to infinity, and warned readers not to pay more than the limit of infinity. The paper also claimed to be published 'Regularly – Irregularly – Submitting to no Censorship'.

The editor was now Eugène van Doren, who owned a cardboard factory and worked from a tiny room in the building, running off 25,000 copies of each issue. Disguising himself as a German officer, van Doren inveigled his way into the offices of the governor general, where he stole documents and left copies of the newspaper.

In one issue the governor general was shown sitting at his desk reading the paper; the caption said that 'His Excellency the Governor' was looking for the truth in his 'dear friend *La Libre Belgique*'. Other issues showed him weighed down by arrest warrants for the publishers. Another showed the Kaiser in hell. Anyone caught working on the journal would be arrested, even carrying it was deemed to be an act of espionage, and the guilty would be fined up to 75,000 francs and sent to prison.

Just after Christmas a trusted friend of the princess, Countess Jeanne de Belleville, arrived at Bellignies. She had made contact with a priest in Brussels who had helped her get her nephew into Holland where he wanted to join the Allied army. The countess wanted the princess to use the same route to get Preston and Bushell away. A plan was quickly formed. The princess's brother Reginald had a contact in Mons who was able to provide forged papers and passports. The princess had given refuge to a woman called Charlotte Matha, who was from Paris and had been holidaying with relatives in Bellignies when the German advance had marooned her. Her husband had been captured in the fighting at Maubeuge. Charlotte was now living in the house and had become the princess's maid. She offered to help the two officers.

On 28 December 1914, a message was sent to Louise Thuliez telling her that Bushell and Preston were going to escape and asking if she would act as a guide along with Charlotte Matha. She agreed. First they had to get to Brussels. On the afternoon of 29 December the four set off for the home of the Countess de Belleville, where they prepared the details for their false identity papers – the two officers were described as 'hairdresser's assistants'. Passports ready, they went to bed tense; the next day they would have to catch a tram from Mons that passed through the town of Enghien where all papers were strictly examined.

The tram from Mons did not leave until 2pm. The party now included the princess and Reginald, who had invited them to have lunch in a small, quiet restaurant. As they ate, two German officers came in and conversation became subdued and strained. Preston and Bushell were scarcely able to speak apart from the occasional muttered 'oui'.

Bushell went to the lavatory and was followed in by one of the officers. They stood next to each other to dry their hands on a roller towel. Later, at Enghien all the passengers were made to get off the tram and wait while their passports were examined.

The escaping men had to be kept in safe houses in Brussels while arrangements were made for their onward journey to the border. Reginald de Croÿ was put in touch with Edith Cavell, who had nursed the two soldiers Boger and Meachin, caring for them until they were fit enough to make the journey to the border. Reginald quickly realised that Edith could be trusted and that her hospital in Brussels was an ideal staging post for the fugitives.

And so, by chance, a local escape route was established by a small cell of Belgian civilians, with Thuliez, Croÿ and Cavell at the centre.

Now that they had discovered a means of crossing into Holland, Thuliez and Moriamé began looking for more fugitive Allied soldiers marooned by the rapid retreat. Slowly a routine evolved. In the first stages local people emerged who were prepared to have the soldiers stay for a night or two. Movement was always at night and at first everyone was suspicious of everyone else. On one occasion, the girls stayed with a family that did not know them. They were given a bed to share and became aware that the whole family was outside the door listening to them. The two women were exhausted from walking, covering up to 25 miles a night, and fell asleep. The family decided they were genuine and the next morning took them to a rendezvous with a group of twelve soldiers who had been in hiding. The first step was to get them to the Mormal Forest and from there to Bellignies, where they would stay for a few nights until they could be taken into Belgium and to Brussels, to make a rendezvous with Edith Cavell. The routine after that was to take them via a series of safe houses to the Dutch border.

There were many attempts to disguise the soldiers. One group was disguised as woodcutters, travelling – standing or sitting – on rough carts accompanied by Thuliez and Moriamé wearing peasant cloaks. The most dangerous part of the trip was to navigate a heavily guarded level crossing. Some of the German soldiers would grunt a surly '*bonjour*' as the guards swung open the gates to let them through. Once in the forest the men hid until nightfall and then made the journey to Bellignies. The woodcutter trick worked for a while but eventually the Germans wanted to know why none of the woodcutters came back.

On another occasion a woman who lived with her father on a farm on the outskirts of the forest was preparing a meal for two soldiers who were to wait with her until nightfall. A German patrol arrived. When she saw the patrol enter the farmyard she hid the two men in the large oven of her disused bakery. Then she answered the door.

'Where is your husband?'

'I am not married.'

'We have seen two men entering here. How do you explain that?'

'They are my grandfather and one of his workers!'

The soldiers were still suspicious and demanded to be shown the whole house. The last place they looked was the bakery but did not think to open the oven.

By now the woman was shaking and white. The officer said, 'Are you ill or what? Why are you so upset? You have turned very pale.'

The woman summoned all her courage and replied, 'I am neither ill nor upset. I am a Frenchwoman and I love my country. When I see your spiked helmets I want to cry.' She pushed her way out of the bakery and the soldiers followed her. By now they were satisfied that there were no fugitives hidden in the house and demanded that she cook for them. Soon they were sitting eating every egg that she had, twenty-eight in all, scrambled.

When at last the Germans left, the two men were released from the oven, shaken, fearful and desperate for water. By nightfall they were on their way to Bellignies.

Another incident occurred when two soldiers whom they were trying to help, one of them a Canadian, disappeared, leaving a note saying they did not trust the women. The men wandered the countryside for several weeks. They eventually turned up again and agreed to be helped. Thuliez took them to Edith Cavell. When she got back everyone was anxious to know how it had gone. She said the Canadian had a loaded gun with him and had said that if there'd been any difficulty en route he would have shot her.

Thuliez and Moriamé's area of activity grew as more and more marooned soldiers were located. They stayed whenever they could in the houses of friends and each morning had no idea where they would be spending the night.

By the new year both Bushell and Preston had crossed the frontier into Holland, disguised as carpenters.

To the disappointment of the civilian population and most of the soldiers, the war was not over by Christmas 1914. At the front, the troops lived in trenches, cold, muddy and frightened. The opposing forces were separated by 'no-man's-land' – a desolate blasted area that resembled a lunar landscape, covered in thousands of miles of barbed wire.

In London the streets were blacked out but the shops were brightly lit, warm and full of shoppers buying presents for friends and family. The theatres too were busy, putting on shows for the children.

The 'Christmas truce' in the trenches of the Western Front brought a strange silence along the line as a series of unofficial ceasefires was established. Soldiers from both sides shouted 'Merry Christmas' to each other, climbed out of their dugouts, exchanged gifts, sang carols, buried their dead, and some even played football.

In some of the churches in Belgium the Christmas sermon was a message from the Archbishop of Malines, Primate of Belgium. In it he described the fury that had accompanied the occupying Germans, the deaths of thousands of citizens, the deportation of thousands more to Germany and the destruction of cities, towns and villages. Later, priests who had read the sermon to their congregations were arrested.

In the cellar of Edith Cavell's hospital that Christmas Day escaping British soldiers enjoyed a Yuletide dinner of roast beef and plum pudding made from a recipe cooked in peacetime by Edith's mother. At one point Edith came down the steps to see how they were. One of the soldiers described her as a kind woman who got things done without anyone noticing what she was doing. He also found her very clever. In the room above their heads was another party, for thirty poor children, refugees who had found themselves in the city. The children gathered round a Christmas tree decorated by the nurses. They were given chocolates and sweets that had arrived on a ship from America. The highlight of the party was the distribution of presents: toy trains and cars for the boys, dolls and clothes for the girls.

Edith had converted her office into a room where the nurses could relax. Her desk had been moved into another place. In the converted office the nurses too ate their dinner, enjoying roast beef and plum pudding surrounded by empty shell cases holding huge bunches of chrysanthemums.

As darkness fell people dropped into the hospital, among them Stirling Gahan, an English clergyman. The company chatted, shook hands and wished each other a happy new year. Moving among the group were some of the soldiers from the cellar. Gahan thought that this boded well for the new year and relished the spice of danger that the Tommies brought to the party. The children and the adults were now enjoying currant buns, jam tarts and weak, milky coffee. Sister Wilkins had organised the sewing of the dolls and clothes and now nursed her own fingers, sore from all the work. For a few precious hours the war faded into the background.

1915

CHAPTER SEVEN

RESISTANCE BEGINS

In January 1915 the war came once more to Marthe Cnockaert's home in Westrozebeke, which was near the front line. The village was again subjected to high-explosive bombardment and the inhabitants, including Marthe, were evacuated. They left on foot and in carts that sank up to their axles in mud, the wheels squelching over straw, old curtains, carpets, bales of wool, cloth and broken furniture, all stripped from the houses by the soldiers and thrown into the tracks in an attempt to make a surface over which men and machines could travel. The sad group watched the village disappear into the distance, as they jolted away from the doom-laden booming of the guns towards the comparative safety of the town of Roulers.

The underground newspaper *La Libre Belgique* was now being distributed by Philippe Baucq who, acting as circulation manager, made his rounds at first on bicycle and later, when bicycling was forbidden, on foot. Baucq was a flamboyant architect and a devout Catholic, who wore a long black cloak and a wide-brimmed hat, like a cartoon version of an artist. He was a handsome man of medium height with a generous moustache and close-cropped bushy hair. He used the nom de guerre 'Monsieur Fromage'. He lived in Brussels with his wife and two daughters. He also lived with the fear of what would happen to him and his family if his undercover activities were discovered by the Germans.

Among the others involved in the production and distribution of the newspaper was a priest, the Abbé de Moor, who was in touch with both Edith Cavell and British Intelligence.

In Lille, Louise de Bettignies, operating as Alice Dubois, set about organising her train-watching network, known as the 'Alice Service'. She reported to Colonel Wallner, a French liaison officer based in Folkestone, and also to an English officer, Major Cameron, whom she called 'Oncle Édouard'. She masqueraded as a dressmaker, a lace saleswoman and a language teacher. She carried a letter recommending her for employment by the Cereal Company, a business that had been set up by GHQ as a cover for resistance activities. She was arrested and the letter she carried found – it was in English. Under interrogation she said that the director of the Cereal Company was French and spoke English but not Dutch. The Dutchman it was addressed to spoke English but not French. She pretended that in any case she was French and could not speak English so had no idea what the letter said. In the end she was released.

One of Louise's early recruits was a woman whose house overlooked the railway station in Lille. The woman managed to operate even though she had German officers billeted with her. They saw the quiet woman passing the time sitting by the window, knitting. What they did not know was that she had devised a code using her knitting. The troops, their movements, the trains and their equipment and anything else she saw could be recorded by changing the stitching. Only she could read it. To the billeted soldiers they were just patterns of wool. Later the information could be written down for transmission to the Allies. Other people invented codes using household food as counters: beans could be troops, garlic bulbs trains; again, the code was invisible.

Louise had also recruited two men, one of whom was a photographer with a printing press and the other an expert with ink and paper. Between them they could forge and produce documents and passes.

Louise de Bettignies had a quick temper and could get into

arguments with the occupying powers. On one occasion, after having an argument in the street with a German officer, she was followed by a plain-clothes policeman whose attention she had attracted. After a while she realised there was someone tailing her and began to panic. She turned a corner and ahead of her she saw a large house; she crossed over to it, banged on the door which opened and, without being asked, she pushed her way in. The policeman arrived at the corner just in time to see her light-grey skirt and the back of her jacket disappear into the house. He waited for her to come out.

Inside, Louise stood in front of the owner, a well-to-do middle-aged woman, explaining the danger she was in and hoping that the woman was a patriot. The woman listened then said, 'Follow me.' She headed across the hall and hurried up the stairs. They climbed to a small bedroom at the top of the house. Hanging from hooks on a wall were clothes. 'Put these on, they belong to my maid. She is out, her name is Marie. Hurry, come down when I call you.' Someone was banging on the door, the noise echoing through the house. The woman disappeared. Louise pulled the maid's long baggy dress over her clothes, tied an apron over it and crammed the maid's bonnet onto her head.

She crept down the stairs to hear a man's voice demanding in heavily accented French to see the woman 'in the light-grey skirt'. 'I am sorry, monsieur, but there is no one here of that description. Why are you asking?' The man became angry, his voice raised, demanding to search the house. Then the woman shouted, 'Marie! Come down at once.' Louise walked down the stairs looking fat and frumpy. At the bottom she curtsied, her head lowered in respectful deference. 'Madame?' 'Have you allowed anyone into the house wearing a light-grey skirt and jacket?' 'No, madame.'

The policeman insisted on searching the premises. The owner looked at him with contempt. 'Show this gentleman whatever he wishes to see.' Then the woman turned and swept back into her drawing room. For the next hour Louise showed the man round. He started in the attic and ended in the cellar. He searched everywhere, opening cupboards, tapping walls for secret hiding places. He found nothing and, very disgruntled, left, slamming the front door with an echoing boom.

Louise collapsed onto a sofa and apologised to the owner of the house for putting her in such danger.

Louise's network quickly grew and she became overwhelmed with work, sitting up late into the night writing her reports on rice paper in tiny handwriting. She often took the notes herself to England or Holland, a very risky enterprise.

The British Intelligence Corps that had been so hastily thrown together at the beginning of the war was not taken seriously by the military establishment. They found it amateur and often ignored the intelligence it gathered. A report on the size of the German forces heading for Mons had been rejected by the French commander-in-chief, General Joffre, as 'greatly exaggerated'. For his part, the commander of the British Expeditionary Force, Field Marshal French, thought that at Mons the Germans would have 'very little ... except cavalry supported by small bodies of infantry'. All in all the size of the enemy forces ranged against the Allies was under-estimated by 300,000 men.

One junior intelligence officer was Sigismund Best, who by now was attached to GHQ. He could speak French and German, had a good understanding of Flemish, and had travelled all over Europe by both car and motorcycle. After being rejected by the army at the beginning of the war because of his eyesight, he had then spent the next week travelling from recruiting office to recruiting office only to receive the same verdict: 'Poor eyesight? Rejected!' Even the lowly Service Corps would not have him. Then, out of the blue, a telegram arrived ordering him to report to the War Office. He joined a queue of men, none of whom had any idea why they were there. Eventually Best was shown into a room where he was interviewed by a friendly man in civilian clothes who said he was a major. They talked for a while and then the major said, 'Well, if your languages are all right and you can ride a motorcycle, you'll get a commission as second lieutenant ... We'll give you an allowance of £50 to buy your uniform and equipment.'

Later that day he was interviewed in both French and German by army interpreters, and that evening was in Kensington Gardens driving a motorcycle up and down the wide Broad Walk. A few days later he collected a brand-new Rudge motorcycle from Euston station and by 24 August was in France. He had no idea about army life; he did not know whom to salute or even how to salute. He admitted he was very frightened and thought that if he came under fire he would run away in a 'funk'.

By October, Best and his motorcycle were in Antwerp. His orders were vague; he was to act as liaison officer to an under-equipped naval brigade sent by Winston Churchill, First Lord of the Admiralty, to support the Belgian army. Best had started on his mission with another officer. They had stopped at a restaurant in Reims where his companion, before sitting down, took off his Sam Browne belt and accidentally shot himself in the foot with his service revolver, which hung in a holster from the belt. Sigismund went on alone.

After Antwerp he went on to Bruges where he climbed the thirteenth-century Belfry. From his perch he could see German troops entering the outer suburbs of the town. At the Bruges GPO he found a telephone and rang the number for GHQ in France. By a miracle he got through to Major Walter Kirke, a senior intelligence officer. Best told him about the German advance. He then set off to get back to France, heading west along the coast. By the time he reached Ostend he was filthy and his uniform was in tatters. He ran into a German cavalry unit but bluffed his way through. At Ypres he ditched his motorcycle in the canal and swam across. When he reached the other side he was naked except for the identity tags round his neck. Even so he persuaded the inhabitants that he was a British officer and by evening Kirke had rescued him, found him a new uniform and taken him to GHQ. From then on, whenever he saw an opportunity he took it without the slightest idea of whether he was doing the right thing, relying on trial and error. However, he admitted that at the beginning there was 'nothing for any of us to do ... they seemed to have no use for us'.

Best wanted to set up an intelligence-gathering network in Belgium. At Christmas he was invalided back to London. He recovered and in the opening months of 1915 he took it upon himself to question Belgian refugees arriving at Tilbury on the ferry from Rotterdam. He was arrested by the police who suspected him of being a spy. Once more he was rescued by Walter Kirke. Best protested that, as a lowly lieutenant, he was powerless without some sort of organisation to give him authority. Kirke responded by setting up an office in Basil Street, Knightsbridge, under the command of Major Ernest Wallinger, a big handsome gunnery officer who had lost a foot in one of the opening battles of the war. Wallinger had married a rich woman and lived above the Knightsbridge office with a housekeeper and a batman. Best was made his second-in-command.

With his new power Best went every day to meet the ferry at Tilbury and to usher Belgian passengers into a waiting room for interrogation. His Flemish was not good and he soon recruited one of the refugees, Joseph Ide, to help him, giving Ide the codename 'Monsieur Emil'. At the end of each day Best and Ide travelled back to London, had dinner and discussed the information they had collected during the day's interrogations. Then Best typed up a report which he sent to all interested parties, including the War Office and GHQ. In the course of this exercise Best began to recruit refugees, persuading them to return to Belgium as agents.

Meanwhile, in Roulers Marthe Cnockaert had been seconded as a nurse by the Germans. She had been granted a pass that allowed her to move around the town during the curfew in case there was an emergency.

Early one morning, just after dawn, and after a long night shift dealing with wounded Germans, Marthe sat, exhausted, in her kitchen when there was a knock at the door. She opened it to reveal Lucelle Deldonck, the friend from Westrozebeke who had disappeared when the Germans overran the village. She now looked old, tired and haggard, her grey hair hanging in wisps. She crept in and put her finger to her lips.

'No one must know I'm here, I have had much difficulty in finding you.'

She explained that she had come from the Allied side of the front and said, 'Marthe, you are young and strong. Would you like to serve your country?'

Marthe nodded without understanding what Lucelle was talking about.

'You realise that in this occupation your life will be at stake every day? What do you say?'

Marthe paused then said, 'I am waiting for my instructions, Lucelle.'

'Brave girl, Marthe. I cannot give you instructions. I am a member of the British Secret Intelligence Commission. I can tell you nothing until you have communicated with them ... in a few days' time expect to receive a summons from me and in whatever manner this arrives show no surprise. For the next few days I shall be not far from Roulers.' Then she was gone, leaving a puzzled Marthe wondering what would happen next.

Three days later, in the early morning, a 70-year-old woman arrived in Roulers. She led an old horse pulling a four-wheeled cart carrying vegetables. She had a contract to supply her produce to the German canteen in the town and was allowed to sell anything left over to the locals, who nicknamed her 'Canteen Ma'. Marthe spotted her as she was on her way to work in the hospital.

'Good day, mademoiselle,' called the old woman in a high, cracked voice. 'It is cold but a beautiful morning to be out early. I have some nice beans, cheap today.'

Marthe bought the beans and found that Canteen Ma had slipped a piece of paper into her hand.

'Read in private,' whispered the old woman, before continuing on her way.

In her bedroom Marthe read:

Come to the second farm on the right-hand side of the road to
Zwevezele. Ask for Lisette, who is expecting to see you at nine
o'clock tonight.

Marthe wondered whether it was a trap; the area was full of plain-
clothes agents known as the Berlin Vampires. She decided to take the
risk and that evening made her way across the frozen fields, hoping
that if stopped she could say that she was visiting a sick woman, a
natural enough thing for a nurse to do. From the fields she could see
German patrols moving along the roads carrying lights. Eventually
she found the farmhouse, knocked at the door and, after a long
silence, heard a voice mutter, 'What do you want?'
    'I have come to see Lisette.'
    The door opened and she was dragged into a dark passage with
a stone floor and led up some stairs into a dark room, heavily cur-
tained and lit only by the glow from a small, dying fire in the grate.
In the gloom she could just make out the figure of her friend Lucelle.
    'Child, I rejoice to see you.'
    Lucelle told her that by coming Marthe had agreed to become a
spy. Lucelle reminded her that she would hear many things in her
work among the German soldiers in the hospital and she was to
report whatever she heard. It would not always be obvious whether
what she heard was important, that was not for her to judge; her job
was simply to listen, remember and report.
    'To British Intelligence you will be known as "Laura".' Marthe
asked how she was to transmit her reports.
    Lucelle handed her a piece of grubby folded paper.
    'You will use this cypher to encode your messages – learn it by
heart and destroy it.'
    Marthe started to hide the cypher in her stocking top when
Lucelle warned her that it was too obvious a place, much better to
conceal it in her hair.
    'You will receive instructions through the old vegetable woman
who first made contact, Canteen Ma.'
    Lucelle then told her where she was to take her coded messages

and warned her to get rid of any incriminating material as soon as possible.

She then told her about the 'Safety Pin Men', a group of patriots who had formed an anti-German espionage system. She would meet them in due course and know it was them because they had two metal safety pins attached to the back of their jacket lapels. She said that a man would appear in a few days and if he showed her the two safety pins she must do anything to help him.

Finally, she explained to Marthe that the next person in the chain of agents of which she was now a part was known as 'Number 63' and told her where the contact was to be found. If the Safety Pin Man appeared, he might have material he wanted to pass on to intelligence and she, Marthe, was to take such stuff to Number 63.

Then Lucelle stood up, said she thought the Vampires suspected she was in the area and that she had to leave at once.

'Be careful, my dear. Goodbye, Marthe, and God be with you.'

By now the daily reports from French, British and Belgian intelligence services were being analysed, collated into one document and sent by telegraph to GHQ. The British section established itself in a house on the Folkestone seafront under the command of Major Aylmer Cameron, to whom Louise de Bettignies was already reporting. Sigismund Best thought Cameron had a 'foxy look about him'. He was married to a woman of great charm and before the war they had both been jailed for an insurance fraud. Mrs Cameron claimed that a necklace worth £6,500 was snatched from her hand outside a chemist's shop in Oxford Street where her husband was buying a hypodermic needle. Both were sentenced to three years' penal servitude. Later, an expert medical witness argued that the attractive Mrs Cameron was addicted to morphine and lived in a world of 'romance and unreality'. Mrs Cameron was released early while Aylmer served the full term, gaining his freedom in 1914.

Spying was not a question of large discoveries but an accumulation of thousands of small pieces of information. Every detail was important – the ages of the soldiers, how they were equipped, what their morale was like. A key element in this was the observation of movements of men and materiel by rail. Knowing who the troops were, where they were going and who was holding any particular sector might enable the intelligence officers at GHQ to make informed guesses about how the enemy was deploying and what his intentions were. Rolling stock, schedules and identifying signs could all supply vital details.

There were still many Allied soldiers stranded behind enemy lines. Edith Cavell, the Princess de Croÿ, Louise Thuliez, Henriette Moriamé and their immediate friends continued to operate their improvised but well-run escape organisation. Fugitive soldiers found by Thuliez and Moriamé were first taken to a refuge in the Mormal Forest then moved on to the princess's chateau at Bellignies, where they were hidden until they could be taken across the border into Belgium.

The routine was simple but time-consuming and made use of the lessons learned the year before. When a group of about twenty or so fugitive soldiers had been assembled in the forest they were taken to Bellignies, where they waited until they could be sent on to Brussels. The moves were planned in great detail and with precision. The women took into account routes, distances and the phases of the moon. A full moon was the enemy, while the three nights when there was no moon at all were all friends. In peacetime the trip on foot from the forest to Bellignies took about four hours, but in wartime, with the country watched by German patrols and German army service vehicles, the journey could take seven or eight hours. The escapers travelled after dark, their faces and hands camouflaged with mud. Louise Thuliez and Henriette Moriamé wore dark-grey clothing to blend into the shadows. They moved with caution, avoiding paths and keeping close to hedgerows. One of the women always walked ahead, with the men creeping slowly behind. If the leader saw a German patrol, or anything suspicious, she dropped a white handkerchief, which was the signal for the whole party to crouch down and hide. Sometimes they spent hours in ditches on the edge of the forest, hating the dogs that barked. Often the party was too big to move in a single body and the men were split into two groups. They made many detours, and every hour or so rested, hiding where they could and taking the opportunity to drink from any water that was available, including rain from puddles.

When at last they approached the chateau, the party halted by a woodshed where they could be hidden. Louise Thuliez left Henriette with the men and went ahead to find the princess, who was waiting for them, hiding in bushes near a gate into the chateau grounds.

The waiting made the princess tense; the slightest noise – the cracking of a twig, even the sound of dew dripping from a branch – made her jump with nerves. As Louise approached where the princess was concealed, she ran a stick along the iron fence that surrounded the park, the signal that she had arrived and that the coast was clear.

The two women then went to the woodshed. On a few occasions, German deserters had infiltrated the group, so the princess questioned the men to reassure herself that they were genuine fugitives. In the shed the men found strips of carpet with which they were instructed to bind their feet so that they did not leave telltale marks or tracks on the soil, the flowerbeds or the lawns.

Once the women were certain that it was safe, the men were led across the lawns into the house and into the great hall, which had been converted into a sort of hospital. Here there were beds with clean sheets onto which the exhausted fugitives flopped and fell asleep. Then the princess went to her bedroom and slept while Louise and Henriette went to a room which was set aside for them and where they too fell into a deep sleep.

The move did not always go smoothly. One night the party had been split into three groups. Louise was in the lead when a soldier came panting up beside her with the news that the third element had disappeared. She ordered the men to wait by a hedge and to keep silent. Then she walked back along a dark road until she met a woman she did not know but whom she had passed earlier on. The woman said that the missing soldiers had taken the wrong path but not to worry as her husband was now escorting them. Fearful that she might be a collaborator, Louise denied knowing anything about the men. As the two women argued the soldiers appeared out of the gloom, led by the husband. Much relieved, Louise took them back to the others who, to her annoyance, were now strolling about in the road and smoking cigarettes.

The day after arrival the men had their photographs taken so that false identities could be prepared for them. One by one they were led out into the garden where they found the princess standing by a table on which was placed a camera. In front of the table was a chair on which each man sat in turn. They were now all in civilian clothes. As each took his place in front of the camera members of the household kept watch on the roads in case the Germans appeared for an unannounced spot check.

The princess handled the camera and the plates with great care. She had been a keen photographer before the war. The plates were originally for a larger device but she had cut them down to size using diamond cutting equipment supplied for her by a glazier. Once the pictures had been taken she developed them in her darkroom. The last stage was to stick the photographs onto blank identity cards. At first the princess's brother Reginald had stolen these from the Germans through a clerk working in the Bureau de Population in Mons. Later, the passes were provided by Herman Capiau, the director of the local mine who had converted some of his factory buildings into a makeshift hospital and who had first brought fugitives to Edith Cavell's facility. He stole them from a German office in Wasmes.

Each card had a name that could be pronounced by its English-speaking holder. The last act was to stamp each with 'Commune de Saint-Jean, Hainaut' – a place that did not exist. Each stamp was countersigned with an illegible signature.

The work was painstaking, tiring and took all day. Trapped in her darkroom the princess was especially vulnerable to discovery and she hoped that the watchers would remain alert. At last, when the work was finished, she took the pile of cards through the house to the great hall for distribution to the men, who saw the cards as a good omen, proof that they were going to get home.

If a German search party paid a surprise visit the men could be concealed in the secret staircase in the tower, the one that the princess's brother had discovered and opened up, disguising it as a store cupboard. If the Germans appeared, the fugitives were bundled into what they called the 'black hole', where they had to stay until the raid was over. One soldier later described the ordeal:

> If she got the wire that her place was to be raided she brought us into a beautiful room which was all carved and panelled wood all round and not a sign of a door. The next thing she did was to bring in a table with a bottle of medicine on it, saying that she was going to bed and pretending to be sick. To our great surprise she opened a door with her fingernails and we went through about nine yards, when we came up against a wall about twelve feet high, and against this wall was a ladder, and up we all got, the last man pulling the ladder after him. This place brought us underneath the stairs of the castle. It was a terrible place, and not even a candle could remain lit. When we all started to cough, the princess would knock at the wood where she lay in bed, a double tap warning us that the German raiding party had arrived. They searched every part of the house; they passed the princess and took no notice of her. The last place they came up was the castle stairs on the outside, and when they started tapping the walls we shifted from one side to the other, and when the all clear was given we came staggering down, as we were properly gassed and our lips were like a blue rag. The princess had a good laugh saying, 'See what women can do for men, and they won't give us our vote.'

As well as the dangers in the chateau, greater dangers lay ahead. The trip to Brussels meant crossing the border from occupied France into occupied Belgium. Once in the city they stayed with Edith Cavell in her hospital or in safe houses. There they had to wait for guides to take them on the home run to the Dutch border. Edith kept meticulous records of all the men who stayed with her. She treated them as patients, inventing illnesses and recording their names, date of arrival and departure, and often, unwisely, kept photographs of them.

In the middle of March 1915, in Roulers, Marthe Cnockaert had a stroke of luck – her father was given the chance to take over the Café Carillon just by the church in the Grand-Place in the centre of the town. The house had been hit by shells which destroyed the upper floors at the back, but the bar plus a private room and some bedrooms were still usable.

Marthe thought that if she was careful she could help in the café in her spare time from nursing and might overhear useful intelligence from the soldiers relaxing there. Marthe's work as a nurse had won her the goodwill of the men. She played the part of a Belgian woman who was in sympathy with the Allies and felt sorrow for her country-men but had no bad feelings towards the individual German fighting men. She even agreed to wash and mend their clothes. Her system was to 'never encourage anybody, never speak to anybody, just let them know you are there and wait for them to make overtures'.

One day a young German officer appeared who was to be billeted with Marthe's family. He was very friendly, had lived in Paris and spoke good French. He told her that conditions in Berlin were as bad as anything the Belgians were experiencing.

'However, we Germans know how to put up with a lot, so it does not matter. We are bound to win.'

She replied, 'You may win great victories, but I do not believe that in the end you will emerge from this war the victors.'

He told her that a sudden crushing victory was going to come and it would come soon. In spite of this cocky arrogance she liked him. She noticed a new type of cargo arriving at the railway station: big, black, heavy iron cylinders. At the same time she learned that one of the café regulars was a scientist and that part of his job was to record the weather in the area and especially the wind direction. All the officers and men she spoke to agreed there was soon going to be a big victory which would bring a rapid end to the war.

She sent all these details via Number 63 and soon got a message from GHQ saying, 'Recent reports of yours of a highly speculative nature. Repeat, troop movements, designation of units, trains etc of more value.'

Although downcast when she received this rebuke, she went on with her work.

On 22 April 1915 it was a beautiful day at Ypres, with a light breeze. In the early evening at about five o'clock French troops, including elements from Morocco and Algeria, saw a strange, low, yellow cloud, looking like mist, rolling across no-man's-land. It slowly enveloped them and within seconds the men were tearing at their clothes, throwing off their greatcoats and scarves, running about screaming for water, spitting blood and writhing on the ground. German soldiers with white gauze pads strapped to their faces came behind the mist, shooting and bayoneting the fear-crazed Allied soldiers.

Ambulances poured into the hospital where Marthe was working. As well as Germans there were French, Canadian and British soldiers. Men whose lungs had flooded and who were drowning. Men suffering from splitting headaches and terrifying thirst. Men who, if they drank water, would die immediately. Men who vomited green froth and whose stomachs contracted as if being cut by a knife. Men who, when they died, turned green then black and yellow, their tongues lolling from their mouths and their sightless eyes staring 'like dead fish'. Word went round that this was a 'gas attack' but nobody knew what that meant. Then orders came through that protection could be had from cotton pads soaked in urine. Some soldiers used their socks and flannel body belts.

The attacks continued for a month. Allied reinforcements arrived and were shocked by what they found. One soldier wrote that the roads were blocked with civilian refugees, along the sides of the Ypres railway lay dead and dying soldiers and civilians, writhing in agony. The faces of the casualties turned black.

By the end of May nearly 100,000 men were dead, gassed or wounded. Some of the gassed victims took months and even years to die.

Had the officers at GHQ taken Marthe's reports more seriously they might have guessed that the heavy, black, iron cylinders described by her contained the gas and would be used in an attack.

CHAPTER EIGHT

THE WIRE OF DEATH

At the beginning of April 1915, in the towns and villages along the border between Holland and Belgium, houses were requisitioned. Then squads of labourers arrived. Some were third-class German soldiers, others were Belgians drafted into the workforce, and yet others were Russian prisoners of war, wild-looking men who frightened everyone. They cleared trees and undergrowth along a wide path stretching along the border as far as the eye could see in both directions. Lorries and horse-drawn carts delivered thousands of yards of barbed wire, copper wire, fence posts and white porcelain insulating formers. Electricity generating plants near the border were requisitioned and, where there were none, new ones built.

Along the centre of the cleared path 10-foot-high poles were rammed into the ground. Engineers stretched the copper wire between the poles, tightening it round the insulators. Wires were run out from the generators, the current turned on and tested by throwing scraps of paper onto the now electrified copper – the scraps caught fire. Sometimes stray cats and dogs were tossed onto the cables and died burning, as the high-voltage current spasmed through their bodies. Finally, barbed wire fences were put up on either side of the electric fence, and units of armed men arrived to man newly erected watchtowers, guarding the lethal barrier through which ran up to 2,000 volts of electricity.

Signs warned that anyone attempting to approach the fence would be shot. Foot patrols guarded it night and day, and from the watch-towers powerful searchlights illuminated the wires.

By the end of August work was finished and the fence stretched in an unbroken line between Aix-la-Chapelle and the river Scheldt, almost completely sealing off Belgium from the Dutch border. In some places it had cut whole villages in half. At regular intervals along its course there were huge gates through which the locals with special passes were allowed to cross. The passes were difficult, almost impossible, to get hold of. It was common to see funeral processions approach the wire so that mourners on the other side could view the coffin of a loved one and pray. The fence was nicknamed the 'Wire of Death'.

Several ingenious ways were developed to cross the barrier. The most dangerous was for agents wearing protective rubber clothing to crawl under the wire or climb over it using wooden ladders. Peasant farmers who worked the land adjoining the fence could be bribed to throw messages over, wrapped in mud. One of the most successful methods was the use of carrier pigeons.

Myths quickly grew up around the birds and their role. One was that it had been noticed that the pigeons followed the Rhine, or the railway between Amsterdam and Thorn. It was rumoured that the British had developed tiny cameras that were light enough to be attached to the birds' tails. The cameras were fitted with clockwork mechanisms that were timed to expose film at regular intervals. In this way, it was thought they could obtain an almost continuous set of photographs of the Rhine and the railway. Another myth put about by Sigismund Best was that he had succeeded in crossing the pigeons with parrots and that the resulting offspring were able to give verbal reports. Best intended this as a joke but the general to whom he told it became furious and reported him for divulging information that was 'most secret'.

As well as the activities of the leading spies, there were many other acts of courage along the fence. For example, one 14-year-old peasant girl called Marie used her age and innocence to become a messenger, in full view of the guards. She was the daughter of Belgian farm labourers who lived near one of the official crossing points in the electric fence. The crossing was guarded by a middle-aged soldier who had not seen his family for a year. Marie reminded him of his own daughter and he befriended her. Marie told him that she had an uncle on the Dutch side who wanted to give her food to supplement her family's meagre rations. The guard could see no harm in granting the child's request and allowed her to meet her uncle. She returned with food, some of which she gave to the guard. What he did not realise was that Marie was also acting as a courier for the underground. For two years, Marie smuggled messages twice a week under the affectionate and trusting eyes of the guard. In the end she was caught, tried and condemned to death. The sentence was commuted to life imprisonment. The young girl survived the war and on her return home she became a local heroine.

By May 1915 Marie Birckel was in Laon, in northwest France, where to her astonishment she found herself on a list of people who the German Kommandantur had agreed should be repatriated to unoc-cupied France, a journey which would take her through Switzerland. After a journey of five days she arrived in Geneva and for the first time came into contact with a member of the French secret service. The officer was impressed by the amount of information that she appeared to hold in her head. She could remember enemy positions, munitions dumps, transit camps and airfields near her village of Variscourt; she could identify the numbers of regiments, where they seemed to be going and what they appeared to be doing. Much of her information was now out of date, but it was remarkable, he thought, that she could remember all the things she had seen in nearly six months of travelling as a refugee.

She was also interrogated by the head of the German secret service in Switzerland, a clever man skilled at detecting agents. She told him she could remember nothing, had seen nothing; in fact, she was so wearied by the months of moving about that she had forgotten almost everything that had happened to her. She wondered whether perhaps the sheer joy of being free from the occupiers had caused her to lose her memory. He was fooled; all he could see was a petite young woman with attractive dark eyes who had been a governess and had the wit to get herself out of occupied France.

From Geneva she went to Paris where she made contact with two senior Allied secret service officers. She fell ill and was forced to spend a fortnight in bed. When she recovered she became impatient to serve her country and help bring the war to an end. She felt she was wasting her time, idling in Paris. She asked her intelligence contacts why they did not send her back to occupied France as a spy. They revealed that this was exactly what they were considering. The area they had in mind was Hirson, one of the most important railway junctions in Europe, now being used by the Germans to transport troops, supplies and ammunition along the front line. Allied intelligence services had so far failed to set up a train-watching unit there. She was, they said, the ideal person to establish a surveillance network, but the problem was: how were they going to insert her?

A plan to send her in by aeroplane had been refused. Other ideas followed, including going to Switzerland to ask the German consul to let her back into occupied France to look after members of her family. This was tried but the Germans turned the application down. Later the intelligence officer reported that he admired her courage and the fearless way she faced the mission she was to be sent on.

A 27-year-old woman, Louise Derache, was regularly crossing the border from Holland into Belgium. She sold butter and was allowed to travel between the two countries. She carried the butter in a large, heavy wicker basket. The basket had a false bottom in which were concealed passports. She was an agent working as part of a group known as the 'Lenders Service', named after the man who had started the organisation, Justin Lenders. The group, seven people in all, monitored German troop movements and the information they gathered was taken to British Intelligence by Louise in her basket.

The group had been penetrated by a double agent, working as a courier. One April day Louise was followed by the police and arrested. All the other members of the group were arrested at the same time and taken to the Saint-Léonard prison in Liège. On 5 June they were tried, found guilty and condemned to death. That night they were taken to the prison block at Fort Chartreuse outside Liège. The Germans were worried that there might be demonstrations or a rescue attempt so the prisoners were taken in covered lorries normally used to transport rations.

Early on the morning of 7 June 1915 they were taken from their cells and led through a white-painted arch to the execution ground, where they were blindfolded and tied to wooden posts. The firing squad had not been told that one of the victims was a woman and the discovery upset them. On command they fired; the men slumped forward, dead. Louise had been shot in the leg and was still alive, writhing in agony. She was then shot in the head. A priest performed the last rites; the bodies were placed in coffins and buried in the grounds of the fort. The eight dead Belgian citizens were the first to be executed on the charge of espionage. Louise Derache was the first woman to die in front of a firing squad. On the night before her execution Louise wrote to her mother asking her to look after her 6-year-old daughter.

More posters appeared on the walls of the town declaring that the dead were 'members of an organisation that transmitted to the enemy regarding movement of German troops on the railways under military control'. The intelligence officers at GHQ were shocked by the executions. The Lenders Service had been under their jurisdiction.

In June Edith Cavell wrote to her mother saying that Jack, the stray dog she had adopted, was 'well and more attached to me than ever. He won't leave me now even to go for a walk with Gracie – he takes no notice of the Germans but passes them with a sublime indifference like all the Belgians.' While a young woman Edith had worked as a governess to a well-to-do Belgian family. As a diversion she wrote a pamphlet on dogs and illustrated it herself with watercolours. The pamphlet was detailed and comprehensive. In it she asserted that a dog will respond to small kindnesses and instinctively 'take upon himself the duty of protector'. When writing the pamphlet 28-year-old Edith could have had no idea that her future self would own a dog that would prove the truth of her words in such dramatic circumstances.

Edith was now having difficulty with the soldiers who passed through her hospital. They were lodged in a room at the top of the house, which was 36 feet long and 9 feet wide and lit by a single skylight. The furniture was simple, scrubbed wooden tables and benches, with heating supplied by a stove standing in the centre of the room, which housed about eighteen men. Edith visited them regularly in the evenings and was known to them all as Sister Edith.

She told the soldiers that they could go out in the evenings provided they left the hospital singly or in pairs. She warned them to stay away from the main thoroughfares and not to speak English within earshot of strangers. She told them that she could not enforce these rules because they were soldiers, not prisoners.

She emphasised the danger they were in by turning out the lights and pulling up the skylight blind. On the other side of the road they could see German officers relaxing, playing cards and drinking. The building housed their command post.

One evening she heard a noise outside and was shocked to realise that it was the voices of drunken Irish soldiers singing 'It's a Long Way to Tipperary', their nailed boots clattering on the road. One of the doctors got them back into the building and locked the doors. The next day they were taken out of the hospital and sent to houses around the district.

The hospital was partly funded by the efforts of Edith's close friend Marie Depage, whose husband had asked Edith to set up the school. Early in 1915 Marie got permission to travel to America to raise funds for the Red Cross. Marie's message to the Americans was that the biggest conflicts of the war lay in the future. She was convinced that there would be tens of thousands of casualties from all sides and that Belgium would be devastated, a ruined country with nowhere to even shelter the wounded. She called for the Red Cross to prepare hospitals equipped with beds, linen and equipment, and to have transport ready, plus a fund of money to buy emergency supplies and fuel. Her work in the United States raised $150,000 in cash and supplies, nearly $5 million in today's money. Her trip had been a success and she set off back across the Atlantic to Belgium.

She boarded the *Lusitania*, nicknamed the 'Greyhound of the Sea', heading for Ireland. She had planned to travel on another ship, the SS *Lapland*, but had changed her mind at the last minute. Indefatigable, she continued to raise money from among the passengers.

All the passengers had been warned by the German embassy that a state of war existed between Germany and Great Britain and that the zone of war included the waters around the British Isles. The imperial German government had given formal notice that vessels flying the flag of Great Britain, or any of her allies, were liable to destruction and that travellers sailing into the war zone on the ships of Great Britain or her allies did so at their own risk.

At 2:10pm on 7 May, 10 nautical miles off the Old Head of Kinsale in Ireland, a German U-boat commander, Captain Schwieger, ordered his crew to surface to perform a routine battery recharge. As the vessel surfaced he saw the starboard side of the *Lusitania*, the ship heading east for home and safety. He fired a torpedo which hit the vessel just behind the bridge. After the detonation of the torpedo he heard another boom and imagined that it must be a boiler blowing up.

He did not know, and nor did most of the people on board the *Lusitania*, that there were millions of rounds of .303 ammunition stored in the hold disguised as crates of butter and tea. After the two explosions the great ship rapidly lost power and began to list. In the radio room the wireless operator transmitted the Morse code for SOS, asking for immediate help. Water poured in, shorting the electricity. The lifts stopped, trapping hundreds of people below decks in pitch dark, struggling to escape the freezing water that rose up through the ship. The crew struggled to launch the lifeboats but the ship was now at such an angle that many of them were smashed to pieces against its side. Six were launched in the eighteen minutes it took the liner to slide beneath the waves. Schwieger watched as the stern vanished, carrying the ship's name in golden letters: *Lusitania, Liverpool.*

Nearly 2,000 passengers and crew died in the screaming chaos of those last minutes. Marie tried to jump into a lifeboat as it swung from the davits but she tangled in the ropes, struggling to save herself as the ship pulled her down. By 2:35pm the ship had disappeared, leaving the survivors bobbing in the spring sun. A rescue tugboat sailed from nearby Queenstown, County Cork. Among the bodies it picked up was that of Marie Depage. Her death caused Edith deep sorrow but her work with the fugitive soldiers could not stop.

Towards the end of 1914, Gabrielle Petit's fiancé, Maurice Gobert, had been wounded and taken to Antwerp. He escaped from hospital and went into hiding, planning to get back to France to rejoin his regiment. Somebody wrote a letter to the German authorities denouncing him; it was signed 'Gabrielle Petit'. No one knew whether she had written the letter but in revenge Gobert's sister wrote to the authorities saying that Gabrielle had helped her brother escape and gave them the address in Brussels where Gabrielle was staying. On the evening of 12 July 1915 Gabrielle was arrested. When she was told that if found guilty she was to be sent to prison in Germany she retorted that at least in Germany she would see Belgian soldiers and that the German soldiers in Belgium were trash.

The officer who arrested her took a locket from around her neck in which she kept a picture of herself. When she asked him why he had taken it, he refused to answer. She told him, 'When you return to Sauerkrautland you should show the picture around because it shows a Belgian woman who has guts.'

She was also wearing a brooch with a portrait of King Albert and she asked her close friend Marie Collet to take it away as she did not want her king to have to spend the night in the Kommandantur. Two days later she was released for lack of evidence. At home she found that her room had been ransacked and that all her letters had been confiscated.

In spite of this, by 20 July Gabrielle had received permission through the Red Cross to travel from the Netherlands to France via Folkestone in Britain. She claimed her journey was to raise money for the Red Cross, but actually she hoped to be reunited with her fiancé and to become a nurse in a field hospital. She sailed on 22 July. On the boat she was approached by a tall man in his late twenties. His name was Joseph Ide, the agent working for British Intelligence who had been recruited by Sigismund Best.

By the time she arrived in London, Petit too had agreed to work for British Intelligence. Later, Ide visited her at the Empire Hotel in St Martin's Lane, Covent Garden. To her surprise he told her that she would be reimbursed of all her travel expenses. Then she was taken to the Basil Street offices where her training began. Ide was very impressed with her dedication, finding her intelligent and with a keen desire to learn.

Earlier in her life Gabrielle had written to her godfather asking him to contribute to her education:

For six years now I have had in my mind the unsinkable desire
to study, but there is no money for that and I feel that if I cannot
study, life for me will be nothing but misery.

She asked him for 2,400 francs to cover her classes for four years and said that 'you have my *formal* promise ... I will pay you back ...' She also promised that she would work hard and be an exemplary student. In the end she did not receive any education after she turned sixteen. Now British Intelligence were helping her realise her dreams.

For the next fortnight Gabrielle Petit packed her notebooks with details of military units, insignia, and the loading and identification of troop trains. Her training included the identification of units by their regimental badges; methods to assess the strength of units travelling by train. She knew that a carriage could carry fifty men, eight horses or six field guns. She had been told how to identify fuel depots, powder stores, the different sorts of artillery, howitzers and field guns; what sort of readiness the troops were in – were they active reserves or second-line reserves? – their health and their morale. For the first time in her life Gabrielle was respected, getting the education she had so craved, and was properly paid.

She wrote to her fiancé, Gobert, who had now escaped Belgium and was in the Netherlands, saying she no longer intended to enrol in a field hospital because she had found something much more useful to do. She could not tell him, she wrote, what her role was but soon he would know everything and would be proud of her. She asked him as well to pray that nothing bad happen to her because there was danger everywhere. She promised that if she succeeded in her work she would ask his superiors to give him leave and that they would spend it together. She ended, 'Dearest fiancé, be brave, very prudent, and pray for us.'

On 2 August she took a written examination in which she did well. The next day she left London on her journey back to Belgium. She again wrote to her fiancé reminding him to be brave and prudent and to remember the ever-present danger. She signed off as she usually did:

> My good and dear little one, be brave, think of she who aspires
> to see you again and who kisses you with all her soul,
>   Your faithful and devoted fiancée, Gaby.

Her future husband was not impressed. He thought she had joined 'some English special service'. He ignored the letter and never contacted her again.

Gabrielle wrote one last letter to her fiancé, again asking him to 'pray for me as I pray for you' and signed it 'Your future wife who loves you with all her soul ... Yours only for life.'

She proudly announced to her godmother Hélène Ségard, who was also her aunt, that she had received 'military instruction' and had passed out of the impromptu course at 'spy level', adding that she now knew how to write intelligence reports and that what had been required of her was the ability 'to sacrifice yourself usefully'.

CHAPTER NINE

CIVIL DISOBEDIENCE AND THE POLICE

By the summer of 1915 Brussels was described as 'a beautiful, impulsive, edgy, hate-filled capital' and its inhabitants were 'full of absolutely blatant hostility, wearing the national colours large as saucers on hats, buttonholes, umbrellas and cravats'.

Independence Day in Belgium, 21 July, was a public holiday. In the weeks before, the German governor general, von Bissing, had ordered posters to be pasted to the walls of the city forbidding all celebrations, including the hanging of national flags and the wearing of ribbons in the patriotic colours of red, yellow and black. The Germans claimed that the population of Brussels had 'in many cases actively aided enemy intelligence'.

The citizens adopted a new symbol, an ivy leaf bearing the slogan *'Je meurs où je m'attache'* – 'I die where I grow'. They also decided to make the 21st a day of mourning. In the clandestine paper *La Libre Belgique* the city was invited to a Te Deum in the cathedral. Leaflets went from hand to hand asking people not to work, to lock up the shops, to pull down blinds and to close shutters. Von Bissing countered by declaring that such actions were illegal and would be punished.

At dawn on Independence Day the city lay silent, all but a few German-run hotels and bars were closed. There was an increased military presence and armoured cars spent all day driving round the streets. People walking to the cathedral were greeted by women handing out ivy leaves and tiny bouquets in the national colours. In the packed cathedral the congregation sang the 'Brabançonne', the national anthem. The same thing happened in churches all over the city. The Belgian colours of red and yellow appeared everywhere. Thousands of red and yellow flowers were sold, fixed on a black background. Three girls, dressed respectively in red, yellow and black, appeared on a balcony in the boulevard Anspach. They waved while the crowd cheered and clapped, then, before the soldiers could intervene, they vanished.

In the centre of the city, the place des Martyrs was suddenly full of people. The police were called out and, in the crowded rue Neuve, German soldiers were posted at 5-yard intervals. Some 250 men formed up in the place de Brouckère. People stared into the sky. High above them a huge toy balloon floated in the air. Written on its sides were the words '*Vive la Belgique*', along with the French tricolour and the Union Jack. The crowd roared its approval, tram drivers beat a tattoo on their bells. Furious German soldiers fired at the balloon, which was hit, deflated and sank to the ground, its job done. A report of the demonstrations appeared in *La Libre Belgique*, Issue 37.

Meanwhile, millions of men lived, suffered and died in the line of trenches that now stretched from the Channel to the Swiss border. An enormous amount of supplies was needed to keep them fed, clothed, watered and equipped with ammunition. All stores for the German army were brought up and held in what was known as the 'rear area'. In Belgium, this huge complex occupied about a third of the entire country. Here soldiers lived in comparative peace, and although the rear area was regularly bombed and shelled, it was nothing like the misery of the trenches.

Belgian civilians living in these areas were under military authority. Their houses and crops were requisitioned to help supply the troops. For the military, civilians were a burden and all were potential spies. They were controlled with fierce local laws, strict curfews and harsh punishments.

As the front line changed with the ebb and flow of battle, so did the rear area. Moving about was difficult and got progressively more difficult the nearer to the trenches one came.

Away from the front line, the rest of the country was governed by German authorities, both civilian and military, known as the German Government General.

By now resistance in Belgium was pitted against three forces: the secret field police, the military police and the political police. The secret field police were responsible for the front line, the staging posts and naval installations in occupied northern France and western Belgium, and the naval installations along the coast.

The military police were responsible for the rest of Belgium, which included Brussels where over a thousand officers were stationed. There were large numbers of troops patrolling the railways.

Smaller, more dangerous and much more difficult to detect were the political police. By July 1915 there were just over one hundred officers, supplemented by German civilians who had lived in or knew Belgium. The political police also used a large number of Dutch, Belgian and French informers. Among other things the political police were on the alert for movement across the frontier with Holland, the hiding of Allied soldiers, smuggling, and the distribution of subversive material like *La Libre Belgique*. By the end of 1915 forty-five Belgian agents had been captured and executed, and many more arrested.

The undercover satirists of the subversive newspaper *La Libre Belgique* soon became the subject of an investigation by the political police. At the centre of this organisation, in an office in Brussels, was a tall, red-faced, 40-year-old lieutenant called Bergan, the head of espionage. His eyes glared out from under his dark, bushy eyebrows which hovered above his large, fleshy nose. His second-in-command was the chief officer of criminal investigations, Sergeant Henri Pinkhoff, a sinister-looking man with a purple birthmark across the left-hand side of his face. Bergan spoke no French but Pinkhoff was fluent, and he also spoke nearly perfect English. After spending some time in the British Army he had lived in Paris for fifteen years posing as an umbrella salesman while actually working for the German secret service.

Bergan and Pinkhoff spent much of their time making lists of suspects, which included the de Croÿs, Louise Thuliez, Herman Capiau and especially Edith Cavell, with whom they had become obsessed. They said of her, '*Die Cavell müss an die Mauer gehen*' – 'Cavell must go in front of the firing squad!' They were soon joined by another agent, Otto Mayer, who had worked at the Café Royal in London. He had spent eighteen years in India, and for a while was employed as the catering manager to the maharaja of Baroda. Mayer was another linguist, speaking French, English and Hindustani. His wife was Belgian and worked as a governess in Brussels, and it was this that had brought him to the city. Bergan immediately assigned Mayer to watch Edith.

Mayer's first ploy was to visit Bellignies and call on the Princess de Croÿ. On meeting her he claimed to be an escaped British soldier and that he had heard she could help him get out of Belgium to rejoin his regiment. She told him that he was quite wrong, she knew nothing of escaping soldiers, was concerned for the future of her country, and besides he would only bring trouble upon her. His best course, she advised, was to give himself up to the German military police.

Later, another German undercover agent appeared, this time at Edith's hospital. His name was Georges Quien, masquerading as an officer with a wounded foot. His orders were to draw up a list of people working in the resistance. Quien had once spied against the French and at the start of the war had been a prisoner in Saint-Quentin in Picardy. He was freed by the Germans and began working for them. He was tall, thin, blue-eyed, soft-spoken and charming. He was also a fantasist, devious, cunning, a liar and a thief. He seduced everyone with whom he came into contact, including Edith's staff. He stayed in the hospital for two days and, on the day he left, three strange men were seen talking to employees working in the kitchen garden. In the days that followed several more German agents called at the hospital, all pretending to be prisoners of war on the run and asking for help.

Cavell and her comrades were aware of the risks they were taking. Edith summed it up, saying, 'If we are arrested we shall be punished in any case, whether we have done much or little. So let us go ahead and save as many as possible of these unfortunate men.' The number of 'unfortunate men' arriving at the hospital was growing every day.

Soon, yet another agent appeared at the hospital. This one was called Jacobs. He claimed to have escaped from a prisoner of war camp near Maubeuge and that he had heard from people living near Mons that he could expect help from Cavell. She took him in, looked after him for a week and then sent him off with a group heading for the border, unaware of his true identity and intentions.

In mid-June Otto Mayer reappeared. This time he called at the hospital and showed his police badge. As Edith was away, he was received by Sister Wilkins, the French-speaking English nurse who had joined Edith in 1912. He asked her if she had any Tommies on the premises. She told him she had no idea what he was talking about, knowing that above their heads was a room in which four British soldiers were hiding. She said, 'If you don't believe me you had better come into my own room, and you can search my desk if you want.'

This he did and found nothing. Then he ordered her to show him the patients. Wilkins knew that on Edith's desk there were records of the soldiers they had helped. As she led Mayer into a ward with genuine patients she managed to whisper to a nurse that the man with her was a German secret policeman. While Mayer toured the ward the hidden soldiers were bundled out of a window, one in slippers and shirtsleeves.

Unaware of what was happening, Mayer demanded to see the hospital medical records. As he slowly sifted through them he did not notice Wilkins leaving him, unaware that she had gone into Edith's office, scooped up all the papers on her desk and taken them to the lavatory on the landing where she stuffed them into the cistern. She then rejoined Mayer, who now ordered her to show him where Edith worked.

When he had finished his examination of the building and its records he ordered Wilkins to come with him to his headquarters and there questioned her for three hours before releasing her.

When Edith heard what had happened she burned her diary, address book and records of the men she had helped. The next day Mayer appeared again, this time with four officers who searched the premises and again found nothing. After that the hospital was searched time after time but nothing was found.

Edith wrote to her mother, whose birthday was coming up on 6 June. In the letter she said:

> Do not forget if anything very serious should happen you could probably send me a message through the American Ambassador in London (not a letter).

The constant harassment and the feeling of being watched began to tell on everybody. One of the doctors noticed that Edith was jumpy, tense and preoccupied, even in the operating theatre, often going to the window and peering round the curtain into the street. At Bellignies the princess too complained that she was disturbed by the slightest noise, even the falling of a leaf in the garden. She came to the conclusion that they had to stop and went to Brussels to inform Edith of her decision. When she arrived Edith was dealing with patients. Eventually her dog Jack bounded in, followed by his mistress. Edith spent a moment staring at her visitor, who noticed that the matron was standing very straight, her large earnest grey eyes seeming to penetrate into the princess's very soul. Then, in a quiet, dignified and authoritative manner, Edith said, 'I wish you hadn't come. I am evidently suspect. Look at those men cleaning the square in front; they must have been there several days and are scarcely working at all. They must be set to watch the house.' Her hushed, gentle voice stopped and silence fell between the two women.

Then the princess told Edith that the chateau at Bellignies had been searched and that she had come to tell her they must stop the work. Edith said, 'I also had a search party yesterday. I heard the footsteps downstairs and only had time to throw some papers in the grate, pour alcohol over them and set them alight. Then the Germans came in and began searching the room. Now all my records are gone. How shall I explain to Dr Depage how I have spent his money?'

The princess told her not to worry, she would vouch for her, and said that in any case no one could possibly doubt her integrity. But they must, she insisted, stop the work.

Edith hesitated, about to agree, then asked: 'Are there any more hidden men?'

The princess replied that Louise Thuliez had found thirty more.

'Then we cannot stop, because if a single one of those men is taken and shot that will be our fault.'

When the princess left, Edith described the precautions she must take on leaving the hospital. She was to go to the end of the street to the patisserie next to the tram stop. She was to hesitate outside the shop as if deciding whether to go in. When she heard the tram bell announcing it was about to leave she must jump on at the last minute. That way, said Edith, anyone following her would be thrown off guard. The princess did exactly as she was told.

Later, Edith found more incriminating evidence which she took to a nearby café, Chez Jules, where the owner was a friend and where the refugee soldiers used to go and pass time in comparative safety. Together they hid the papers under a floorboard near the bar.

The flamboyant distributor of *La Libre Belgique*, Philippe Baucq, was also feeling the net closing in on him. On 27 July 1915 he went to his favourite bistro, Chez Oscar, five minutes' walk from his house, to play cards with his friends. When the game ended he rose to leave, turned to his friends and said, 'I don't think you will see me in here again.' On 29 July he told his daughter, to whom he was very close, that he would like to take her for a walk. He explained that things were not going well and that he expected to be arrested in the near future. He explained how she should behave if she were questioned about him. She must plead complete ignorance, nothing must interfere with her studies, and especially her music.

A few days later, on 31 July, Louise Thuliez arranged to meet six metalworkers in a café near the Gare du Midi in Brussels. The men wanted to leave Belgium and needed her help to cross the border with Holland. She had made a reservation for a room in a small hotel where she planned to take the men before sending them on their way across Belgium to the frontier. Earlier in the day she had met Baucq to finalise the arrangements for the crossing. Their meeting took longer than she'd planned and he invited her to come and stay the night at his house once she had dealt with the metalworkers. She agreed, then made her way on foot back to the Gare du Midi to wait in the bistro. Time passed slowly; by ten o'clock the men had not appeared and she gave up. Tired, she took a tram outside the pillared entrance to the station and in a few minutes was knocking on the door of Philippe's house. He opened it and ushered her in. She was astonished to find his wife and niece packing up thousands of copies of Issue 37 of *La Libre Belgique*, which had a full account of the events in the centre of Brussels on Independence Day.

When she asked him why he was taking such a risk he laughed and assured her that it was perfectly safe. Much safer, in fact, than keeping them in the secret room where the journal was printed.

Baucq decided to take his German shepherd dog, Diane, for a walk. At the door the animal began to growl. As he opened it, Baucq was confronted by Henri Pinkhoff and a band of undercover police-men. They looked like grotesque parody gangsters, wearing hats pulled down over their eyes and scarves tied round their faces. The men barged past him. Diane snarled and snapped. The house was suddenly full of burly, aggressive men. Pinkhoff shouted for Baucq to pay attention, yelling that there were soldiers in the street. Louise Thuliez panicked and ran up the stairs carrying her handbag, which contained evidence that could get her shot if it were discovered. A man stormed after her, grabbing the bag as she tried to hide it behind the iron bath. He gripped her by the arm and forced her downstairs, where she found Baucq had been arrested.

In the attic Baucq's 13-year-old niece had forced open a window and was trying to hide copies of *La Libre Belgique* on the window ledge. Some were bound in bundles which slipped and fell three storeys, thudding onto the road among the soldiers who were guarding the outside of the house. The men were astonished to be bombarded by great lumps of newsprint. They looked up and saw unbound copies fluttering down like giant confetti. A member of Pinkhoff's gang flew into the room, grabbed the girl and dragged her struggling from the window. She too was dragged downstairs to be interrogated. Pinkhoff shouted at her to tell him her age and, when she said that she was thirteen, he demanded to see her birth certificate. She showed it to him and to his exasperation it confirmed her age. She was a minor and could not be arrested. Pinkhoff was furious, screaming at the girl that she was very rude.

The men continued to search the house, breaking furniture and scattering books and possessions. Pinkhoff took Baucq into another room to interrogate him. He tried not to admit anything. Thuliez was questioned; she claimed that her name was Mme Lejeune and that she had left her husband and could not remember her new address. The men said, in that case they would be happy to find her accommodation in the prison of Saint-Gilles.

Just before one o'clock in the morning Baucq and Thuliez were thrown into a car and driven through the dark, genteel suburbs to a police station where they found an angry Lieutenant Bergan waiting for them. He barked that his men had found copies of the illegal newspaper, plus other seditious literature and lists of names. He told them that, in Louise Thuliez's handbag, they had found a receipt for sixty-six francs for the 'lodging of six men for four days'.

The disorientated pair were placed under arrest, forced into another car and soon were driven through the forbidding entrance to Saint-Gilles prison. There they were formally charged with espionage, circulating seditious literature and prohibited newspapers, and helping Allied soldiers.

As dawn broke the next day another raid was mounted on Baucq's house. More incriminating evidence was found. Meanwhile, the coded messages in the notebook in Thuliez's handbag had been deciphered, revealing the addresses of many of the people associated with her activities.

Two days later Baucq was taken to be interrogated by Pinkhoff and Bergan. They told him that his niece had confessed and threatened that he should do the same or face the direst consequences. They shouted at him to take his hands out of his pockets and to be polite. Then they demanded to know if the name Reginald de Croÿ meant anything to him. They bombarded him with more names. When they'd finished he was dragged back to his cell, feeling as though he had gone to bed drunk and woken bewildered, with a bad hangover.

At Bellignies, the princess's brother heard what had happened and went to Brussels to warn Edith Cavell. She had now destroyed all remaining incriminating evidence, including newspapers and the diaries she had filled with her activities, written in tiny letters. Cavell warned the prince himself that he too needed to escape. He thought she looked exhausted.

On 4 August a German officer arrived at the hospital. He searched Cavell's office and asked her if she was in touch with London; they were particularly interested in any letters she had received. Then he left. The next day Henri Pinkhoff and Otto Mayer arrived. Again they ransacked her office; all they found was a letter from England that had been sent through the American legation, but it was enough. Edith and Sister Wilkins were arrested.

They were taken, in separate cars, for interrogation at the Kommandantur. Sister Wilkins watched Cavell walking ahead of her, her slight body erect, her demeanour calm.

CHAPTER TEN

INTERROGATION

Sister Wilkins was told that there was no point in her denying anything. They knew that men – soldiers and agents – had been using the hospital and that Edith Cavell had been paying for guides to lead the way across the border into Holland. To her amazement, Wilkins was allowed to go back to the hospital. When she found out that Edith Cavell was being detained at the Kommandantur she became hysterical. From then on Wilkins and the other nurses were kept under armed guard. They were allowed to carry on with their nursing duties but needed permission to leave the building.

Edith was held in a crowded women's cell in the Kommandantur. The day after her arrest she wrote a letter telling the women to carry on with their hospital work and enquiring after Sister Wilkins. She asked for a red blanket, a napkin, cup, fork, spoon and plate, two towels and her toothbrush. In a day or two, she said, perhaps she could have some clean linen. She warned that they should not send any of the best plates. She also asked after her dog Jack. Finally she asked for a book, some embroidery, her nail scissors but nothing much else as she had nowhere to put things. She wished everybody well and hoped for the best.

When Sister Wilkins arrived at the Kommandantur with the blanket and other things Edith had asked for, the Germans laughed at her and insulted her. She felt, she said, 'as though we were engulfed in darkness'. On 7 August Edith Cavell was in a prison van heading for Saint-Gilles jail, where she was put in solitary confinement in cell 23.

In the quiet of the garden at Bellignies the princess and her brother were walking with their grandmother. The air was still and the period after lunch was one in which the Germans rarely visited the house. After a while they sat by a charming small lily pond. They stared at the large flat leaves that glistened in the sun and talked about a bud that had been growing for several days and which they hoped would flower any day. The grandmother said, 'It won't live; the lotus only grows where there is happiness.'

A few days later, on 24 August 1915, the princess saw an open car passing the gates. In the back were two armed German soldiers; sitting between them she was shocked to see Countess Jeanne de Belleville. The princess knew that her friend had helped nearly four hundred soldiers escape across the border. Whatever the danger, she seemed 'indefatigable . . . and exuded goodness'.

The princess began to look for places to conceal the false identity cards, letters and papers she had accumulated over the previous year. She hid the cards in her easel. The rest she put in tin boxes which she secreted in the ivy covering the old tower. At the same time it was decided that Reginald should go into hiding. He was taken in, under an assumed name, by the nuns of the nearby Clinique de Linthout.

Within days a search party of four men arrived. In a panic the princess took the cards from her easel and shoved them into a velvet cushion in the basket where her fierce little terrier, Vicky, slept. The soldiers searched the princess's painting equipment, squirting the coloured paints from their tubes, watched from her basket by the snarling Vicky. While three of the soldiers searched, a fourth took her into the hall. His French was perfect and his manner confidential. He shrugged and said it would be better to confess everything. The princess said she had no idea what he was talking about. In a low voice and in Walloon he advised her to disappear as soon as possible. The soldiers found nothing. They left and sealed off the village.

The next morning a long, open-top military car arrived. From it descended Pinkhoff and Bergan. They ordered the princess to accompany them to Brussels. They assured her that she need not pack anything as she would return that night; they raised their hands and declared to the princess's grandmother: 'We give our word she will return tonight.' Nevertheless, the princess asked her maid to pack some overnight things.

They drove her to the station where they caught the express to take them across the border into Belgium and on to Brussels. The two men gave her no peace, interrogating her for the whole journey. They insisted that many of her associates were already in custody and had confessed everything. The princess struggled to stick to the story that she knew nothing, had no idea what they were talking about, all the while trying to keep a clear head and fighting off fear.

When they arrived in Brussels they were met by another car and driven to the prison of Saint-Gilles, where she was taken to a waiting room. To her dismay she was greeted by other prisoners who broke the cardinal rule that they must not, under any circumstances, acknowledge each other.

Later, Jeanne de Belleville was brought in and her calm courage again impressed the princess. The day wore on and the princess asked if she could go home. She reminded them of their promise and pointed out that, as they had cross-examined her, what else was there for her to do? Pinkhoff told her that she was now implicated in crimes so serious that there was no question of her leaving. She was allowed to write a letter of protest to the governor general and then shown to a room with a bed which was made up with the linen she had brought.

A guard was placed outside her room. Below was the officers' mess from which drifted the deep male notes of men singing and laughing, getting drunk. Food was brought to her but she could not eat it. Worried sick about her old grandmother she tried to sleep. In the corridor the guard stamped up and down. All through the night she was disturbed by the sound of cars and police vans coming and going, discharging new prisoners. Eventually the princess gave up trying to rest and watched the sad scenes unfolding below her window as more new prisoners were led into captivity. In the morning she was told that the governor general had refused to accept her letter.

The prison itself was huge. From the courtyard a flight of broad stone steps led to a mock Gothic vestibule lined with granite pillars and balustrades. The building had five wings, each three storeys high, radiating out from a central hub and surfaced with black and white flagstones. The prisoners were led down these vaulted tunnels and locked in small cave-like cells. There they could only wait, their nostrils filled with the stench of stale cabbage and urine and their ears assailed by the constant clanging echoes of iron doors slamming shut, the rattle of keys and the sobbing of terrified inmates.

Each cell measured 3 yards long by 2 wide. To the left of the door was a tap with a metal bowl under it. In the opposite corner was a small cupboard holding another bowl and a beer glass. Almost everything in the room was made of metal, including a tin slop bucket. The floor was oak and the room was painted a grey paste colour. A window opposite the door could be opened a couple of inches, while an iron spike in the wall could be pulled to sound a bell to call for a doctor. The only decoration was a crucifix above an iron pull-down bed, which during the day turned into a table.

The prisoners were woken at five in the morning and at seven were given a half-bowl of coffee and a lump of bread. At eight they were visited by a sergeant who asked if everything was all right. The same man was allowed to sell them postcards and approved newspapers. At noon, lunch was served – a bowl of soup, potatoes, meat and beer. The knives, forks and plates were collected an hour later. At five in the afternoon came supper, another bowl of coffee, a lump of bread and a piece of cheese. Prisoners were also able to receive food delivered to the prison by friends or relatives. At eight forty-five in the evening a bell rang to signal that it was time to prepare for bed and a quarter of an hour later another bell rang to mark the end of the day. The corridors were patrolled through the night and the guards shone torches through spy-holes in the doors. When prisoners were taken from their cells they were led through the stone corridors wearing rough linen hoods over their heads with two holes cut for the eyes.

So the days passed. The princess watched as more and more people were arrested, many of them soldiers and young men of military age. In the courtyard a ridiculous figure strutted about, the *Feldwebel*, the sergeant major of the prison. In their cells the young men sang patriotic songs and one day they held up a large sheet of paper at a window with the words 'PRINCESS DE CROŸ?' written on it. When the princess nodded they clapped their hands without making a sound and began to hum the Belgian national anthem.

The princess did not know that after taking her away the Germans had visited her chateau several more times, searching, stealing and trying to intimidate her staff and grandmother. Eventually the old woman had a stroke and fell senseless to the floor. She never spoke again but lay in her bed staring at the door. Within a few days she was dead.

The princess herself began to haemorrhage small amounts of blood from her lungs. A German doctor visited her and asked her what she had been doing. She replied, 'Nothing but my duty, doctor, you would have done the same thing in my place.'

'No,' he shouted, 'women should have nothing to do with war; women should remain in their homes.'

'I was in my own home looking after my own people. It was your people who tore me away.'

The doctor stared at her and the princess realised that he expected her to receive the death penalty.

Edith passed her days in solitary confinement, worrying about her nurses, penning letters of encouragement, and on several occasions wrote, 'I am quite well and more worried about the school than my own fate.' She gave orders about the care of her dog, Jack, and was concerned that her students would fail their exams. Most of all she found comfort in the book that she had asked Sister Wilkins to bring her: Thomas à Kempis's *The Imitation of Christ*, for Edith the most important devotional work after the Bible. Edith had kept a copy by her side for the whole of her adult life. The same book had influenced John Wesley, and General Gordon had carried it into battle. It was described as 'an inspiration to sacrifice and humility and to the severest self-examination'. Anyone not under its influence would have missed a chance to become more humble and 'ambitious for purity of life'.

While Edith and her comrades endured their imprisonment and interrogation, Gabrielle Petit was on her way back to Belgium, her head swimming with the information that she had been made to learn. She had been told that, like Louise de Bettignies, she would report to the Cereal Company, the Allied intelligence cover organisation. Her area of responsibility stretched from Tournai to Lille. She must monitor German troops arriving at rear area staging posts and organise a communications network that could take the intelligence out of Belgium and into Holland, from where it could be analysed, collated, edited and sent on to GHQ in France. What she was not able to watch herself she must organise others to do. It was a huge task.

The girl who had once been so poor that she had lived on the streets and gone without food or clean clothes; whose family had found her angry and disorganised and had hinted that she had taken to prostitution in order to earn money; and whose employers had found her chaotic and impossible to work with, was now, for the first time in her life, trusted and respected, and had been given a vital job with a guaranteed income. She had become a small but significant player in the war.

On 17 August she headed for Brussels, to the home of her unofficial mother, Marie Collet, whom she asked to help her, making Marie the first part of her organisation. Gabrielle remembered how Marie Collet had looked after her before the war and taken her in when she was poverty-stricken. It was Gabrielle's turn to be able to say, 'Now that living becomes expensive, your daughter will be able to help you out a little.'

She told Marie Collet that her role was to become a receiving post for the orders that were soon to start arriving by courier from British Intelligence. Marie was also to hand over to the couriers the intelligence reports that Gabrielle would write twice a week. Marie agreed and enrolled her two sons to help.

The older woman was at first anxious for her young friend. The dangers, she insisted, were grave. Gabrielle blithely waved aside the problem. In London, she said, she had undertaken to be 'totally loyal'.

Her godmother Hélène Ségard also tried to talk her out of the dangerous world she was entering. This time Gabrielle shrugged, laughed and said, 'You only die once.' She knew that if any of them were caught they faced the death penalty. They all knew about the undercover cell that had been penetrated in Liège. Its members had been executed and they included a woman. No one was safe from the firing squad.

Gabrielle now set off for Tournai, her home town. The trains that civilians could travel on were few and far between. German military police patrolled the platforms and corridors demanding to see identity papers and travel permits. The 60-mile journey took hours. Trains were cancelled at the last minute and Belgian civilian passengers were forced to get off and wait for the next one, while German troop and military movements took precedence over everything.

At Tournai station, military police guarded all the exits and the queues to get past them were long and slow-moving as the sometimes semi-literate soldiers examined passes and identity papers. There was a constant flow of trains chugging in and out, steam hissing from cylinders, smoke belching from the coal-fired boilers. The pale faces of uniformed men stared from the windows, new arrivals from Germany not knowing what awaited them at the front. Soldiers swarmed everywhere, embarking, disembarking, swearing and being sworn at. The cacophony of train whistles, shouted orders, doors slamming was overwhelming and frightening. Eventually, Gabrielle found herself in front of a uniformed and armed man who took an age to examine her pass. Then she was through, hurrying out of the station onto the cobbled streets of the ancient town which had been captured the year before without too much damage to its many churches, its Baroque and Art Nouveau buildings. The winding streets all led to the Grand-Place, a huge square overlooked by a soaring, heavily built cathedral.

Her destination was a shop selling glassware run by the wife of her cousin Georges Delmeule. Again, risking all, she told him that she was now an agent working for the British and asked him for his help. Georges and his wife had lived in the town for years and were popular figures in the community. Many of their relations lived in the area and some knew and liked Gabrielle. Georges agreed to help her and the two began to make a plan of operation. Georges would cover for her when she was away. In return she would run errands for him and the wider family in Brussels. Georges thought that his 10-year-old son, also called Georges, could sometimes accompany Gabrielle as she roamed the country, playing the part of her young and ingenuous nephew being looked after by his doting aunt, a picture of innocence.

By the early evening everything was settled. Georges led her back to the station, opposite which was a small café with rooms where she could stay. From one of those rooms she could watch the comings and goings of the trains. She spent most of the night making notes and then set off on the most dangerous leg of her journey – the road to Lille, which meant moving deep into the rear area and approaching the lethal zone of operations, the front line.

In spite of the difficulty of moving about in the rear areas, Gabrielle claimed, 'I can weave my way through anything.' She took whatever transport she could, from the trams that crisscrossed Belgium and northern France, to farm wagons, bicycles and her own two feet. Eventually, via back roads, country lanes and fields, she reached Lille, a huge railway junction, and sent her godmother, Hélène Ségard, a message telling her, 'I have arrived.' Her work as a spy had begun. Her first mission was a triumph; she had found her way into areas that other agents had found impossible to penetrate.

Meanwhile, the network set up by Louise de Bettignies was flourishing. She was making twice-weekly visits to British intelligence officers, sometimes in Holland and sometimes travelling to England. The intelligence she gathered took a small team of officers several days to analyse. One British officer reported that her work was precise, and unsurpassed by any other network in Belgium. Her work included recording not only the exact position of gun batteries but thousands of other highly important details. He added that he and his colleagues admired and revered Louise; in fact, they adored her.

By August 1915, 'Oncle Édouard', actually Major Cameron, was pressing her to enlarge her network. Louise told Léonie Vanhoutte, whom she now called 'Minou', that the work was hard but was of real value and that they must try to do as asked. But the strain was beginning to tell. In September, Louise went to see her mother, her sister and other members of her close family. As she left she said, 'I wanted to see you all for the last time, for I feel the end is coming. I shall be arrested and shot.'

At the end of September Léonie Vanhoutte received a letter asking her to come to a café carrying a newspaper. There she met two men she did not know who talked to her about 'Alice', de Bettignies' codename, and asked her if she had any message she wanted taking to Holland. The men appeared friendly and to know all about her. They offered to help and arranged for a rendezvous the next day. Disturbed, Léonie went home to sleep.

At five the next morning three armed men broke into her room, and shone a torch in the sleeping woman's face, shouting, 'Wake up! Don't move or I fire.' They then turned the room upside down, hurling the contents of drawers onto the floor and examining her clothes in great detail. They pulled open her wardrobe, which contained her clothes and those of Louise de Bettignies. These too were pulled out and searched. Nothing was found and the men had no idea that the clothes belonged to two different women. Nor did they discover that, under her nightgown, Léonie had a small incriminating square of folded Japanese tissue paper tied on a ribbon round her neck. Finding nothing, they arrested her and took her to Saint-Gilles prison. She was interrogated for several days but revealed nothing. Then, unexpectedly, she was shown a photograph and asked if she knew who it was.

'No, I don't know this person.'

It was Louise de Bettignies.

*

On 23 September Gabrielle Petit's godmother received a message from a Van Tichelen, head of the Cereal Company, saying that he was surprised not to have heard anything from Petit. A courier had called three times and received nothing. She was ordered: 'Please give your correspondence to the bearer of the present message, or I will otherwise be forced to break off all commercial relations to my regret.' The next day she received a message telling her that three of Gabrielle's 'order forms' had been received and that 'let us hope that things will go much more smoothly from now on ... happy to hear that nothing fatal will happen to our friends'.

By now Petit had worked out a form of private shorthand which she would write onto cigarette papers, rolling them round tobacco to smoke if caught, or hiding them in the locket she wore round her neck, a present from her late mother. She covered the sheet in her small, neat handwriting, describing the presence of troops in the area, their uniforms and the number of wounded soldiers. In a diary entry which she mistakenly dated '31 September' she reported that there were almost no soldiers in Tournai, just a few reservists and small units guarding bridges. On the other hand, vehicles with red crosses painted on their bonnets were pouring in from the front full of very badly wounded men. Among the 'mutilated Boches' were British and French, 'they are very badly hurt'. She saw one officer who had lost his nose, his right arm and left leg. On one evening she reported that there had been a violent dogfight over the town with the pilots chasing each other towards the front.

In another report, dated 1 October, she described the citizens of Tournai making money by helping the Germans to fill sandbags. She also noted that every day trains full of wood and ammunition, especially gas-filled mortars, went off heading for Lille. Some of the reinforcements, she said, were just young boys.

By 2 October her report noted that almost all the military in Tournai had vanished and that the same was true of other nearby towns. Guns, ammunition and observation posts had all but disappeared. All that remained were soldiers burying the dead to the sound of military bands playing in the town square. She overheard some men saying that they thought they would soon be heading for the front line in the direction of Lens; others thought they were headed for Vimy. She noticed that they all had very full packs. Allied aeroplanes flying over Tournai were driven off with ack-ack fire.

What Gabrielle witnessed was caused by the battle that had been started by the Allies on 25 September at Loos. The British commanders wanted to break out of the trench system and bring mobility once more to the Western Front. Many of their soldiers were new, inexperienced conscripts. They had been tempted into the army by Lord Kitchener's campaign, with posters showing his face adorned with a huge handlebar moustache and the slogan 'Your Country Needs You'. Now, with only basic training, they waited in the trenches, while deep underground sweating sappers dug tunnels that finished below the German front line. They packed their handiwork with explosives and trailed wires back to the entrances, ready to be connected to batteries and detonated seconds before the advance began. Above ground men prepared cylinders containing 140 tons of chlorine gas. The battle began and the British clambered out of their trenches. The chlorine gas swirled around, engulfing friend and foe alike. British soldiers tore off their gas masks because they could not see through the steamed-up goggles. Rifleman Frank Edwards started his march towards the enemy kicking a football. Edwards fell with a bullet in his thigh, choking on the gas. Men fell in their hundreds, the attack faltered and the reserves were ordered forward. More men struggled, single file, along destroyed country lanes, slipping and sliding in the mud, sweating and cursing as the afternoon wore on and darkness came. The miles of telephone wires were cut by shellfire; now staff cars, motorcycle despatch riders and runners on foot struggled across the battlefield with handwritten orders, the only hope of controlling the fighting. Privates, sergeants, junior officers and generals alike died in the mire.

The battle resumed the following day; 10,000 men moved forward. Four hours later 8,000 of them were dead or wounded. German machine-gunners were sickened by the slaughter and stopped firing. In the air, target-spotter aircraft, equipped with wireless transmitters, directed the artillery while other planes dropped 100-pound bombs on troop trains, marshalling yards and railway lines. By 28 September the British were back on their starting lines; they had lost the battle and suffered 20,000 casualties. One general commented: 'From what I can ascertain some of the division did actually reach the enemy trenches, for their bodies can now be seen on the barbed wire.' The Germans called it the '*Leichenfeld von Loos*' – the field of corpses at Loos.

One hundred and twenty miles to the south stood the ruined cathedral of Reims, overlooking another battlefield. The ancient building's interior was broken by shellfire, its stained-glass windows shattered, its exterior blackened and scarred. Red Cross flags fluttered above its towers. From its ruined heights it was possible for military observers to look over the fields of Champagne, already the scene of one battle and soon to be the site of another.

On 25 September, the same day that British soldiers had trudged through machine-gun fire near Loos, twenty divisions of French soldiers stood hunched in nearly 30 miles of trenches. They were waiting for the artillery barrage to finish and the shrill call of whistles ordering them to climb out of the trenches and into the squalor of no-man's-land. At 9:15am the order came. In some parts of the line the troops were accompanied by their regimental bands, complete with flags flapping in the morning rain. The fighting went on until early November. By the end another 200,000 men were dead, wounded or captured, and almost nothing had been gained or lost by either side. The cathedral saw it all, implacable above the carnage.

By 4 October Gabrielle Petit had decided to return to Brussels. Her right hand was in a bandage and she reported that she had spilled some acid on it that she used to make invisible ink. Her thumb and little finger were the only ones that worked, she said, and added that it might be necessary to amputate her middle finger. Although she tried to joke about it, the acid burns were very painful and she was in agony. When, later in the day, she got to Brussels she was taken to a doctor who gave her some ointment and told her that there were likely to be complications. The next day she woke in greater pain and, as the doctor had predicted, the scarring was covered with an abscess. Gabrielle took the matter into her own hands and sliced the scab off, whimpering with pain as she did so. She redid the bandage and wrote a report that she had 'butchered' herself and expected to be better soon. Her dramatic self-treatment worked; the pain died away and her hand began to heal.

On her next journey to Tournai, Gabrielle was followed by a woman secret police agent. She managed to escape her and set off immediately for Lille. For the next few days she wandered the area in stages, by tram or on foot. She crossed the border into occupied France. There were soldiers everywhere. By 7 October she was back in Lille. Soldiers thronged everywhere, too many for her to guess the number. She reported that they were young and fit. There were machine guns sited in trees along the boulevards and even on the tower of one of the town's churches; wounded were pouring in, some from a railway accident, others from the front. All the villages were taken over by the troops, who were requisitioning food. The locals were short of everything.

The next day Gabrielle Petit was again in Tournai. She saw troops arriving from Lille on three-day passes before moving on to the front line at Ypres. Ammunition trains were also on the move. Each had fifteen wagons, expertly covered so that it was impossible to see what they contained. The church of Saint-Brice in Tournai now housed an observation tower. Every night trains full of troops arrived, officers stumbled out of their quarters to supervise departures and arrivals and were themselves sent off. Gabrielle found that the troops had been instructed not to talk to anybody about who they were or where they were going. The Germans were in the grip of spy fever, imagining that there were agents everywhere, and often they were right.

Getting her reports out of the country was difficult. The early ones went by barge along the Scheldt–Brussels canal steered by a Dutchman, a drunken river boat captain. The reports were hidden in the toilet, pushed behind a wall. The room was small, dark, hot and disgusting. So filthy that soldiers looking to search it could not enter without retching. After a while the captain disappeared; no one knew whether he had been arrested. His disappearance disrupted the message service.

Soon after he vanished, Marie Collet, whose house acted as a post office for incoming instructions and outgoing reports, was warned that a new courier had been recruited. Later she heard the sound of hobnailed boots on the stairs outside her apartment. She opened the door to reveal a 34-year-old peasant farmer. He told her that he had been hired to bring orders and take messages and that he would do this by crossing the Wire of Death, near which he lived. She said she was expecting him and let him in. He was soaking wet. She fed him, dried his clothes and then gave him the reports. These were written on flimsy rice paper which he hid in matchboxes, or even in the bowl of his pipe. After he had eaten some food, one of her sons took him across Brussels to pick up other reports and then he set off on the long journey back, about 70 miles. This ramshackle arrangement worked well for several weeks.

In Roulers Marthe Cnockaert's walk to work took her past the station, a large Edwardian building. She noticed that once a week an ammunition train stopped to be unloaded. It took twelve hours to unload the shells and bullets and transfer them to trams to be taken to the front. The train arrived on a different day each week. Marthe's work regularly took her to the station to supervise the loading of the wounded men she had been treating, sending them on their way to hospitals in Germany.

One day, as the train Marthe had helped to load pulled away, she told the ambulance driver who was waiting to take her back to the hospital that, as it was such a lovely day, she would walk home. The German officer in charge of the station, a small pudgy man in a smart uniform and highly polished boots, heard her saying this and offered her a cigarette. She refused, saying she could not smoke outside in public. The officer invited her to join him in his office and perhaps take tea with him. In the course of their conversation she saw a railway schedule indicating the date of the next ammunition train. On her way home from the hospital that evening she left a coded message with this information for Number 63.

Later she was visited by three officers from the military police. They followed her into her kitchen where they asked her to sit.

'Fräulein Cnockaert, we would like to know the whereabouts of Lucelle Deldonck. You know her, do you not?'

Another of the three leaned very close to her and said, 'Do not be afraid, Fräulein, just tell us what you know.'

She explained that she had not seen Lucelle since the day of the invasion when she had been taken from the cellar by the Germans; for all she knew, Marthe said, Lucelle might be dead.

The men pressed her: Had Lucelle been in this very room recently? Was Marthe sure? They protested that they did not want to arrest her, especially as she was doing such valuable work tending to the wounded. Finally they left.

The ammunition train arrived, on schedule, in the middle of the night. Marthe watched from the doorway of her house as searchlights probed the clouds and the ack-ack guns surrounding the station began to fire. Far above she saw a single aeroplane, caught in one of the lights. The firing increased; the building shook with the concussion.

A sudden flash of light from the station lit the whole sky, followed by the rumbling roar of a huge detonation. Marthe could hear screaming voices, shouted orders, running feet. The ammunition train had taken a direct hit. In the sky the plane climbed away and then lurched, flames coming from the fuselage. Marthe watched it plunge towards the ground, disintegrating as it fell. The station burned all through the next day and at the hospital Marthe bandaged the wounds of those who had survived the blast. She wondered if among them was the officer who had offered her tea and cigarettes.

The British aircraft appeared every day for a week to bomb Roulers, which was now an important camp for soldiers who had been on the front line. These aircraft earned the nickname the 'Seven

Sisters'. A rumour spread that soon the civilian population would be ordered to evacuate.

Through Canteen Ma, Marthe received a request to provide information about the naval defences in Bruges on the coast. Getting a pass to travel there was impossible; even the area near the coast was heavily guarded. Marthe thought it would actually be easier to travel to the Congo. Then she remembered that earlier in the war one of her uncles had received permission to move to a small farm he owned near the coast at Ruddervoorde, near Bruges.

One of the men staying at her father's café was a German captain who commanded a machine-gun unit. One night she gave him a piece of black-looking cake and some of her hoard of coffee. As he munched away on the near-inedible gift, she told him that she might have to be evacuated and that she was going to apply for permission to stay with her uncle at Ruddervoorde, but she had no way of transporting her possessions.

As she had hoped, he offered to take her stuff on one of his machine-gun carts, all she had to do was give directions. Marthe said the farm was very difficult to find, perhaps she could accompany the carriage? She could leave the furniture with her uncle and then return. He said this was impossible; it was already illegal for him to transport civilian goods on a military vehicle and he categorically refused to try to get her a pass. Then he had a brainwave – she could travel disguised as a German soldier.

The following night a wagon arrived driven by a soldier whose nickname was 'Silent Willy'. He had a uniform for her and some heavy ammunition boots. The uniform did not fit but was covered by a greatcoat. She coiled her hair under a forage cap.

As she changed, her father helped load the wagon with some of their possessions, a few innocent bits of furniture, some sheets and crockery.

The drive to Ruddervoorde took all night and involved passing several patrols and checkpoints. The dark and the disguise worked. At her uncle's farm they were fed and the driver said he was going to brush the horses and then sleep. With the furniture safely deposited they could return whenever she wanted. Marthe said she would like to spend the day with her uncle and asked if they could leave after nightfall.

Marthe spent the rest of the morning talking to her uncle and her two cousins, getting them to tell her as much about the area as possible. The Germans requisitioned a proportion of his produce, which he took to a depot outside Bruges and even onto the docks themselves. As a result he had been able to observe the Germans turning the city into a fortified naval complex.

He explained that since Bruges had fallen to the Germans the year before many people had fled the city, but that had been stopped and now they were virtual prisoners; food was short, tuberculosis had broken out and morale among the citizens was very low. Civilian traffic was virtually banned in the city, bicycle permits had been suspended and even loitering in the streets was forbidden. A recent edict demanded that owners of carrier pigeons must shoot them or themselves be shot. Most newspapers were forbidden, and there was a 10pm curfew. In the dock area the curfew was even earlier, starting at eight o'clock in the evening. As he talked, she realised just what a risk she had taken entering the Bruges area.

He went on to tell her that the enemy was building a huge dock connected to the canal system. One of the installations appeared to be for submarines. Her cousin had been there several times and was able to draw a sketch map of the installation. A lot of military equipment, including heavy guns and bridging material, was being brought by railway into Bruges. Artillery was also being set up in the surrounding woods.

By dawn the next day she was back in Roulers and that evening handed in a coded report of all she had learned about Bruges and the massive construction works. Later she was summoned to the office of the German town mayor. She was to come immediately and she wondered if she had been betrayed. An hour later she sat with an officer who had been joined by the mayor. They offered her wine and raised their glasses, toasting her and congratulating her on her award of the Iron Cross for her work in the hospital.

Later, one of the officers who was lodged in her parents' café told her that he had something very important to discuss with her and said: 'Will you come to my room, we can be sure of being alone there at any rate. Come, you can trust me, we have always been friends.' She followed him up the stairs, worried that she had been found out and that this was a prelude to arrest. Once in the room he offered her a cigarette and she sat on the bed.

He told her that he was a member of the German secret service. He said that as she had already won the Iron Cross for her work in the hospital, would she consider working for the fatherland? She did not know what to say.

He went on: 'I will trust you. Fräulein, have you ever had cause to suspect anyone of your acquaintance as a spy against Germany?' He went on to tell her that there were at least three Belgian agents working in Roulers and that one of them had been shot the night before. She wondered if he was referring to Number 63. He declined to tell her more.

She hesitated and then asked him what he wanted her to do. The officer then gave her instructions about whom she should watch.

'Understand, Marthe, I want results, and we are prepared to reward handsomely those who produce them.' Roulers, he said, had become a hotbed of espionage and he wanted her to help stamp it out.

Marthe stood up and said, 'I am going to bed now and I shall think about what you have said and the ways in which I can help you.'

In her room she thought about her dilemma. How could she provide enough information to the Germans without betraying her comrades and yet which was useful enough for them to trust her? Within the month the problem was solved; the officer who had approached her was dead, assassinated by the resistance.

One evening a stranger asked her if she could direct him to the Café Carillon. He was dressed like an agricultural worker but did not talk like one. She told him that the café was her home. He paused for a moment then said, 'So you are Laura?' He showed her the safety pins behind his lapel. They arranged to meet that night in a farm-house, where he told her that he was a Belgian officer and that his mission was to find out about the Lengenboom gun, a huge cannon, sited outside Moere, that was firing at targets 30 or 40 miles behind Allied lines. He had been dropped in by parachute and had got a job as a labourer on the emplacement. He now had plans of the site but had been wounded. He wanted her to help him destroy the gun. He had explosives and needed Marthe to organise a bombing raid as a diversion. Before the plan could be put into operation he was discovered by the German secret service and killed trying to escape.

CHAPTER ELEVEN

SUCCESS AND FAILURE

A few weeks after the arrest of Léonie Vanhoutte, Louise de Bettignies stood by a checkpoint outside the town of Tournai. She was with a companion and, although they both carried identity cards, they had only one passport between them. The passports were cardboard documents without photographs. They were difficult to acquire and were needed for almost every journey in the rear areas and in the zone of operations. While her companion waited behind, Louise approached the checkpoint, presented the passport and was waved through. A little further down the road she made contact with a scruffy boy whom she knew. The boy's father was a smuggler and the lad knew how to cross checkpoints and borders unnoticed. He was now part of Louise's network. Out of sight of the German guards she gave the boy the passport which he took back past the checkpoint without being seen. Then he gave it to Louise's companion, who in turn presented herself to the guards and was waved through. Minutes later she was reunited with Louise and, arm in arm, the two women started down the road into Tournai. They had not gone far when a voice ordered them to stop. They turned to see two men approaching; one was pulling a German police identification badge from his jacket pocket.

'German authority! Your papers please.'

'But we showed them over there.'

'If you have them I want to see them.'

Within minutes the two women were under arrest. Very soon Louise de Bettignies entered Saint-Gilles prison. As she passed through the arch she saw a black marble tablet fixed to the wall. The inscription read:

However great the Trials that Your
Sins have brought upon You,
Don't abandon Yourself to Despair,
Open Your Heart to Repentance.
Your Courage will return, Your
Sufferings will abate, and You
Will once more become Worthy
Of Esteem, of the Forgiveness
Of Men, and the Mercy of God.

On entering her cell she saw a crucifix on the wall which she took down and laid on the cell's simple table that doubled as a pull-down bed. Then she waited for her interrogation to begin. For the next few weeks she was threatened, beaten, confronted with Léonie Vanhoutte and told that her case was hopeless and that she and Léonie would be found guilty and shot. In spite of all this the two women revealed nothing.

In the solitude of her cell in the prison of Saint-Gilles, Edith Cavell pored over her copy of *The Imitation of Christ*, marking passages even though she knew them by heart. She paid especial attention to the passages concerned with the Christian life, self-discipline and patience, and some that dealt specifically with her own predicament. The book told her that she must live as a pilgrim on earth for 'this earth of ours is no lasting city'. It told her she must moderate longings and desires and submit herself to the will of God, and that like Jesus she must endure the loss of comfort and take up the cross. 'All flesh is grass', it said, and 'all glory shall fade like the flowers of the field'. It told her that when 'one is lost, that is when victory is close at hand'. In the silence of her cell she sought God's support, praying to him to help her endure and overcome the crisis she found herself in. She clung onto her faith as now, like her Lord Jesus who had led her all her life, she was to be sacrificed, her cell a new Gethsemane.

When it came to her turn to be interrogated, she was taken from Saint-Gilles prison back to the Kommandantur, where she was confronted by Lieutenant Bergan, the head of espionage, and Sergeant Pinkhoff, the chief officer of criminal investigations, plus two others, Sergeant Neuhaus and the agent Otto Mayer. The questioning was tortuous. Edith spoke French but not German, Bergan only spoke German. Sergeant Pinkhoff, therefore, acted as the translator and Neuhaus wrote everything down and served as a witness. She was questioned and answered in French; her replies were translated into German. The eventual deposition was presented to her in German, which she signed without properly understanding what it said. Part of the statement read: 'My statements which have just been read over to me, translated into French, conform to the truth at every point. They are perfectly intelligible to me in every detail and I will repeat them before the tribunal.'

First she was asked her name, job, place of birth. In the deposition she was described as 'well off'; questions about her character and credibility were annotated with a question mark. The document asked if she had a criminal record, beside which the words 'probably not' were written. Later, Lieutenant Bergan attached a notice to her statement which read: 'All our suppositions were confirmed by the deposition of the woman Cavell. In order to achieve this we made use of the trick of pretending that the information is already in the hands of the law.'

In her deposition she confessed that Prince Reginald de Croÿ, Louise Thuliez and several others had brought soldiers to her hospital, for whom she had made arrangements to cross the border into Holland. She also mentioned working with Philippe Baucq and many others.

She did not know that Bergan and Pinkhoff had arrested several of the others. Each was questioned separately. Baucq was fluent in French and German and knew what the interrogators were up to, 'the trick'. For six weeks he admitted nothing and refused to sign anything. In desperation Bergan placed a double agent in his cell who tricked him into talking about the people he had been working with.

Over the next few weeks Edith was interrogated twice more, each time signing a confession that she could not understand.

Soon Edith and all the people who had been arrested with her and her comrades had been interrogated and had signed confessions – there were thirty-five in all. A date was set for the trial, 7 October. Edith wrote to Sister Wilkins asking if she would bring from the hospital her blue coat and skirt, a white muslin blouse, her pair of thick reindeer gloves and her grey fur stole. These were the clothes she proposed to wear in court, not her matron's uniform.

When Louise Thuliez was questioned by the same men, she claimed that she had worked alone. She signed her deposition but later regretted having done so, especially as she had no idea what the German text said.

When the prison bell sounded at 5:30 on 7 October, the thirty-five accused prepared themselves. Edith put on the clothes that Sister Wilkins had brought her. In another cell, Albert Libiez, a lawyer, washed and dressed and read the notes he had prepared for his own defence. As seven o'clock approached he heard doors being opened on his corridor and names being called; he knew that the time had almost come. His cell door was thrown open with a clang, his name was called, and he walked out to join the others as they were led outside.

The corridor was lined with warders who came to attention and saluted, causing some of the prisoners to giggle nervously. Outside in the morning air stood a Black Maria, nicknamed *'panier à salade'*; a bus was parked next to it. Edith was told to get in the Black Maria; inside there were already several others. Finally, two armed men climbed in, pulled the doors shut and ordered them not to talk. The convoy moved off, heading for the Parliament building.

After about half an hour it pulled up at the rear of the huge ornate building. The accused were led out through heavy doors and along a maze of stone corridors and staircases. Soldiers guarded the route while court officials darted about. The passage through the building was dizzying and bewildering to the defendants, who had spent most of the last two months in solitary confinement, in narrow dark cells.

The back-stairs passages gave way to larger, grander corridors; the low murmur of a large crowd could be heard. The disorientated prisoners were finally confronted by high, polished wooden doors that swung open, and they walked into an enormous chamber, two storeys high and covered in gold, surrounded by pillars and larger-than-life oil paintings of dignitaries wearing the gilded trappings of power. All round the room sat men, many in German uniform, some peering through binoculars. The floor was covered in thick ornamental carpet, the air was hot and heavy. The prisoners were split up and grouped according to the severity of their crimes. The noise of chatter died away.

The six with the gravest accusations, the Princess de Croÿ, Philippe Baucq, Edith Cavell, Louise Thuliez, Herman Capiau and Jeanne de Belleville, were led to a line of gilded seats in front of the presidential dais. Several German men bowed to the princess as she passed. Then the prisoners were told to sit, each accompanied by two soldiers carrying rifles with fixed bayonets. The others were placed in two rows to the side, at right angles to the presidential dais, their defence lawyers sitting in front of them. The accused stared around the chamber, seeing some of their co-defendants for the first time. The noise in the court slowly grew as spectators began to mutter to each other, pointing to the accused, nodding, making observations about their terrible crimes and the even more terrible punishments that awaited them.

After a pause the sharp sound of a gavel hitting wood echoed round the colossal room. The spectators fell silent and the whole court – spectators, clerks and magistrates – rose to its feet in a rustling of gowns, and stood in respect for the judges who processed in. Five elderly men, wearing beautifully cut uniforms and all with the Iron Cross at their throats. Then came the chief military prosecutor, Dr Eduard Stoeber. One of the defence lawyers thought that Stoeber looked as though he was going to a military ball, with his

The people involved in the resistance came from all walks of life. Gabrielle Petit had worked as a shop assistant and a waitress.

English nurse Edith Cavell was asked to set up a teaching hospital in Brussels. The hospital became a rendezvous point for escaping Allied soldiers.

A centre of resistance was established by the Princess Marie de Croÿ at her home, the Château de Bellignies.

The Château de Bellignies dates from the Middle Ages. Its round tower contains a secret room where Allied soldiers could be hidden.

At the outbreak of war more than half a million German troops flooded into neutral Belgium heading for France. They were described as 'the steamroller'.

All over the country people became refugees. These women are fleeing from Westrozebeke, a village in West Flanders.

After their defeat at Mons, many British soldiers were marooned behind German lines.

Agent Marthe Cnockaert was a nurse.
The unwitting Germans conscripted
her to care for their wounded.

Marie Birckel and Émile Fauquenot
were sentenced to life imprisonment.
Even from prison Marie sent intelligence
to the Allies. The two later married.

Louise de Bettignies reported that a
massive German attack was about to be
launched at Verdun. She was ignored.

LA LIBRE BELGIQUE

FONDÉE
LE 1er FÉVRIER 1915

BULLETIN DE PROPAGANDE PATRIOTIQUE — RÉGULIÈREMENT IRRÉGULIER
NE SE SOUMETTANT A AUCUNE CENSURE

Gabrielle Petit used the satirical underground newspaper *La Libre Belgique* to torment the German High Command.

Mme Rischard and her husband ran a railway monitoring network from their home in Luxembourg. This photograph shows the house in 1950, largely unchanged since 1918.

In 1917, Mme Lise Rischard became a reluctant but highly effective agent in Luxembourg.

115. La Prison de SAINT-GILLES

In 1915, a group of thirty-five resistance workers, including Edith Cavell, Louise Thuliez and the Princess de Croÿ were arrested and taken to the prison of Saint-Gilles.

At her trial, Edith chose not to wear her nurse's uniform. Some of her comrades thought this was a mistake and that the Germans would have respected her more had she done so.

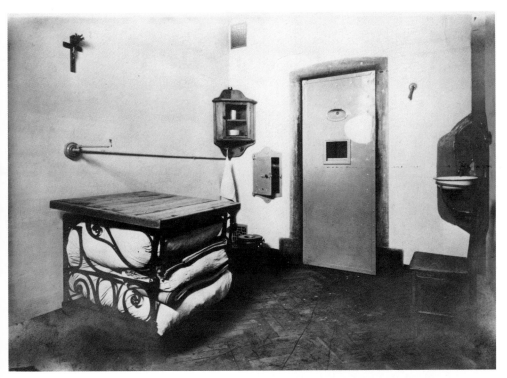

Edith's cell was number 23. On her last night at the prison she received Holy Communion and just before dawn was led to the firing squad.

Louise Thuliez and the Countess de Belleville were sentenced to death. They asked that they might spend what they thought would be their last night together in the same cell, praying. Edith Cavell was not allowed to join them.

145. Bruxelles Monument à Gabrielle Petit
fusillée par les allemands le 1er Avril 1916
et aux femmes belges mortes
pour la Patrie

After the war Gabrielle Petit received
a state funeral and monuments were
erected in her memory, like this one in
Brussels. She is now largely forgotten.

On 17 March 1920, this
memorial in central London
was dedicated to Edith Cavell.
Carved on it are the words she
spoke in her cell the night before
her execution: 'Patriotism is not
enough. I must have no hatred or
bitterness for anyone.'

immaculate uniform, monocle and waxed moustache. He was followed by the senior clerk of the court and the official interpreter. Stoeber reached his seat and placed his shining helmet on the desk before him. Then the clerk placed several large files on the desk along with a copy of the German military code.

Next, with great ceremony, the judges were sworn in. A roll call of all the prisoners was made, each answering as best they might, intimidated by the grandeur and pomposity of the ceremony. Stoeber then read the charges in German, his voice rising and falling with the skill of an actor, controlled, authoritative and firm. The policeman, Lieutenant Bergan, was called to make a long statement to the court in German. At the heart of his statement was the assertion that the accused had contravened paragraph 90 of the German military law, which defined 'conducting soldiers to the enemy' as a treason against Germany.

Few of the defendants could follow what he said. The German was laboriously translated into French for them. The opening formalities over, five of the main defendants were taken out of the court, leaving Edith Cavell alone. In deference to her status the Princess de Croÿ was taken to a room on her own and offered refreshments which she refused, worrying that anything she took, even water, might be drugged. As she sat waiting she thought about Edith and was disappointed that she had chosen not to wear her matron's uniform which might have impressed the Germans. Louise Thuliez thought the same thing as she was led from the court; the nurse's uniform, would, she thought, have made Edith into an emblem of charity and mercy in a place where there was none.

Edith was summoned to a chair in the centre of the proceedings. Stoeber rose to begin his examination. The matron was his star defendant. He deployed all his physical and vocal skills as he questioned her. A beautifully modulated and confident voice, pauses for reflection on the dishonesty and vileness of her crimes, sudden flashes of righteous anger followed by a change of tone to one of momentary sympathy as he tried to work out how a woman devoted to good should descend to such depths. Again he spoke in German and his words were translated into French. Edith answered in French with a marked English accent. Her answers were translated into German. As she spoke she stood quite still, and calm, her voice low and unafraid.

Stoeber asked her with whom she had collaborated and she answered honestly, naming four people including Louise Thuliez and Herman Capiau. She told the prosecutor that her organisation had no head. She said that she had begun her work because two wounded men had come to her and she thought they would be shot if captured. She was acting, she said, on humanitarian grounds. She admitted that she had helped about two hundred men escape from Belgium. Nobody asked how an English nurse living in Belgium could be accused of treason against the fatherland. Stoeber's questions done, Edith returned to her chair. The whole process had taken less than ten minutes.

It was now Louise Thuliez's turn to be led into the court and to sit in the chair that had been occupied by Edith. She knew that when she was arrested the Germans had found a lot of incriminating evidence. Her handbag had contained coded addresses and a forged identity card. Now she was asked to explain why she was in possession of these things. She was also asked to describe the structure of the organisation for which she worked and to identify its chief. She answered that there were no chiefs, each person operated out of a desire to help the soldiers caught in the chaos and destruction created by the advancing German army. Her questioning over, she stood, waiting to be led to her place in the court. Stoeber stopped her and asked, 'What was your motive in acting as you did?' She replied, 'Because I am a Frenchwoman.'

When her turn came to be cross-examined the Princess de Croÿ too was ordered to sit in the centre of the court. Since her arrest she had denied everything. Because of this, she was told she was just making her case worse and would incur the utmost rigours of the law. She had decided that she would not take any oath and that she would only admit to the things that she knew could be proved. She said, yes, she had housed fugitive men and, yes, she had photographed them because they would need photos for the identification cards required to travel to Brussels. When Stoeber asked her what her motives were, she lost her temper and snapped: 'One must do one's duty without thinking of the consequences.' Her clear voice drifted over the heavy carpeting; the heat in the court was stifling.

Stoeber dealt with all the witnesses in the same theatrical and ruthless manner.

At the end of the morning's proceedings the court broke for lunch. The senior officials disappeared, while the soldiers brought in an enormous pot of hot soup, their lunch. Nothing had been prepared for the prisoners, who were tormented by the smell of the hot food the military guards were slurping down. The soldiers who had finished eating offered the dregs from their bowls, but these were declined. A few of the accused men had managed to bring some food in with them which they shared with the others. The Countess de Belleville persuaded one of the soldiers to go outside and buy some rolls. Then the thirsty prisoners presented their cupped hands into which the guards splashed water.

While this was happening Louise whispered to Edith, 'Baucq, Capiau, you and I stand a bad chance, but what does it matter so long as we are not shot?'

Just before two o'clock the room was brought to order in preparation for the return of the judges and lawyers. Louise noticed that now several of them had copies of the green-covered book that contained the German military code, which they kept looking at and then whispering to each other.

The afternoon wore on as Stoeber cross-examined the witnesses with forensic efficiency, giving each only a few minutes to reply, determined to process them all that first day. They were ordinary people: a farmer, several labourers, a student, a shopkeeper and a housewife were among those who stood before him. Some spoke the local dialect, which added to the confusion of languages.

Then Lieutenant Bergan was called, who assured the court that his interrogations had been carried out in front of two witnesses, Pinkhoff and Neuhaus. No violence or pressure had been used and his written reports were models of accuracy and fairness. He told the court that in his opinion all the accused were part of an organisation that was working against the occupying powers and that the leader was Edith Cavell, whose hospital was the headquarters.

The last witness of the day was a 14-year-old boy, Philippe Bodart, the son of one of the accused. He stood before the judges, a small, thin figure, his face pale, his hair and clothes black. The child was warned that if he lied he would be liable to ten years' forced labour. He was questioned about Baucq, who shouted from his chair that Philippe did not understand French and spoke English at home. Baucq was ordered to be silent. The child's questioning went on and his answers incriminated Baucq. Yes, Baucq had copies of *La Libre Belgique* and, yes, he had heard Baucq talking about mapping a route across Belgium to the frontier. The princess watched as Baucq leaned forward, his head in his hands, his shoulders shaking with emotion. Some of the accused wept as Stoeber finished and told the child to say farewell to his mother, who faced a long sentence.

The court rose at 7pm and the weary defendants were driven back to the prison, bewildered by the change in their lives which, before the invasion just over a year before, had been so ordinary.

The next day, Friday, 8 October, the court met in another building, the Chamber of Deputies, and was convened with the same theatrical pomp and splendour. Stoeber spoke for two interminable hours. He began by emphasising that all the accused had willingly signed their confessions and that they were a ruthless organisation working against the fatherland.

He went on to describe each of the accused in turn, starting with 'the head' of the organisation, Edith Cavell, then moving to Louise Thuliez, Philippe Baucq, the Princess de Croÿ and all the rest. He stated that they had all worked in tandem. He outlined the methods they had used, including forged documents, safe houses, bribes and escape routes. On and on he went, his German incomprehensible to almost all the defendants, who were again desperate for water as the room got hotter and hotter.

He reached the point where he outlined the sentences that the treasonous bunch deserved. His words were now translated into

French. The crime was treason and the leaders deserved the death penalty, the others long terms of hard labour. He spoke Edith's name, followed by the word 'Todesstrafe' – death penalty. Edith stood motionless, 'imperturbable and calm', Baucq collapsed as if broken; the watching German officers nodded in approval. When Louise Thuliez heard her name and the demand that she should be executed she found herself at first in a state of stupefaction, then surprise, followed by doubt and finally resignation. She hoped that if this was to be her cross, then like her Lord Jesus she would find the courage to bear it.

It was now the turn of the defence lawyers, who had not met their clients nor knew what they were accused of and were given no time to prepare. There was little they could do or say and anything they did say in the brief time allowed was ignored.

The proceedings came to an end. Cavell was asked if she had anything to add and she replied that she had nothing. The princess stood and said she took full responsibility for everything and that she wanted the court to know that Mme Cavell was a nurse and not the head of an escape organisation, and that she had been brought into danger when she was asked to shelter wounded and fugitive men. In the half-light the normally frail-looking princess raised her hand and drew back her shoulders; she looked beautiful as she said that she would like to make it clear that she wanted to take Edith Cavell's place. One man in the room wanted to applaud her and regretted to the end of his days that his courage failed him. The accused were told that they would hear their fate on Monday.

The court spent Saturday reviewing the case and deciding the sentences. For the prisoners, Saturday and Sunday passed with agonising slowness. On Sunday night, when Louise Thuliez turned out the gas-lamp in her cell, a warden opened the wicket in her door and passed her some matches, telling her to relight the gas on the orders of the governor, who wanted the prisoners to be inspected every five minutes. One of their number had hanged himself. Thuliez found the continual squeaking of the cover to the peep-hole a torment and in the morning she tried to protest, but was ignored.

At about three in the afternoon of Monday, 11 October, Louise Thuliez's cell door was opened and the warden said, 'Get ready to come and receive your sentence.' She dressed formally, thinking that she was to be taken to the governor's residence. She was led towards the central hall of the prison and as she arrived saw that her fellow defendants, except for the princess, were already there, bare-headed and dressed as they were when they had been arrested.

Five men appeared, led by Stoeber. The prosecutor began to read from a paper in his hand. First he read five names, Louise Thuliez, Philippe Baucq, Edith Cavell, Jeanne de Belleville and Louis Séverin, who was not one of the six main defendants, but had helped raise money and had harboured fugitive soldiers. After each he uttered the word 'death'. For a second Thuliez thought, 'At last I am going to see my mother and father.' The Countess de Belleville wondered how she would face her maker and hoped that her imperfections would be balanced by the sacrifice she had made for her country. Thuliez turned to the countess and in a terrified whisper said: 'We are condemned to death, it is appalling.' Thuliez saw that the countess's complexion had taken on a strange violet colour. When Baucq stepped forward and began to protest that the sentences were too harsh, he was shoved back. The chaplain said they could write to the governor general and appeal for mercy. Thuliez asked Cavell if she would make such a plea and the nurse answered, 'No, it is useless. I am English, they want my life.' Then she was led away. As the rest of the small group were taken back to their cells, the governor and prison wardens took off their hats and bowed deeply.

Stoeber and his party next visited the cell of the Princess de Croÿ, who, in spite of her guilty verdict, continued to be shown greater respect than the other prisoners. The men crowded into her tiny room and the lawyer announced that he was going to read the sentences. The list was long and started with those condemned to death. Stoeber droned on and the princess was vaguely aware that she was condemned to ten years' hard labour. While the voice intoned she wondered if she would be allowed to appeal on behalf of all the condemned. Stoeber behaved with more grace than he had in court and said that though she could not consult with her lawyer, if she was going to appeal she must write *at once*. He was emphatic about the need for urgency.

Meanwhile, Jeanne de Belleville and Louise Thuliez arrived at the corridor where their cells were located. They did not know for certain when their death sentences would be carried out, but thought it could be the next day. Thuliez turned to her warder and said, 'Monsieur, we are destined to die together, may we please pass our last hours together?' The warder ignored her and Thuliez repeated her request to the chaplain, who agreed. Their cells were adjacent and, as Thuliez pulled her mattress into de Belleville's cell, she asked if Edith Cavell too might join them; her cell was next to theirs. This request was refused.

When they were alone the two condemned women threw themselves into each other's arms and prepared to spend what might be their last night on earth comforting each other, reading their prayer books, talking quietly, reflecting on what was about to happen, and all the while the gas-lamp flickered and every five minutes the spyhole in the door rasped, sliding open to reveal the eye of a warder ordered to check on them.

The day ended and two nurses from the hospital, Sisters Elizabeth Wilkins and Beatrice Smith, arrived at the prison, desperate for news. They were met by the deputy governor who told them that five death sentences had been passed and that Baucq and Cavell were to be shot at 7am the next day. Events were out of his hands; the only person who might be able to help was the American ambassador, who, for the duration of the war, was responsible for British interests in the country. Perhaps, the deputy suggested, they should approach the American legation's lawyer, Gaston de Leval. He gave them the address and the two women hurried off into the gathering gloom and the drizzle.

By now Stoeber had received some of the appeals from the prisoners and had passed them to Traugott von Sauberzweig, the military governor of Brussels, who replied:

... I deem that the interests of the state demand that the sentence
against Philippe Baucq and Edith Cavell be carried out immediately [underlined in red ink] ... I adjourn the death sentence on
the other prisoners until a decision has been reached concerning
the appeals for clemency ...

In the light of this command the governor of the prison ordered
that the sentences of Cavell and Baucq be carried out at dawn
the next day.

In their cell Thuliez and de Belleville heard the rattle of keys as
Edith's door was opened, then voices murmuring and the noise of
shoes walking into the distance, echoing slightly on the stone floor
of the corridor.

Edith was led along the dark corridor, following the prison chaplain, Pastor Le Seur, dressed in his officer's uniform. He took her into
another room. For a moment they both stood in silence, looking at
one another. Then he told her, stuttering and almost unable to speak,
that she was soon to be executed. Another silence, then Edith asked,
'How much time will they give me?'

'Unfortunately only until tomorrow morning.'

The nurse stood, her face slightly flushed, her eyes glazed, not
seeing. The priest asked her if he could serve her in the hours ahead,
and pleaded with her to think of him as a man of God, not a German
officer. She asked if he could contact her mother with the news of
her trial and execution. He promised to do his best.

Then he offered to contact the Anglican chaplain in Brussels, the
Reverend Stirling Gahan, who had been a guest at Edith's Christmas
party; he could ask him if he would come and give her communion.
She appeared overjoyed at this idea. Then Le Seur asked if she would
like Gahan to be with her at the end; he would stand aside. This she
declined, saying Gahan was not used to such things.

The priest replied, 'Miss Cavell, I too am not used to such
things ...'

Then he agreed to accompany her on her last journey. The interview over, they prayed and Cavell was taken back to her cell.

In another part of the prison Philippe Baucq was visited in his cell by his wife. He handed her a wodge of lavatory paper on which he had written a diary of the events since his arrest and a description of life in the prison.

Across the city the Reverend Gahan arrived home to find a note from Le Seur. It read: 'An Englishwoman is about to die.' This puzzled him; he had no idea to whom it referred. He hurried to Le Seur's lodgings where he was informed of all that had happened since the death sentences had been announced. Gahan returned home to fetch his communion set. When he told his wife Muriel what was happening she too set off, heading for the American legation. Gahan went to the prison.

Gaston de Leval, legal adviser to the US ambassador in Brussels, sat in his lodgings listening to the two nurses, Sister Wilkins who was in tears, and Sister Smith who was more composed. They were all stunned at the speed of events. De Leval sat down and wrote a plea for clemency. It was addressed to the governor general of Belgium and it would be signed by the American ambassador, Brand Whitlock, who knew nothing of what had happened and was ill in bed. Then they set off for the legation, where a small party of women had assembled, none of whom believed that their friend Edith would not see another sunset.

Rain pattered against Whitlock's bedroom window. De Leval stood in front of him, white and shaking, holding the two pleas he had written, one for the governor general and a second for Baron von der Lancken, head of the Politische Abteilung, the political department. Whitlock had only to sign the two documents, but he added the lines: 'My Dear Baron, I am too ill to present my request in person, but I appeal to the generosity of your heart to support it and save this person from death. Have pity on her! *Votre bien dévoué*, Brand Whitlock.'

Whitlock then ordered that his first secretary, Hugh Gibson, should present the pleas in person; ideally he wanted the Spanish ambassador in Brussels, the Marquess de Villalobar, to add his support to the pleas. De Leval went on his way, leaving the women to wait and pray.

Edith wrote two letters, one to her nurses and one to her mother. She finished the letter to the hospital saying, 'If any of you has a grievance against me I beg you to forgive me; I have perhaps sometimes been too strict but never knowingly unjust, and I have loved you all much more than you can ever know.'

At 9:30pm a figure appeared outside the prison and rang the bell. A guard opened the door to reveal Stirling Gahan carrying his communion set. Edith received him in her dressing gown, ushering him into her simple, clean cell decorated with the flowers her nurses had sent.

They discussed her life and she told him that the last ten weeks in prison had been like a fast, allowing her to contemplate life free from the distractions and diversions of the world. It had been a time of rest and mercy. She had one thing she wanted, above all, to say, 'standing as I do in the view of God and eternity: I realise that patriotism is not enough. I must have no hatred or bitterness towards anyone.'

Then Gahan gave her communion. After she had drunk the wine and eaten of the bread, he said, 'We shall remember you as a heroine and a martyr.'

'Don't think of me like that. Think of me as a nurse who tried to do her duty.'

Then they quietly recited the hymn 'Abide with Me', finishing with the words: 'Where is death's sting? Where, grave, thy victory? I triumph still, if Thou abide with me.'

Finally the pastor said, 'Perhaps I had better go. You will want to rest.'

'Yes, I have to be up at five. We shall meet again.'

'Yes we shall. God be with you.'

Then he was gone, leaving her to ponder the fact that by the following evening she would understand the many mysteries that had guided her.

Finally, at the end of the last complete day of her life, Edith copied some words from Book 4, Chapter 4 of *The Imitation of Christ*:

I am racked with grief of heart, I am burdened with sins, I am troubled with temptations; I am entangled and oppressed with many evil passions; and there is none to help me, none to deliver and save me but thou, O Lord God my Saviour, to whom I committed myself and all that is mine, that thou mayest watch over me, and bring me safe to life everlasting.

A small group of women had now gathered in de Leval's office, waiting for news. They had been there for nearly four hours and included nurses from the hospital, Mrs Gahan, the English chaplain's wife, and 'a little wisp of a thing who had been mothered by Miss Cavell, and was nearly beside herself with grief'. Hugh Gibson appeared, with the news that he and de Leval had failed. They had arrived at the German Politische Abteilung to find the offices empty. Baron von der Lancken was at the theatre, the governor general was in Berlin. When von der Lancken finally emerged from the variety show, he listened to what de Leval had to say and told him not to worry, assuring him that it was all rubbish, Cavell would not be put to death that morning. 'Come and see me tomorrow.' Even so, de Leval persuaded him to telephone the presiding judge. When von der Lancken returned he admitted that what they were saying was true. He rang his superior, the military governor, who angrily said he would not change his mind. There was talk of telephoning the Kaiser.

The women in the room began to sob as Gibson continued with his tale of failure. They were given sherry and then they left.

At five in the morning Sister Elizabeth Wilkins and Sister Beatrice Smith walked in the dark and the rain towards the gates of Saint-Gilles prison. They were depressed that the squabbling men who held power, influence and sway over the lives of millions of people had achieved nothing to help their condemned matron.

As dawn began to break the gates of the prison opened and two cars manoeuvred slowly out, driving through puddles that glistened in the beam of the headlights, water softly splashing round the tyres. The nurses glimpsed Edith staring ahead and then she was gone as the cars accelerated into the streets which the sun was now beginning to reveal, heading for the shooting range at the Tir National, where a large contingent of men was already drawn up. Standing in two rows stood the twelve members of the firing squad. In front of them the stakes to which the condemned would be tied. Near the stakes lay two yellow coffins. To one side stood a group of senior men that included the prosecutor, Stoeber. He broke away from the official party and walked towards the soldiers, who snapped to attention holding their rifles. Stoeber stood immaculate and erect, his shiny boots stained with small splashes of yellow mud. In his loud, theatrical, confident voice he assured the firing party that they need have no qualms about shooting a woman and a man who were traitors to the fatherland, and who had committed the gross sin of treason.

The car with the condemned bounced towards them and drew up. Soldiers moved forward and opened the doors, escorting the prisoners to the two stakes. Baucq waved his hat at the soldiers and declared, 'Good morning, gentlemen, we are all comrades before death.'

This enraged Stoeber, who barked at him to be quiet and then, in German, read the sentences. The prison governor translated these into French. As his voice rose into the damp morning air Le Seur, the prison chaplain, held Edith's hand. She asked him to let her mother know that she died with a clear conscience for God and her country. Then a soldier quietly took her arm and led her to her post, her dress dragging in the mud, her shoes squelching in the wet. Next, she was tied and blindfolded. The young soldier was the last man she saw on earth, her eyes filled with tears.

Then it was Baucq's turn to be bound to his post. Under command the soldiers raised their rifles and fired. Edith's body jerked upright three times, her face streamed with blood from a wound in her forehead, another bullet punched a hole in her heart. Baucq died instantly.

The soldiers lowered their rifles, the bodies were cut down and placed in the coffins ready for immediate burial. One of the officials present thought that 'she went to her death with a bearing which is quite impossible to forget'. Uneasy at what he had been a part of, he knew that she must be buried quickly, in silence and secrecy. The world must not know what they had done.

Two days after Edith's execution, Elizabeth Wilkins, who was also the accountant for the hospital and Edith's executor, made an inventory of her effects. Some furniture, a chest of drawers and a trunk, and five miscellaneous objects: a carpet, a pillow, a shawl, a cushion, a clock. They were carefully stowed away against the day when the war would end.

The news of Edith's death reached the War Office in London and an official was told to ring her mother with the news of her execution. When he got through he asked if he was speaking to Mrs Cavell. The woman on the other end confirmed that indeed he was.

'I rang up to tell you that your daughter in Brussels has been shot by the Germans.'

There was a pause and Mrs Cavell then replied, 'When you get in touch with the right Mrs Cavell, you won't put it quite like that, will you? She's a very old lady and she isn't very well.' When she eventually heard what had happened to her daughter, old Mrs Cavell sat silent and dignified.

The execution of Nurse Cavell turned into a propaganda disaster for the Germans. In England, Prime Minister Asquith told the House of Commons that Edith had 'taught the bravest man amongst us the supreme lesson of courage'. There were calls in the press for German cities to be flattened by bombing, that there should be an Edith Cavell Machine Gun Regiment, and the words 'Remember Edith Cavell' were used as a recruiting slogan. On 23 October, the writer H. Rider Haggard recorded in his diary: 'Emperor Wilhelm would have done better to lose an entire army corps than to butcher Miss Cavell.'

In America, the *New York Times* wrote that 'every Neutral Nation has heard with a shock of horror the news of the execution of Miss Cavell. The world at large prays that Germany's enemies may triumph.'

In Germany, the Kaiser ordered that no more women were to be executed without his approval. In the German press, Cavell became a monster at the head of a vicious spy network and a recruiting agency for soldiers. Von Bissing wanted to know why 'when thousands of innocent people have died in the war ... should anyone become hysterical over the death of one guilty woman?'

One of the few lawyers who had been allowed to defend those brought before the German military tribunals was Sadi Kirschen. He had tried to defend Edith Cavell and was shaken by her death. He thought a lot about who the agents were and how they were led. He came to the conclusion that most of the sacrifices the Belgians were making were wasted. He thought their leaders, safe in the Netherlands, were amateurs, undisciplined and incompetent. Heavily influenced by the suffering of the imprisoned men and women and the executions, he developed the view that spying was for the experts, military people who knew what they were doing and what they were looking for. Civilians, he thought, could only produce 'derisory reports and ridiculous statistics'.

On 'the other side of the hill', some German counter-intelligence officers were impressed by the spirit of sacrifice shown by the Belgians. They were also impressed by their ability to recover once a network had been blown. They found the Belgian underground to be run by men and women with a fanatical sense of patriotism, duty and sacrifice that was unequalled anywhere in Europe.

One Belgian politician wrote: 'Let us admire! Let us admire without reserve! ... think of the number of actions undertaken – trifling in appearance, but enabled by the goal! How they testify to the valour of a country that is determined not to die, that mobilises all its resources and bravely resists the boot that wants to crush it.'

CHAPTER TWELVE

LIVING WITH THE INVADER

On 5 November 1915 the Princess de Croÿ was taken from her cell and led, under armed guard, out of the prison and into a car. A few minutes later a young officer, tall, unsmiling and silent, got in. He stared at her through his monocle and the car moved off. Not one word was spoken as they sped through the streets of Brussels towards the Gare du Nord, where they drove straight into the station and onto a platform where a train was waiting. The princess did not know why, but lined up near the train were porters from some of the hotels in the city who, very politely, saluted her. She boarded the train and was placed in a second-class compartment with another woman, also a prisoner. The officer and the sergeant both sat in the carriage with them. The train pulled out and she fell asleep.

The princess woke when the train stopped at Louvain, where her brothers, Reginald and Leopold, had been students. The town she had known was almost unrecognisable, many buildings destroyed by the fires deliberately started by the invading Germans. The next stop was Aix-la-Chapelle, where some women from the German Red Cross gave her a tin mug of lukewarm ersatz coffee and a dry sandwich. Then the journey continued until, finally, they arrived in Cologne, which had recently been bombed by the Allies and where they had to change trains. The exhausted princess sat on her suitcase. It was now only the sergeant guarding her. He was going on leave and carried mountains of food he had stolen in Brussels.

After the long and slow journey they arrived at Siegburg, where she was ordered to go on foot to the prison, a walk of more than half an hour. The princess was too ill to attempt it, so she and the sergeant waited for a tram. Finally, in the bitter cold and pouring rain they arrived at the looming, dark gateway. The sergeant pulled on a bell rope and after a wait the night guard opened the door and let her in. A female warder carrying a guttering candle led her to her cell. They walked down corridors that had grey paths marked down each side. A prison regulation insisted that the inmates must walk on the grey areas. The warder opened the door and pushed the princess in, saying, 'Your bed is on the left.' She then closed and locked the door, leaving the princess in the pitch dark, fumbling for the bed and collapsing onto it, feeling like a trapped animal.

She could hear a guard tramping up and down the corridor. The walls echoed with the stifled shouts of her fellow prisoners and above it all a child's voice crying, '*Maman, maman.*' The princess finally fell asleep. Just before dawn her cell door swung open to reveal two prisoners carrying a slop bucket. The stench wafting in from the corridor made her retch.

She could now see that her cell was the standard 3 yards long and 2 wide. It had a cupboard with a mug, plate and bowl. A metal pan hung from the wall in which she was to wash not only herself, but her eating utensils. Later that day she was taken to a medical room where she was weighed and examined, the doctor listening to her heart and lungs through a stethoscope. She was then taken back to her cell where she sat in silence. Later, the inspector of the prison burst in with the directress. He demanded to know why she was there. Before the princess could answer, the directress said, '*Affaire Cavell.*' The inspector pointed to a card screwed in a frame to the wall and said, 'Have you read that?' She peered at it, vaguely taking in its message:

You are now a prisoner. Your window is barred, your door is locked, the colour of your clothing indicates that you have lost your liberty.

The notice went on to declare that it was God's will that they were there and that he was punishing them for their sins by taking away their freedom. It continued: 'If you do not obey willingly, your spirit will be broken.' Again, the notice insisted, this was all God's will. The princess thought it a 'pharisaical lucubration'.

She was next taken to an accountant's office where her sentence was read to her again and she was told that, with good behaviour, 'you may deserve the clemency of our emperor and see this sentence curtailed'. Then she was stripped of all her clothes, her possessions and her money and taken to the bathhouse where she was washed. Next came the issue of regulation prison clothing. For those sentenced to hard labour the dress was brown, for everyone else it was grey. The garments were made of rough wool and consisted of a blouse and a floor-length skirt. Undergarments were made of cotton, with blue and white cotton stockings and a white cotton neckerchief.

The prison was shaped like two Ts, one for women and one for men. The female section was run by a woman called Frau Ruge, a widow whose husband had been an army officer. She was refined and sometimes seemed to care for the women in her charge, although she was frightened of the prison governor.

The cell walls were whitewashed and on one there was an oil lamp that was allowed to be lit for one hour during winter. Electric light was turned off in the early evening before the last meal, which had to be eaten in the dark. In the winter the prisoners could spend fifteen hours in total darkness, moving about and eating their meals by touch alone.

The princess's dreary day began at seven o'clock with the ringing of a bell; a few minutes later the cell doors were opened and the prisoners put their water jugs and slop buckets outside. The stench from the buckets filled the prison. Within fifteen minutes they had been collected and emptied by prisoners. At eight o'clock breakfast was distributed, four ounces of black bread and a hot black liquid with no sugar – artificial coffee. The prisoners were allowed two exercise periods of forty-five minutes each. For the rest of the day they sat in their cells, some sewing garments, others stamping trouser buttons with a machine that was brought, daily, to the cell. At eleven-thirty a disgusting liquid masquerading as 'vegetable soup' was given to the prisoners. At the beginning of the war this had the odd piece of meat in it, but as the conflict went on this too disappeared. At 6pm another bowl of liquid was dished out, after which the cells were locked until seven the next morning.

Bread was made with potato meal and the soup was made almost entirely of beetroot. As the war wore on and rationing in Germany became more severe, the food in the prison deteriorated. There was very little medical care and the sanitary conditions were disgusting. The prison doctor was nicknamed 'Dr Getout'. Most prisoners who joined the long file outside his office were not diagnosed and were given the same pills irrespective of the symptoms they were showing. Dysentery, typhoid and tuberculosis stalked the cells. Some prisoners died in the night and their bodies were taken out in coffins.

Pregnant women often gave birth alone in the night. They were allowed to keep their children for nine months, after which the babies were removed and sent to homes. After this the children were brought to see their mothers once a month, on Sunday.

While the princess was being admitted at Siegburg, Louise Thuliez sat in the prison of Saint-Gilles in Brussels, waiting to be executed. On 10 November a copy of the German propaganda paper *La Belgique* was pushed into her cell. She opened it and was astonished to read that her sentence, and that of the Countess de Belleville, had been commuted from death to 'Hard Labour for Life by the gracious action of His Majesty the Emperor'. Later, this news was given to her officially by the commandant of the prison, who flew into a hysterical rage when she told him she already knew. When she told him she had read it in *La Belgique* he became apoplectic, shouting that the newspapers had no right to publish such stuff without proper authorisation. Thuliez stood in silence as he raged on; *La Belgique*, after all, was written, printed and published by the German authorities.

Two days later the countess was also sent to Siegburg, while Louise was taken to Cambrai to face more charges carrying the death penalty. The conditions in the prison at Cambrai were very bad; her cell was freezing and had no light and everything was filthy, including her plate and tin bowl for drinking. She was accompanied everywhere by a soldier carrying the usual rifle with a fixed bayonet. Visits to the lavatory were especially humiliating as the guard followed her into the latrine bloc, which was in the prison yard and open to observation. The guard looked on impassively as she tried to find a free cubicle, often having to push open several doors.

After three days, she and six others were taken for trial in the town hall at Cambrai. In the corridor she met the two men who had arrested her – Bergan, whom she called the 'Diable Noir', and Pinkhoff. Bergan was friendly and held out his hand as if to shake hers. She looked him full in the face and put both her hands behind her back. He frowned and said, 'We know for certain that your sister was one of those who distributed La Libre Belgique; we will meet again in Brussels.' Louise had no idea what he was talking about, her sister had played no part in the underground activities. The trial took all morning. The statements she had given before were used against her and she again regretted signing them, remembering that they were written in German and she had no idea what they said. The death penalty was demanded and on Christmas Eve she and the others were summoned to hear their sentences. Thuliez was not to be executed but was once again given hard labour for life. She spent Christmas Day alone in her cell, listening to the Germans singing carols and getting drunk. A few days later she followed the princess to Siegburg.

Like the others she was taken under armed guard to the station. She was warned not to try to escape, to which she replied that she was too proud of being a prisoner to want to make a run for it. At the station she sat in a compartment with the armed soldier sitting opposite, his knees pressing against hers. The journey was long and tedious and went via a stop in Brussels. At one point a Frenchwoman tried to enter the carriage. The guard could not speak French and the woman tried to argue until Louise warned her, 'Madame, it is useless to insist, you cannot get in here.' Later, she heard the woman complaining that it was disgraceful to see a Frenchwoman travelling alone with a German soldier and refusing to let anyone else in the carriage.

When her guard delivered her to the prison she asked him if he would really have shot her and he confirmed that he would have done, adding that if she'd escaped he would have been court-martialled and faced up to ten years in prison.

By Christmas 1915 food shortages were severe in Roulers and smuggling food was treated by the Germans as a serious crime. House-to-house searches were a regular occurrence, with gendarmes knocking people up in the middle of the night. Anyone found keeping undeclared animals risked a long prison sentence. Coffee, butter and jam became expensive black-market items and were usually unobtainable. Food substitutes were used. Roasted oat chaff mixed with roasted pea shells served for coffee. Potato pulp mixed with beetroot served for jam.

Drapers' shops had their stocks requisitioned and people improvised clothes from anything that came to hand; blankets, tablecloths, curtains and even canvas blinds suddenly appeared as suits, skirts, hats and dresses. One woman, Madame Veldock, kept a goat in her cellar. She had knocked a hole in the wall to connect it to the cellar next door. Whenever a house-to-house search was under way the goat was led into the next-door cellar until the gendarmes had left and then brought back again as the men moved on. Mme Veldock was never caught.

People could be arrested for the smallest offence and it became almost a badge of honour to have spent time in Roulers' civic jail. Three young girls, all under twelve, were sentenced to ten weeks for picking up bits of coke lying along the railway leading into Roulers station. An old couple in their seventies were given the same punishment for hiding a few pounds of potatoes and some maize.

Many of the women left in the town found ways to smuggle food to prisoners in the small civic jail. It was discovered that ventilation holes had been drilled in the glass of some grated windows that protruded a few inches above street level. Food could be rolled into long cylinders and slipped through the holes. By this means, bread and meat could be passed to the prisoners. At night only a sergeant and an enlisted man were on duty, and only one patrolled the outside walls at a time, making it easy to evade them. As the year progressed they had become lazy and they too were hungry. In the end it became possible to bribe the two men with food and get them to turn a blind eye. Marthe Cnockaert too helped smuggle food into the prison.

As the year 1915 ended it became harder for Marthe to operate. Her contact, Number 63, had disappeared and security was generally much tighter than it had been at the beginning of the war. A new German battalion of a thousand men had arrived and were quartered in the town. Marthe Cnockaert's contact, Canteen Ma, was now the only way in which she could get information to the Allies.

Nevertheless Marthe continued with her double life. She and her parents lived 20 miles from the front, hearing the constant noise of heavy gunfire and at night seeing the horizon lit by explosions and Very lights arcing into the dark sky. Even so they thought that life so near the front line was worth it, hoping that when the Allies finally won they would be among the first to be liberated.

At Christmas 1915 the town filled with drunken soldiers carrying Christmas trees which they had cut from the surrounding woods. They danced arm in arm, sang sentimental songs and set fire to the Christmas trees. Even though it was snowing some of the drunken men were nearly naked. Military policemen tried and failed to keep some sort of order. A sergeant in a machine-gun company appeared wearing his helmet at a drunken angle, his tunic buttoned to the throat, no trousers on his legs, just an old pair of worn-out long johns. Tied outside one of the houses in the main square was an officer's horse. Whooping with delight the sergeant clambered on top, cantering off into the night followed by men from his company, shouting, laughing and firing their weapons into the air.

Later that night Marthe found out that the commotion had been caused by the arrival of news that Serbia had fallen several weeks before. It was rumoured that Russia itself had fallen too. The revelry went on until dawn on Christmas morning. The next day a garrison order appeared:

AMMUNITION, WASTE OF

It is strictly forbidden to use ammunition to celebrate any National Feasts of Victories of our Glorious Armies in the Field. Commanders will see that this order is strictly adhered to. It is understood that certain officers encouraged men by personal example in the demonstration on the night 24/12/15. In future such conduct will be severely dealt with.

It was rare now that injured Allied soldiers appeared in Roulers, but Marthe still had two in her care. Both had been badly wounded. Marthe took advantage of the Christmas chaos to get them away.

She was still in contact with Canteen Ma and trusted her implicitly. She arranged with the woman to have an agent waiting in a nearby village at midnight on 25 December. The village was about 14 miles away and on the way there was a derelict house which could be used as a refuge. In it had been constructed a small secret room with an escape hatch, where fugitive men could hide.

Marthe organised for civilian clothes to be left by a shed in the hospital grounds. The men were to put these on and then to walk out of the hospital mingling with the civilian workers. The plan worked and they set off on the road towards the deserted house. They arrived at about 7:30pm, just before the curfew, and were joined by Marthe. They found the secret room and hid, lighting a candle and sitting on the straw-lined floor until late in the night when it would be safe to continue their journey.

As they waited two gendarmes came into house to shelter from the snow and cold. One of the concealed soldiers made a noise which the gendarmes heard. First they shouted, demanding to know who was there. Marthe and her charges cowered in the dark, not daring to move, trying not even to breathe. Then the gendarmes began to bang on the wall and finally they began to shoot at the walls.

Rounds tore through the partitioning. Marthe scrabbled in the straw, trying to find the escape hatch. The candle was knocked over and the straw began to burn. They found the hatch and scrambled out, running into the darkness. Behind them the house started to blaze and the gendarmes backed away, holding their hands up to protect themselves from the heat and the glare from the flames, which was blinding them.

The fugitives had only three hours to make their rendezvous, which was 6 miles away. Several times they had to hide in roadside ditches to evade the patrols and the vehicles that were rushing troops to the scene of the fire. After an hour of this they were freezing and soaking wet from the water in the ditches. The shoulder wound of one of the soldiers began to bleed.

As they neared the place where they were supposed to meet the guide who was to take them to the frontier, the dark shape of a man appeared in front of them.

'Friends for the frontier,' he murmured.

Marthe gave one of the soldiers a packet with a small amount of money.

'You're a sport, nurse, you are.'

'Lady, you're the right stuff.'

And they were gone into the night.

Marthe made her way to her aunt who lived in the village, who dried her and gave her some food. Later Canteen Ma appeared; Marthe crawled onto her little donkey cart and fell asleep under a tarpaulin, lying among the pots and pans and old vegetables it contained. By the next morning she was back on duty in the hospital, exhausted.

In December 1915 the German general Erich von Falkenhayn wrote an appraisal of the campaign he was about to embark on. It was read by the Kaiser.

The string in France has reached breaking point. A mass break-through – which in any case is beyond our means – is unnecessary.

Within our reach there are objectives for the retention of which the French General Staff would be compelled to throw in every man they have. If they do so the forces of France will bleed to death.

A letter appeared in the *New York Times* describing what life was like for ordinary people. The letter reported that:

... with German permits, [we] have ridden all over our country to see what might be done for the people whose husbands, wives or children have been shot and whose houses have been burned. It was a sad pilgrimage, indeed almost a calvary ... In many instances we have stayed days at certain places where immediate relief was necessary and through the kindness and timely efficiency of the American Committee for the Relief of Belgium, and the American Legation with which we have always been in touch, the necessary and primary relief was generally obtained. We rode over 2,000 kilometres on our bicycles: sometimes we were tired out and almost daily moved to tears by what we saw and heard ... the sufferings of this winter will be terrible.

1916

CHAPTER THIRTEEN

THE POLICE CLOSE IN

As the winter set in Gabrielle Petit was evicted from her rooms, the landlord claiming she was behind with the rent. She took new lodgings in a nearby area of narrow streets.

Gabrielle had taken on a great deal of work, some of it above board, such as working for the Red Cross, raising money for Belgian prisoners of war. She worked undercover and, as well as spying, she helped a secret organisation, Le Mot du Soldat (The Word of the Soldier), which kept the families of Belgian soldiers fighting on the Allied side of the front line in touch with their families. She helped distribute *La Libre Belgique*, the clandestine underground newspaper. She took great delight in the fact that she could get the paper into the hands of the German High Command. She called the German governor general of Belgium, Moritz von Bissing, 'Von Beau-Singe', a play on words meaning 'Pretty Monkey'. She said that if necessary she would deliver the paper in person to him and 'make him see red'. She told her comrades that she would do this because the 'Boche detests being made fun of'. As well as all this, she was recruiting guides to get people across the border into Holland. She described herself as always being at 'full gallop'.

But the stress was beginning to tell. Marie Collet worried that Gabrielle was going to be arrested. Gabrielle herself began to suffer from exhaustion. Her controller had the codename 'Aunt Anastasia', and she complained that the Aunt was burying her in work and that she was not allowed any more to visit her home town of Tournai. But she added, 'I will shut up from now on since the more I gripe, the more work is piled on ... otherwise, all goes well, as I am being assured every day.'

On 1 January 1916 she waited for her courier, whom she had nicknamed 'the Peasant'. When he arrived he was in a state because the day before a friend had been arrested. He took her reports and set off on his long journey. Then he vanished into thin air. After the disappearance of the Peasant a new courier appeared, a Dutchman. Gabrielle did not like him. He was slapdash about security and arrived in daylight hours. She found it strange that he told her not to fold her reports but to roll them up. Gabrielle decided that she would not give him all her reports and tried to find another way of getting them into Holland. She was frightened that the Germans were closing in on her. She told Marie Collet that she was exhausted and at the end of her tether and could only do a few more spying trips. She wrote that the controllers in Holland 'are safe behind the border and betray us and steal from us'. She also told one of her closest friends that if things went wrong she was determined not to betray anyone. 'I will be arrested alone; I will be shot alone ... Everything must continue; if I fall I will be replaced.'

In a large mansion in the expensive rue de Berlaimont in Brussels, once home to a part of the Belgian government, sat the young Paul Schmitz, head of counter-intelligence operations for the German Police Bureau A. Sitting opposite him was his second-in-command, Hans Goldschmidt, described by his secretary as being intelligent, devious, deceitful and dishonest, and having very good French. He courted favours from his staff, including introductions to pretty women. He was well dressed and always wore a buttonhole and sported gold-rimmed glasses. Goldschmidt was in charge of the everyday dealings with the Belgians.

His boss, Schmitz, ran a very successful department. In the offices around him were the twenty-one detectives under his command. Moving in and out of the offices were informers, some full-time, others part-time. At first Schmitz had recruited them from the working classes of Brussels. Now these had largely vanished, to be replaced by people on the make, including commercial travellers, small-time accountants and clerks.

The detectives themselves were a mixed bag of intelligent men. They drank, invented nicknames for themselves, often spoke several languages and could banter with each other in Parisian slang. They also hung out in underground nightclubs where they found many contacts and picked up information. One had run a gunpowder factory, another had sold cars, one had stolen the prototype of a new French machine gun, yet another posed as a Dutch broker selling coffee, an expensive and rare commodity. They were well-dressed, elegant men who could move with ease among the Belgians.

One agent, called Burtard, was a big, dark, blue-eyed man with a strong personality. He was married with three children and had mistresses whom he kept in apartments all over the city and would disappear for three days at a time on drinking sprees.

Police Bureau A had a genius for penetrating the amateur Belgian resistance networks that had formed soon after the invasion. They also had men in the Netherlands monitoring the couriers carrying intelligence out of the occupied country.

That day, Schmitz and Goldschmidt were talking about Gabrielle Petit. In their cells they held Gabrielle's courier, the Peasant. They had enjoyed interrogating him, forcing him to reveal, among other things, where Gabrielle lived. The time had come, they agreed, to arrest her.

Across the city in her new rooms Gabrielle sat with a neighbour, Auguste, who had a room in the same building. She and her neighbour were talking and drinking coffee, a rare treat. They heard the sound of powerful motor cars drawing up outside and heavy shoes thumping on the stairs. There was a sharp rap on the door. Gabrielle stood, walked across the room and opened it. In front of her was Goldschmidt and behind him a group of well-dressed detectives. Several had cigarettes dangling from their mouths. Goldschmidt asked her in a quiet voice, 'Are you Miss Legrand?'

This was Gabrielle's cover name.

'Yes.'

The man standing next to Goldschmidt stepped forward and punched Gabrielle hard in the stomach, sending her staggering back into the room. The men charged in and dragged Auguste to her feet. Gasping for breath and doubled over, Gabrielle saw that one of the men was a Belgian whom she recognised. She began to shout at him: 'These men are Boches, but you are a Belgian. You should be ashamed of yourself.'

The men ransacked the room, opening drawers, throwing papers on the floor, pulling up carpets and finding nothing.

'You poor Boches,' said Gabrielle, 'you can't find anything, how very sad.'

Then one of them found some cards she had made with drawings of German military uniforms and notes about the colours of the badges and insignia. In spite of the pain from the punch in her stomach, she laughed. One of the agents was grinding his cigarette out on the carpet. Auguste grabbed an ashtray and Gabrielle shouted at her not to worry. 'These people feel themselves at home in a stable.'

Outside, cars were waiting; in one of them was Marie Collet, already under arrest. Through the glass windows of the vehicle she saw Gabrielle being pulled from the house, stumbling on the stairs, losing her balance and then being dragged across the pavement. The front door of the car was pulled open and Gabrielle thrown in, falling against the driver. The car pulled away. Gabrielle wound down her window and shouted, 'I have been arrested by the Boches!' The police officer in the back of the car shouted at Gabrielle to be quiet. She gabbled to Collet that she was not to worry; they would all be released by the evening and she must go back to her room and help herself to a ham that was there. The policeman sneered and asked her how she could afford a ham – was it on the back of her spying work?

He then told her to 'shut the fuck up or I will hit you'. Gabrielle pulled a hatpin from her hair and waved it threateningly. 'We will see about you having the nerve to hit me. One has to be a dirty German like you to dare say that to a woman.'

The car drove on, Gabrielle breathing heavily, wild with fury. The destination was the huge, gloomy prison of Saint-Gilles, where Edith Cavell had been incarcerated. She and Collet were hauled out of the car and each marched off in different directions. Gabrielle was hustled along dank corridors and bundled into a cell, alone.

The next day her interrogation began. First it was Goldschmidt who questioned her, always accompanied by a translator, Otto Becker. When Becker first came into her cell he was alone and she asked him whether he was 'as much of a Boche, as much of a brute' as all the others. She called his superior 'a *Schwein*'. Becker was astonished at her insolence. She refused to admit anything. Nevertheless, over the next weeks Becker came to know, respect and admire her.

A day after her cell door had first slammed shut she was visited by an official who, with great punctiliousness, handed her one hundred francs. He explained that they had found the money in her room; they were returning it and required a signature. The next day, in her cell, Marie Collet received a visitor carrying two large ham sandwiches and a comb. In the days that followed, the miserable woman, frightened and alone, was showered with cheese, milk, sugar and handkerchiefs, somehow arranged by Gabrielle. Auguste, the neighbour who had been in her room when she was arrested, received a letter apologising for the upset the incident had caused and asking her to keep an eye on the room 'until I have established certainty about my prospects'.

At first Gabrielle's interrogation sessions were polite but firm and, when pressed to give the names of her associates, she refused. When she was alone she began to sing loud patriotic songs, her voice echoing along the dismal corridors, infuriating her interrogators, who began to lose their tempers with her.

Three weeks after her arrest she was allowed a visit from her sister, Hélène, who found her sitting crying in her cell, holding her head in her hands. As she entered and the door closed noisily behind her, Gabrielle looked up, her eyes puffy from weeping, the side of her face swollen, red and bruised. Gabrielle did not say how this had happened.

In the world outside, in Tournai and Brussels and all the villages through which she had travelled, the people who had helped Gabrielle waited in terror for the hammering on the door that would mean she had cracked and given them away.

By now Louise de Bettignies and Léonie Vanhoutte had been incarcerated in Saint-Gilles for nearly six months. Each cell had a radiator bolted to the wall, connected to the system by an iron water pipe that was held in a metal tube. If anyone tapped on the pipe the noise could be heard in the surrounding cells. The prisoners could talk to each other by whispering into the tube. They called this 'the telephone'. Léonie was aware that a new prisoner had been installed in the cell next to hers and was not surprised to hear a tapping on the pipe. Then she bent down and put her ear next to the steel conduit. A woman's voice whispered, asking her who she was. Léonie did not answer, worried that she was listening to an informer who might try to trap her into a confession. But whoever it was persisted and Léonie began to talk to her. She discovered that her neighbour was Gabrielle Petit and the two women struck up a strange friendship. Gabrielle told her that she had been 'worked over' by her interrogators but had told them that they would not find 'the coward' in her. Léonie described her own, similar experiences and whispered the name of Louise de Bettignies. Petit described how the prison chaplain had called the king of Belgium a 'puppet', to which she had replied that her king was worth a lot more than that 'goose-stepping emperor of yours ... that dirty Kaiser ... at least my king is in front of his soldiers'.

Becker, the translator, became a regular visitor to Gabrielle and was impressed that every day she wrote patriotic slogans on her walls: 'Long Live Belgium', 'Long Live King Albert'. Every day the slogans were washed off and every day she rewrote them.

But after time the pressure, the loneliness and the fear wore her down. On her twenty-third birthday, 20 February, she celebrated alone. She wrote to a friend telling her how slowly time seemed to pass and how she longed for something to happen, some sort of resolution to her predicament. She wrote that she hated things dragging on.

Earlier in the month, on the same day that Gabrielle Petit was arrested, 2 February, Marie Birckel sat in a railway carriage watching Paris slide by as her train pulled out of the Gare Saint-Lazare. In the overhead rack was her rucksack containing nothing but a change of clothes and some washing things. She was heading for Dieppe and the ferry to Folkestone.

By three in the morning, under a bright full moon, she was on English soil feeling dizzy and weak after a stormy crossing. She soon left the port and found the office where the French intelligence officer, Colonel Wallner, was waiting for her with a special passport. It was Wallner who had received Gabrielle Petit. Marie told him she had nowhere to stay and he gave her the address of a bed and breakfast where she could recover. When she arrived she found that the room was freezing, the house unwelcoming and the food disgusting. Here she stayed for the next three weeks while she was instructed in field craft and observation techniques by an expert, a man who had successfully completed a mission in France and been given the Military Medal.

By the last day of February Wallner thought she was ready to be sent back to Belgium. She took a train to Tilbury and a ferry to Rotterdam. On the way, there was a violent knocking on her cabin door. She was ordered on deck with the other passengers and told to put on her cork life jacket. The lookout thought he had spotted the periscope of a submarine. A few days earlier a ferry had been torpedoed off the English coast. The danger passed; the ferry docked in Rotterdam and Marie set foot on neutral Dutch soil, where she was contacted by Allied resistance operatives and arrangements were made to get her back over the border into occupied Belgium.

It was decided that Marie should go across country to a place where she could be put on one of the many barges that had permission to sail between Holland and Belgium. She travelled at night in a small group led by a guide. The weather was bitter; it snowed and the wind howled. The first night they covered 23 miles, the second 25, often crossing ground made treacherous by deep piles of slippery, frozen, pine needles. On the second night Marie lost her balance and fell into freezing water. Several times they boarded a barge, crawling aboard through special hidden access points and lying in the dark on coal covered with mattresses stuffed with straw. Each time they passed the border and entered Belgium, the canal was closely monitored by German patrols and guards mounted in watchtowers. Searchlights followed the barges, every movement was watched. On each attempt they deemed it too dangerous to disembark and the party returned to Holland, the mission aborted.

CHAPTER FOURTEEN

JUDGEMENT

At the end of the previous year, 1915, the German general Erich von Falkenhayn and Kaiser Wilhelm II had sat in a railway carriage staring at maps and discussing how best to bring the war to an end. They decided that an attack in the region of the fortress town of Verdun was the most promising option. Later, the idea was discussed with other generals and was met with great enthusiasm. One said, 'We must take action and bring the war to its conclusion. To this end I believe we must attack and take Verdun.'

General von Falkenhayn's plan was to attack where the French and British armies met. He knew that the year before, in the battle of Champagne, shellfire had caused the French to suffer 'extraordinary' casualties. He ordered a huge build-up of ammunition to make sure that shellfire was the most important component of the attack. He hoped to drive a wedge between the British and the French and provoke a counter-attack in which he would bleed the Allies to death in a war of attrition. He called his plan 'Operation Judgement'.

If he succeeded, the French would collapse and make a peace treaty with the Germans, leading to the expulsion of the British from Europe.

He told one general that if his plan worked the war could be decided in fourteen days. The Kaiser agreed and thought that when the French counter-attacked they would be repulsed with an enormous loss of life and equipment. There were others who thought that the plan relied too heavily on luck.

In the new year 1916, the area around Verdun was cleared of civilians, buildings were requisitioned and thousands of miles of telephone wire were laid. Ten new railway lines were installed and twenty new stations built to carry more than thirty trains a day, transporting the 4 million artillery shells of every calibre that it was planned would be fired in the first fortnight of the attack. The area became one of the biggest store depots and ammunition dumps in the world, manned by 1,200 troops living in underground shelters.

Across no-man's-land, the French and British armies waited in trenches that met at the river Somme. They had no idea that the Germans were preparing an attack.

At 7:15am on 21 February, in the bitter cold, the German Kaiser personally ordered the firing of the first shot to signal the beginning of the battle. A million shells were fired in ten hours. One 210mm shell landed 19 miles from its target and exploded in the courtyard of the bishop's palace in Verdun, destroying part of the cathedral. The firing was carefully controlled and the phenomenon known as *Trommelfeuer*, where the noise of exploding shells merges into one roaring sound, was achieved in the last hour of the bombardment. The thundering could be heard nearly 60 miles away.

One soldier wrote, 'The human presence was reduced to flattened terror.' Another that 'trenches of normal depth in the course of a few minutes were opened up as if by a hidden hand, and turned into deep pits lined with corpses and fragments of corpses'. One hundred miles away a senior officer could hear 'an incessant rumble of drums, punctuated by the pounding of big basses'.

The bombardment went on for days. In the words of one soldier, 'Every particle of ground on which we stood ... was searched by the enemy's fire – the front, the supply line, the rear, the crests, the hollows, the roads, the village, the bridges and the stations – the hills around us smoked like volcanoes. Every second and with every step new holes appeared in the torn ground ...'

On both sides of the Western Front the wounded began to arrive. An eyewitness described 'men holding their intestines in both hands, the broken bones tearing the flesh, the arteries spurting blood as a clot gave away, bared brains ... the maimed hand ... the empty eye sockets, the pierced chests, the skin hanging down in tatters from the burned face, the missing lower jaw ...' And at the hospitals: 'Pasty-faced tired assistants unloaded mud, cloth, bandages and blood that turned out to be human beings ... the wounded lay ... naked in their stretchers while the attendant swabbed them with a hot soapy sponge – the blood ran from their wounds through the stretchers to the floor, and seeped into the cracks of the stones.'

By 25 February both sides had taken 25,000 casualties and at last the French realised that the advance was the real thing. It became a matter of honour to hold the fortress.

Six weeks later the Germans had managed to take the ground that they had planned to capture on day one of the offensive, and in the process had lost 81,000 casualties. General Falkenhayn decided that his plan had failed and wanted to call a halt. However, the battle went on.

On 31 March 1916, while the battle of Verdun raged, British GHQ moved to Montreuil-sur-Mer, a small town surrounded by ramparts on the main route from London to Paris. It was connected to the front and the outside world by telephone and road systems.

Soldiers in the mud and blood of the trenches thought that the officers at GHQ just swanned about in motor cars wearing red tabs on their collars. The reality was that the staff at GHQ, nearly 5,000 men, worked very hard, developing the strategy of the campaigns and dealing with the huge logistical problem of supplying food, equipment and ammunition to nearly 2 million men and 500,000 animals.

The entire Allied operation could be destroyed by a surprise attack. The millions of pieces of information gathered by spies and agents operating in Belgium had to be sent to the Allies quickly, before the intelligence became obsolete. Staff officers in all departments were to be found at their desks by nine o'clock in the morning and were usually still toiling away after ten or eleven o'clock at night.

There were compensations. The main form of relaxation was the 'officers' club'. The subscription was five francs a month. For a small daily charge members were entitled to three meals a day and afternoon tea. Wine was available at nine francs for a vintage claret or burgundy, and five francs for a decent ordinary wine. Champagne was fifteen francs a bottle. Most of the officers were colonels, alongside a few majors, brigadiers and captains.

Smoking was prohibited until after 8:20pm. On one occasion a senior visiting general lit a cigar at 8pm. The mess sergeant major found a ladder, climbed up to the mess clock and altered the time to 8:20. After dinner most men went back to their desks. Apart from waitresses and nurses there were no women at Montreuil.

While GHQ was establishing itself in Montreuil, a young artillery officer called Henry Landau was recovering from German measles, an illness he had contracted while on leave in London. The adjutant of his regiment had given him the address of his sister and Landau took her out to dinner. When he told her that he had travelled in Europe and could speak German and French she said that her 'Chief' was looking for someone like him. A few days later Landau was ordered to report to the War Office, where his languages were tested. Later, he was told to present himself at No. 2 Whitehall Court. There he learned that he had been transferred to the Intelligence Corps and was to see 'the Chief' at once.

At Whitehall Court he was shown through a bewildering series of corridors, stairs and passages, eventually taking a small private lift with a zigzag metal door to an office at the very top of the building. He pulled back the clanking ironwork and stepped into a plain room decorated with two seascapes, a map of Europe and a chart of the trenches. On a large safe stood a mechanical gadget, the reason for which he could not fathom. At the end of the room was an ordinary table and behind it sat a man with a pointed chin and a beautiful bowed mouth. The clean-shaven man was staring at him through a gold-rimmed monocle. This was the legendary 'C', Captain Mansfield Smith-Cumming, head of the Secret Intelligence Service, Foreign Section (MI6). Cumming had a passion for all forms of transport and for speed. He was a rich man who had several houses, and any number of boats, including a 10-ton luxury yacht. He owned a Rolls-Royce which he allowed his 12-year-old niece to steer up Piccadilly. Early in the war he had lost a leg in a motor car accident in France. This was the man who sat at the centre of a number of secret and sometimes overlapping and conflicting intelligence organisations and who was known to all as 'the Chief'. He motioned for Landau to sit down.

After a few words of introduction Cumming said, 'I know all about your past history, you are just the man we want.' He explained that his train-watching intelligence operation had broken down both in Belgium and in occupied northeastern France. No information was getting through. The Chief wanted him to go that night to Harwich and from there to Rotterdam, where he was to make contact with his head of operations in Holland, R. B. Tinsley, codename 'T'. He was to use 'T' as a cover and communicate through him. 'Although I must warn you that he is an absolute scoundrel.' After briefing him about the arrangements in Holland he said, 'You are in complete charge of the military section; responsibility for its success or failure is on your shoulders. I can't tell you how it is to be done – that is your job. You have carte blanche.'

A bemused Landau wondered what 'T' was really like. He would soon find out.

Before the war Tinsley had been the Chief's agent in Rotterdam. Tinsley was built like a boxer, stocky with powerful shoulders and a penetrating, challenging stare. One of his employees described him as being a cross between 'a sea captain and a prizefighter'. The senior intelligence officer Walter Kirke thought he was 'a smart fellow' but that no good agent would want to work for him. Tinsley ran operations in Holland, France and Germany but spoke no Dutch, French or German.

He had been appointed by the station chief in Holland, Ernest Maxse, the consul general in Rotterdam who lived in The Hague. Maxse was a man who waxed his moustache, dyed his hair black, used a monocle that dangled from a black silk ribbon and was described as having 'fiery eyes set in a sallow, hollow-cheeked face'. Some thought he was a cross between a fictional spy and a stage villain. Maxse's position as consul general meant that he was forbidden to contact agents directly. Hence his appointment of Tinsley.

The intelligence gleaned by Tinsley was analysed in The Hague by a tall, highly strung, scholarly-looking major called Oppenheim, known as 'Oppy'. Oppenheim had no idea of life in the field but was brilliant at his work. He could squeeze every drop of information from the reports that reached him. When confronted with scraps of information from the train-watching networks he had an unerring instinct for what they meant in terms of troop movements and volumes of men. Once Oppenheim had made his analysis the work was passed on to the Chief, who forwarded it to GHQ in France. He was an essential link between agents operating in the field and GHQ.

Throughout her imprisonment and interrogation Gabrielle Petit was not allowed legal representation, even though there was a group of lawyers, known as the 'defence committee', who were prepared to represent her and others like her for nothing. The German police hated the committee, often excluding its members from defending spies. Even when they were allowed into court they were not given trial dates and often only learned about the fate of their clients when they had been tried, condemned to death and shot. Gabrielle was interrogated alone, with no lawyer present. Gabrielle's trial took place behind closed doors and began on 2 March.

Her prosecutor was Eduard Stoeber, the officer who had successfully prosecuted Edith Cavell. He now boasted that he might not leave Brussels alive and liked to show his friends examples of the death threats he received. One promised that he would be gunned down in the street.

Early in the morning of 2 March Gabrielle was taken from her cell and led to a horse-drawn cab in the courtyard of Saint-Gilles. She was driven from there to the military hospital to collect her comrade Marie Collet, who was being treated for leg ulcers. When the cab arrived, Collet was waiting outside, under guard. She watched as it pulled up and inside a hand lifted the grey curtains covering the windows to reveal Gabrielle. Collet immediately shouted, 'Look, there's Gabby!' Collet climbed into the cab and the two women hugged and cried together.

Collet asked her where they were going and Gabrielle replied, 'Mother, we are going to our condemnation.' They were taken first to the Kommandantur, the German administrative headquarters. Petit called the soldiers guarding them 'our footmen'. From the Kommandantur they were led on foot to the Senate building, where they were to wait to be summoned into the grandeur of the Council Chamber. Petit took off her hat and pulled the hatpin out of her hair, which fell round her shoulders. She told one of her interrogators, 'See, I am all dolled up for you.'

Then they were led into the chamber, two small figures before the bench of judges and lawyers, all in their regalia, the room soaring around them. The judge sat at a dais draped in veiled flags; one was huge and bore the eagle of the House of Hohenzollern. Collet was terrified, seeing herself as a piteous mouse who had been let out of a trap into a big room somewhere in which there was a cat. Petit told her to be brave and to remember that 'it's *our* Senate, mother.'

The trial began. Just as he had done with Cavell and her comrades, Stoeber spoke in German which neither woman could understand. His words were translated by an interpreter who was cavalier and brutal in his treatment of the prisoners. The lawyer appointed to represent them was allowed to take notes but was forbidden to intervene in the proceedings in any way.

Eduard Stoeber opened the prosecution by asking Gabrielle why she had joined British Intelligence. She replied, 'Because of the atrocities you commit.'

Stoeber asked her what she was referring to and she answered, 'You have the gall to ask me which one. The ones you have committed in Charleroi where you burned people alive.'

Stoeber banged his fist on the bench in front of him and shouted that Gabrielle was lying.

'If you want to come with me I will show where it happened.'

She refused to name anyone with whom she had been working, saying, 'Never ... you commanded hundreds of men, tell us their names.'

When told that some of her friends were already in prison so she might as well name them, she replied, 'You've looked for my name, so now go and look for theirs.'

All her responses were designed to exasperate the court. When asked why she did not live with her parents she said that her private life had nothing to do with her work as an agent. When Stoeber asked her what she saw on the railways at night, she shot back, 'What I see at night? What do you think? It's dark, isn't it?' Asked what she would do if released, she said that she would take up her work where she had left off when she was arrested.

At the end of the cross-examination and after Marie Collet had denied knowing anything about Gabrielle's work, Stoeber summed up the case for the prosecution. The only words of French he spoke were to describe the charge and the sentence that he asked the court to hand down. Stoeber demanded the death sentence for Gabrielle and fifteen years' imprisonment for Marie Collet. At this, Petit sprang up and began to hurl abuse at the prosecutor, calling him a '*Schweinhund*', telling him that he should be ashamed of himself. She refused to sit down and be quiet. Eventually Gabrielle and Marie were taken out of the court. They would return the following day to hear the sentences. As they were led past the crowds outside, Gabrielle repeatedly shouted out, 'Gabrielle Petit, spy, condemned to death!' Collet was silent, her head cast down. On arrival at Saint-Gilles Gabrielle told her guards that she had been condemned to death. They thought she was joking.

The next day, at eight o'clock in the morning, Gabrielle and Marie were taken by prison van to the Kommandantur to have their sentences confirmed. In the van with them was a priest who had started an underground paper called *L'Âme Belge* (*The Soul of Belgium*). She told him that she had been condemned to death and that she was going to ask for her sentence to be carried out and for Marie Collet's to be overturned. At the Kommandantur her sentence was made official: she was to be shot. Collet was acquitted for lack of evidence.

Later, as they waited for the van to take them back to Saint-Gilles, Gabrielle told the priest the verdicts. She was alternately crying and laughing. At one point, she sang some of the words from a song called 'Paris–Berlin', which contained satirical references to the

Germans, including the line: 'We may be Germans / but not for long'. Then she told the priest that in the morning she would be 'Boom!' and mimed aiming a rifle. Finally she settled and asked for coffee and traditional smoked-meat pistolets for herself, Marie Collet, the priest and another man who was with them who was about to serve a ten-day sentence for insulting the Germans. During the lunch the priest offered to hear her confession. She later told the priest that she would show the Germans that 'a Belgian woman knows how to die'.

She told him that any attempt to blindfold her would be met by spitting in their faces.

In the van on the way back to the prison the priest said that she should appeal her sentence but she refused, saying, 'I don't want to owe them anything.'

Back in Saint-Gilles, Gabrielle gave Collet the few valuable possessions she had there, including her rosary and prayer book, plus a fur muff, a watch and a pair of gloves. The two women were then taken to their separate cells and never saw each other again.

Gabrielle thought she was going to be executed the next day, but she was not. For the next few weeks her godmother, Hélène Ségard, tried to get the sentence commuted. A woman lawyer gave her advice on how to do this, but Gabrielle could see from the look on her face that there was little hope. The court had been offended by her lack of respect.

On 8 March Gabrielle was visited by her godfather and her sister. They had the appeal form for her to sign. She was still cheerful despite the challenging conditions in the prison, where things were not easy and it was cold. 'It is a bit hard but I wrap myself in my coat, don't I?'

She told them that life was good. 'We laugh, we sing, especially the "Brabançonne"' – the Belgian national anthem.

As for the petition, she refused to sign it. When her visitors left she wrote by the crucifix hanging from the wall: 'I refuse to sign my request for pardon in order to show the enemy that I don't give a damn.'

She also wrote: 'No one will ever know how much I have suffered ... The days are centuries here and I am so alone.'

When another prisoner told her that the Germans would never

execute a young woman she replied, 'No hope, I can be freed if I denounce my helpers. Never, I prefer to die!'

And all the while she sang and shouted and made 'an infernal ruckus' in her cell and in the exercise yard. On the day after her sentence had been confirmed she shouted for all to hear, 'I have just been condemned to death. I will be shot tomorrow. Long live the King! Long live Belgium!'

She also sang the song from Gounod's *Faust* which contains the line: '*Salut, ô mon dernier matin*' – 'Hail, my last day'.

She let her hair down and wore her long blue overcoat open over her dressing gown, and told her godmother, 'I am at home here, no one should disturb me.'

She made a list of the possessions still left in her room. They included: '1 blue blouse with braids. 1 brown velvet one, 1 green, 1 white shirtwaist, 1 white blouse and 1 pretty carton with faded ribbon.'

A German officer told Marie Collet not to give away any of Gabrielle's things. He said she would be imprisoned until the end of the war because the Germans 'don't shoot women any more'. Gabrielle wrote to her godmother, saying, 'I still believe the death sentence has been commuted to life in prison, otherwise it seems to me I would have been executed already.' In the same letter she wrote, 'Will the death penalty be commuted to life in prison? I don't know but I think so. I'm only twenty-three, I am a bit young, that is probably the reason I am still alive. Do me a favour and spare me some silk and an embroidery pattern so I have something to do.'

She wrote a long letter to the translator Otto Becker and told him about the man she had been going to marry, Maurice Gobert. She said, 'He loved me with all his soul; I tried everything to distance him from me. But to no avail. I tried to love him but I couldn't; I have a great deal of respect for him; but that's all ... He knows full well I don't love him; besides, I have never been able to love anybody ... I will live this life without ever having felt deeply. I only appear animated; when my nerves falter I am quite worthless.' Nevertheless she added: 'Underneath my nerves I possess a very strong will; because I am highly strung, I appear to be something of a hothead and tend to be misunderstood; yet I am quite different from what people think of me ... I like danger to begin with and hatred does the rest.' She ended the letter by repeating that in the case of her fiancé, 'I will not let myself be dominated ... Even if I do not love him, I will respect him.'

Gabrielle continued to refuse to sign the application to be pardoned; even Becker gave up, though he thought that 'we Germans were persuaded that women would no longer be executed after the commotion that the execution of Miss Cavell had made and the delay in Gabrielle's execution only strengthened our belief, which was also shared by the secret police'.

It was now March 1916 and both Louise de Bettignies and Léonie Vanhoutte knew that their trials would soon take place. They were still wearing the clothes in which they had been arrested, which were now worn out, as were their shoes. They both wore detachable linen collars which they washed in an attempt to look smart in court. Their trials began on 16 March. Once again the court assembled with predictable pomposity and once again it was Stoeber who led the prosecution. There were six accused in all, one of whom had been part of Louise's network.

When Stoeber asked Louise for her full name he did so in German; when the translator began to repeat the question in French, Louise said, 'Don't trouble, I understand.'

Stoeber demanded that she speak in German to which she replied, 'No, monsieur. I am French. Make use of your interpreter, but let him be careful to translate conscientiously.'

Throughout the hearing neither Louise nor Léonie would incriminate any of the people they had worked with. At one point Louise said, 'You want me to pay with my life for the harm I do you in saving those you are seeking. Well, kill me – but you won't make me speak.'

At the end of the proceedings the sentences were read out:

'For Louise de Bettignies, death.'

'For Léonie Vanhoutte, death.'

There was one more death sentence and the other three were given varying terms of imprisonment with hard labour.

The next day the two women were taken to the Kommandantur where they were told that Louise was to be shot but that Léonie's sentence had been commuted to fifteen years' hard labour.

Back in Saint-Gilles, Louise wrote several letters, one to the prioress of the Carmelite monastery where she had once thought to become a nun.

MY REVEREND MOTHER

I have been condemned to death by the Council of War ...
My life has been far from perfect and I have never been a model
of meekness and abnegation ...

These last five months of prison have been five months of
retreat, prayer and study ... My brain is not very clear today.
I am still under the emotion of my verdict, and feel weak and
fatigued. Tomorrow I shall be better. I shall partake of Holy
Communion and prepare to go and see God in heaven. I should
like to feel nothing as strongly as the love of God these last days
and a complete resignation to his will ... Goodbye dear Mother;
forgive me all my faults ...

Through the 'telephone' Léonie Vanhoutte gave Gabrielle Petit the news that she had been reprieved. Gabrielle asked her to 'keep a spot for me' and hoped that she too would have her sentence commuted. Léonie left Saint-Gilles on 24 March, heading for Siegburg prison in Germany.

As the days passed Gabrielle slowly lost hope that her sentence would be commuted. Her scissors were taken away from her and her heart medication, digitalis, was withdrawn in case she tried to commit suicide. Gabrielle wrote to her sister saying that she was going to die with her 'honour guard', which was her way of describing the firing squad that she was to face. She joked with her godmother, Hélène Ségard, asking her if she could imagine her 'going off to eat potato peels *chez* the Boches', which was what would happen if she were sent to Germany to a labour camp.

On 31 March a German military policeman appeared on Hélène Ségard's doorstep. He carried a yellow envelope bearing the stamp of the Kommandantur. The letter was in German and Hélène could not understand it. The soldier fooled around, imitating shooting and saying in German 'tomorrow'.

Ségard and her cousin went straight to the Kommandantur, but it was shut for lunch. Then they walked to find the priest, who refused to intercede because the order came from 'my emperor'. The three of them argued, Ségard demanding that he prepare her for death and that they must be allowed to see Gabrielle one last time. He gave them a permit to take back to the Kommandantur where there was another argument. They were asked how they knew about the execution; it was meant to be a secret to avoid a disturbance in the town. A call was made to the prison and the information conveyed that Petit was to be executed the next day, that she must not be told and that her sister would soon be visiting. Becker the translator was so shocked that he went at once to see Gabrielle. When he entered her cell she stared him straight in the face and said, 'I will be shot tomorrow.' Fifteen minutes later her sister Hélène arrived. With her, Gabrielle was very cheerful. As she left Becker told the sister that the pardon had been refused.

There was then an uproar in the prison when an officer arrived from the Kommandantur demanding to know who had broken the news about the execution. Becker was ordered to accompany the officer to cell 23 to inform Gabrielle of her fate. It was, he said, 'the worst moment of my life. I had to announce her death sentence, this heroic woman whom I had admired so unreservedly, whom I had come to respect ... and for whom I had a liking; I [was] her only friend in the prison, the only one who took her mind off her plight.'

After telling Gabrielle that her sentence was to be carried out the next day, they left her cell. Minutes later Ségard and the cousin arrived. It was six o'clock in the evening. They were led to a visiting room where they waited for Gabrielle to be brought in. When she arrived she hugged them, smiling. Then she said, 'My path is at an end ... I know it ... but even if it has all been for nothing I leave without regrets ... I have been condemned alone, I could have sold my people, I have refused. I did well, didn't I?'

Neither woman could speak. Gabrielle said to her godmother, 'It is not such a pity, I have never been strong. Don't be too sad.'

She was laughing. 'I have always been firm in the face of danger, do not fear.'

The visit was over and she was led back to her cell. From the end of the corridor she shouted, 'No blindfold!'

That evening Becker accompanied an officer to her cell. The officer had brought a letter from Berlin which Becker translated for her, although he already knew the message it carried. It said that the request for pardon had been denied and she was to be executed the next day. In the silence that followed, Becker saw that she was flushing and her face was crimson. He felt sick that there was nothing he could do to help this woman through her last hours. She was an enemy of his country but also a heroic woman whom he admired and respected. The officer spoke, telling Gabrielle to make arrangements for her few remaining possessions. Gabrielle recovered her composure and, as the officer left the cell, she sat down to express her last wishes, using a blue pencil to write on card. She handed it to Becker who, unable to speak, nodded his head. She laughed and told him not to be so solemn. Then he turned and left the cell. When he had gone she took the pencil and wrote on the doorjamb: 'They consent to shoot me tomorrow. Farewell to all my unknown and much-tried friends.'

The next morning, 1 April, the prison chaplain came to give her communion, then they left the cell. Outside, Becker was waiting; he saw that her eyes were red from crying. She nodded as she passed him; tears were running down his face. The chaplain followed her as she was led outside to a carriage into which they both climbed. As it pulled away he handed her a rosary and a prayer book, and asked her if, when the time came, she would like a blindfold. She refused, saying, 'I am not afraid of looking into the rifles.' Then she withdrew into herself, holding the rosary and reciting its prayer: 'Hail Mary full of grace ...'

The journey took twenty minutes and, as she was led from the carriage to the stake where she was to be shot, the chaplain again offered her a blindfold, telling her softly that nothing should disturb her thoughts of heaven. She relented and a soldier stepped forward to tie the cloth across her eyes.

In the darkness she could hear the officer in charge of the firing party ordering his men to load and aim. The priest saw her draw herself upright, her shoulders defiantly back like a soldier. The officer's raised sword flashed through the air followed by the shattering noise of the rifles firing. Gabrielle, one of the Allies' most important agents, died instantly.

Four soldiers placed Gabrielle's body in a wooden coffin. Her long blue overcoat torn by the bullets that had killed her and stained by the red of her blood. Like all the others who had fallen before the firing squads, she was laid to rest in an unmarked grave.

At noon dark-pink posters appeared in Brussels, declaiming:

By judgement of the military tribunal of 2 March
1916, GABRIELLE PETIT, saleswoman, living
in Molenbeek, has been condemned

TO DEATH.

For treason on grounds of espionage.

The accused had confessed to having organised, for a
substantial fee, a railway spying service, and to have,
over several months, transmitted to enemy intelligence
the reports drawn up by the agents she engaged.

The Judgement has been executed.

A few weeks later Louise de Bettignies' sentence was commuted to a life sentence of hard labour and she followed Léonie to Siegburg prison in Germany.

CHAPTER FIFTEEN

More Arrests

Later, in the same month as Gabrielle Petit was executed, another agent sat in a cell waiting for the firing squad. His name was Dieudonné Lambrecht and on this, the last night of his life, he was writing to his wife. He wrote in sorrow that he would leave his wedding ring and a small cross she had given to him before the war. He would cover it in kisses for her, and knew they would meet in heaven. Eighteen months earlier he had fled from Belgium into Holland hoping to join the army. Instead, he was approached by British Intelligence and was persuaded to return to his home town of Liège to organise a spy ring to watch the railways and gather information on German troop movements of every kind.

Soon he was running a band of train watchers covering Liège, Namur and Jemelle. Every train that passed through was observed and recorded, the information being sent to GHQ. Lambrecht himself devoted his time to recruiting new agents and spying on troop movements in rest areas behind the lines. He tried, but failed, to establish a similar organisation in the Grand Duchy of Luxembourg, another important German railway hub. He also acted as a courier, carrying documents written on fine paper and hidden in the cloth buttons of his coat.

Slowly, as the Germans made it more and more difficult to get intelligence out of Belgium into Holland, communication between agents in Belgium and their contacts in Holland all but dried up. By

the beginning of 1916 Lambrecht's couriers stopped appearing and
he found he had no way of getting his reports out of the country.
His controller in Holland became frantic, and in turn British GHQ
became impatient, demanding intelligence. Lambrecht's main letter
box in Liège was a small tobacco shop run by a husband and wife
team who were related to him, the Leclercqs. One afternoon Mme
Leclercq was on her own in the shop when a new and unknown
courier from Holland appeared. He told her he had just crossed the
wire from Holland with an urgent letter for M. Leclercq. He knew
the code words, 'The seven boxes of tricolour cigars have arrived
safely.' Something made Mme Leclercq suspicious. She denied any
knowledge of the cigars and told him they were not expecting any
letters from Holland. As soon as the man left she went searching for
her husband and told him what had happened. He was furious; as
far as he was concerned the code words had been authentic. When
Mme Leclercq got back to the shop she found that the man had
returned and left a letter which they immediately took to Lambrecht.
It contained a coded message from his controller in Holland saying
that the courier was to be trusted and that it was essential that he
send, immediately, the reports that had been building up for weeks.

The six-week backlog was too much for one agent to carry safely
so Lambrecht spent the night preparing a résumé of all the information. The next day he went to the tobacco shop and handed over
his work to the new agent, wishing him a safe journey back into
Holland. The courier told him not to worry, he had a foolproof route
that he was going to take that evening. In the meantime, he would
spend the day in the centre of the city. Lambrecht warned him to be
careful, there were counter-intelligence men everywhere. The pair
shook hands and parted.

On his way home Lambrecht realised that he was being followed
and, by jumping on a tram, he managed to throw off his pursuer.
Worried for the safety of the courier he went looking for him in the
Café du Marronier, one of the many cafés in the main square at the
centre of Liège. As he looked through the plate-glass windows he
saw that the courier was sitting with two men who he knew were

German secret policemen, men who had blighted his life since he had begun his undercover work.

Lambrecht went home to warn his wife and to get her to warn the Leclercqs. He opened the door of his house to confront a group of German policemen who grabbed him, dragged him back into the house and told him he was under arrest. They added that his wife was already in custody. He was interrogated and tortured for a month, but did not reveal the names of the thirty agents who operated for him. He managed to persuade them that neither the Leclercqs nor his wife had any idea what he was up to. He was tried and condemned to death.

On 18 April, he stood alone in front of the firing squad. One of the most important communications doors between the Belgian underground and the Allies had been kicked shut by German counter-intelligence.

The next day Lambrecht's cousin Walthère Dewé stared at a poster that had appeared all over the walls of Liège. It blazoned Lambrecht's execution. Dewé was thirty-five, had two children and was chief engineer of the Liège Telephone and Telegraph network. He was tall, thin and dark, with a strong stubbly beard. He was a devout Catholic, with many influential friends both in his social world and in the church. Dewé wondered whether it was his duty to God and his country to pick up the baton that his cousin had dropped.

He discussed his problem with his closest friend, Chauvin, the professor of engineering at the Institut Montefiore in Liège. The two men agreed that they must try to carry on Lambrecht's work. They were in contact with Lambrecht's right-hand man, who was also a close friend of Dewé, Father des Onays. The three men began to analyse what Lambrecht had been doing and where he had gone wrong. Several men close to Lambrecht were contacted in the strictest confidence and they began to formulate a theory. Lambrecht had placed himself in danger on two counts. The first was that he was known to all his agents, his name and contact details. The second was that he always undertook the most dangerous work himself. Thanks to his courage he had not broken under harsh interrogation, but had he done so his confession could have led to the arrest of every man and woman in his network.

Dewé and Chauvin set about reorganising the operation. They divided Belgium into four sectors, each under a head agent, and as far as possible every agent in the group was isolated from the rest. They next approached Chauvin's father-in-law, who was the chief of police in Liège and had to work with the German secret police. They explained what they were doing and he agreed to supply them with photographs of all the German agents in Liège. He also undertook to try to keep them informed of those Belgians who were collaborating with the Germans.

The three founders wanted women to be involved at all levels of the organisation, and worked to ensure that in the event that they themselves were arrested and deported or executed their network could be run entirely by female agents. They planned a reserve of women who knew everything that was going on, and could take over in an emergency and lead the network.

They also needed to identify someone with money who would bankroll the organisation. Most agents were not rich and if they gave up their jobs would need financial support. Like any business, the new network would have running expenses, not least of which were bribes. They knew a banker in Liège, approached him and came away with a promise of financial support, at least for the time being.

On 22 June, two months after Lambrecht's execution, the new organisation began work. They called it 'Service Michelin', naming it after the Michelin tyre company whose advertisements had appeared all over Belgium before the war. Soon, many of the old railway-watching posts in Liège and Jemelle were back in operation; intelligence was pouring in, with the usual, huge, problem – they had no way to get it out of Belgium and into Allied hands.

Dewé decided to send a messenger to Belgian GHQ in France to ask that they organise a trustworthy courier service. A Belgian railway engineer called Bihet was approached to carry out this role. Dewé gave him strict instructions about secrecy, nobody in the Service Michelin must be named. The engineer disappeared towards the electric fence heading for Holland and successfully crossed over. Eventually, a coded advertisement appeared in a Dutch paper indicating that he had arrived.

Two weeks later in the Saint-Denis church in Liège, a woman knelt in a pew, praying. She wore a distinctive green hat. She was devout and was seen to come in to pray every day at 11:30. In reality she was a French agent, and her job was to wait for a person carrying a message from Holland. If he or she appeared, the word 'Yser' would be whispered, and the woman in the green hat would murmur, 'Lion d'Or.' At which point she would be handed a message from Bihet. Every day she appeared and every day there was no sign of a courier. Dewé thought that his plan for establishing communication had failed.

In Flanders, the Germans were strengthening their defensive positions. Sappers dug into the chalk, burying telephone wires 6 feet underground that spread back like spiders' webs linking the rear command centres to the front line. Soldiers sweated, digging dugouts and building concrete bunkers. They knew an attack was coming, but not exactly where the blow would fall. When it did come, though, they wanted to be ready to survive the inevitable bombardment that would precede it.

On the Allied side, observers peered through powerful field glasses, watching the toiling enemy, satisfied when from time to time a shell burst among them. High in the air reconnaissance pilots took photographs of the enemy preparations. All along the Western Front the landscape was scarred with white zigzag trenches and miles of barbed wire. Two miles behind the front line there was another complex of trenches stretching parallel to the front and behind that a third system. The German defensive positions formed a lethal band nearly 30 miles long and up to 5 miles deep.

In their headquarters German planners on the general staff tried to work out the strength of the enemy facing them. General Falkenhayn was in constant touch with the Kaiser, assuring him that the fighting at Verdun had left the French with only six reserve divisions, not realising that they had nearly twice that number. As to the strength of the British, the general staff estimated that they had reserves which would last for months of fighting but were certain that the German troops could hold the line.

Meanwhile, Marie Birckel had arrived in Holland and was sitting in the office of a 20-year-old Frenchman called Émile Fauquenot, who had himself been recruited by British Intelligence. After a short initial training period he was sent back to Holland to establish his headquarters in Maastricht, tasked with organising a network to watch the railway traffic in Liège where he had strong family connections. Fauquenot was a brilliant organiser and soon information about train movements in and out of Liège flowed from his network, with reports arriving two or three times a week. He was helped in his work by a powerfully built older man called Franz Creusen. It was in front of these two men that Marie Birckel now sat.

She explained to them that her mission was to establish a train-watching operation on the prized, and so far elusive, Hirson line. At first Fauquenot was reluctant to help her. He thought it was too dangerous and that she was far too inexperienced. Marie refused to be put off and in the end won both men over.

The battle at Verdun and the impending campaign on the Somme meant that the need for intelligence was urgent. The two men were being bombarded by GHQ with requests for information, especially about the Hirson line. The problem was the usual one of how to get Marie across the border and into Belgium. The electric fence had become a major problem and all the guides with the understanding and skill needed to cross it were unavailable. She demanded to see for herself. At night she and a guide crawled within 30 yards of the high-voltage obstacle. Searchlights sweeping backwards and forwards revealed the body of a man hanging, dead. Marie agreed that crossing it was too dangerous.

They decided that a less complicated route would be to cross a canal that formed part of the border. There was no barbed wire, no high-voltage current, just a very wide stretch of water. There were guides who could help her, men who had been smugglers before the war but who now worked hand in hand with their old enemy, the customs men.

The crossing point was nearly 50 miles away and the journey meant that Marie had to be led across country over two days and always after dark. The journey involved moving in the freezing cold and in pitch black across a landscape crisscrossed with water-filled ditches. Just as before, a thick coating of frozen pine needles made the going slippery and dangerous. At the end of the first leg they reached a safe house in Eindhoven, where they were given hot coffee.

When they set off the next night the snow drove hard into their faces, half blinding them. From the trees great clumps of snow fell, battering them to the ground. When they approached the canal a flooded pit barred their way. Again, Marie slipped and fell in the freezing water. Shivering and frozen, she pressed on. They had now crossed into Belgium; the last obstacle was the canal. There were many more patrols than they had expected, some moving within yards of their position. The nearer they got to the canal, the slower their progress. They were often forced to stop, unable to speak, hardly able to make a gesture for fear of making a noise that would attract the attention of the Germans. Only the dark and the terrible weather prevented them from being discovered. Eventually, they reached the edge of the canal where they crouched, waiting for the guides who had been organised to see them across. They waited for two hours. No one came and they decided, once again, to abort the mission and made their slow way back into Holland.

Three days later they made another attempt at a different spot. The weather had improved; it was not so cold and the snow had turned to rain. But once again the patrols and the searchlights forced them to abandon the attempt.

By now Marie's controller at Folkestone, the French officer Wallner, had located another Dutch bargeman who he thought could be trusted, and who had agreed to take three people in his boat. The cost of the passage was 200 francs per person.

At midnight on 12 April Marie and two others boarded the canal boat *Marie-Elisa*. They scrambled into a small hole cut in the deck and heaved themselves into the bilges, filthy and wet. Charcoal was heaped on the hole to hide it. Inside, the boatman had laid sacks of straw to make it easier to lie still and even sleep. They crossed into Belgium but dawn was breaking and it was impossible for the boat to stop and let them off without being seen. For three days and nights they went backwards and forwards, not able to disembark. Yet again the attempt was abandoned. The boatman could not make another attempt for at least a month and, fearing for his life, he refused to carry on.

Marie's two companions abandoned their mission and she was ordered to return to Folkestone by 15 May. On 11 May she argued with Fauquenot that she should have one more try. In despair he turned to his mentor, Creusen.

Creusen had found yet another guide, going under the codename of 'Bertram'. No one knew him but he had recently arrived with some refugees and he seemed to be honest. He undertook to take Marie into Belgium across the high-voltage fence.

On 13 May, Marie and Émile met Bertram in a café. Émile felt that something was wrong and asked Bertram to postpone the mission. He refused. He said that he knew where the guard posts were but that they might change at any moment. Also, it was the night before a new moon; the darkness was essential to the crossing. Marie said she was not frightened and was going to continue with her mission. Nevertheless, as she and Émile said goodbye to each other she paused and added, 'I have a feeling I will not return.'

The next night Marie and her guiding party of five were within 50 yards of the high-voltage fence. The men had provided her with heavy rubber gloves and boots to protect her against the current. Marie could hear the fence humming in the dark, like a malevolent spirit. Two of the men were hauling a barrel covered in rubber, and two had satchels slung over their shoulders. They too were wearing heavy rubber gloves and boots. The men with the satchels pulled out large balls of coarse twine. Bertram wound an end round each hand and the men crawled away on either side of him into the darkness, unwinding the twine as they went. Their job was to watch for the sentries and guards patrolling the fence. When the searchlights were traversing away from the agents, the men were to tug on the strings, a signal that the crossing party had a few moments of safety.

Marie was behind Bertram, his rubber boots inches from her face.

They waited, searchlights passing regularly over their prone bodies. Suddenly Bertram felt a simultaneous tug on the strings, he pulled on Marie's arm and she crawled forward, following him. The men ahead rammed the barrel through the wire; Bertram scrambled through the drum and Marie crawled after him, the rubber lining snagging against her sides. Then she was through, following Bertram as he slithered under the outer wire and into Belgium.

In the watchtowers two men peered through high-powered field glasses, watching Bertram and Marie as they ran for cover away from the fence. The men were officers from the German secret police and had been given strict orders that the crossing party were to be left alone. They knew all about Bertram and were paying him.

Bertram grabbed Marie and pulled her stumbling into a wood straight ahead. Waiting for them were two Belgian agents, who took her heavy rubber gloves and boots and led her once more into the darkness. The secret police watched her disappear. The telephone lines to German Intelligence in Liège buzzed with news of her movements.

On the trip to Liège Marie became suspicious. Bertram did not seem to know the route and was unfamiliar with the countryside. With only a glance at the map she felt she knew the way better, and yet Bertram claimed to have escorted up to a dozen people at a time. As usual it was raining hard and she was soaking wet. At Visé they met a contact who asked her if she knew anyone in Liège. She replied that she did not and he said that she must stay with his cousin, who would look after her. They arrived at two in the morning. The cousin welcomed Marie, made her an omelette and offered her a change of underwear. They would replace her ruined clothes the next day with an outfit that would not attract suspicion.

Bertram went off to stay the night with a friend and appeared at

eleven the next day carrying the new garments that he had bought for
Marie, including a coat, a hat and a pair of shoes. He handed them
over demanding she pay for them. She knew the price he claimed to
have spent was double the real value, even for wartime. Nevertheless
she paid up, after which Bertram gave her the address where she was
to meet her contact.

The following morning she stood outside the rendezvous. A man
with a key appeared and opened the door. He told her that this was
his house and then hesitated, wondering out loud if it would be better
to go to a local café. He said that the women who lived in the house
did not know what he did but were curious and bound to gossip.
He repeated the warning that there were spies and collaborators
everywhere. He suggested that she should leave the safe house and
take a room at the Hotel Cosmopolitan. They could meet the next
day in a café outside the main station, which would be much safer.
Marie agreed but told him she was anxious to get out of Liège and
on to Hirson, her real destination. That night she slept in the Hotel
Cosmopolitan, her mission under way.

When she reached the café the following morning her contact yet
again warned her that there were 'Boche' agents everywhere. Then he
told her she was to make contact with a certain 'Monsieur' and was
given an address. She arrived there and was let in by a woman who
said that the certain 'Monsieur' was expected soon. She was invited
to wait. Inside the house she found that things were very strange.
On a chest of drawers there were photographs of German officers,
standing with them was Bertram. She was confused and beginning
to realise she might have walked into a trap. She still had time to
escape before the arrival of the strange man and left immediately,
saying she would return later.

She walked to the botanical gardens, checking that she was not
being followed. There she sat for a while trying to work out what
to do. If this contact was genuine she had nothing to fear, but if
he was a collaborator she would be arrested and interrogated. She
had no idea how much the Germans knew and for how long they
had been following her, or even if they had been following her. She

decided to go back to the house and bluff it out, feeling she was in a grotesque comedy.

Back at the house the man was waiting and she blurted out that she had seen the photographs and that it was clever of him to have got so close to the Germans, they obviously trusted him. She said that the two of them needed to make contact with Fauquenot; she needed more addresses from him of people working in the field whom she could trust. The man said it was too dangerous to go back to the frontier, better that she should write to Fauquenot. That was impossible, said Marie, he would think she had been arrested. She had to meet him in person. After a while the man agreed, saying he would prepare everything and they would travel to the frontier together by bicycle the next day.

As they set off at nine the following morning the agent said that he was going to call in at the German Kommandantur; he could use his influence to persuade the occupying authorities to issue travel papers that would make her life simpler. Marie was now very scared and wished that she had fled as soon as she realised the Germans were involved.

In the Kommandantur she was arrested, her rucksack seized and searched; the Germans found nothing incriminating. They accused her of trying to get information for the big offensive that they were now expecting on the Somme. She replied that, whatever they thought, the French would be victorious. Then she was left alone. At midday she was offered potato soup which she could not eat. She no longer thought of her captors as 'Allemands' but 'Boches'. Later she was taken to Saint-Léonard prison, where she was pushed into a tiny cell and the door slammed shut behind her.

The next day she found almost unbearable. She was tormented by the thought that she should have listened to Fauquenot. If she had not been so headstrong she would now still be free.

In the days that followed she was taken several times to the Kommandantur for questioning. They had raided the hotel where she had been staying and showed her all the things that she had left there. At one point she saw Bertram joking with the secret police. She was questioned intensively.

'When were you last in Rotterdam?'

'I don't know.'

'You contacted a man called Mercier. Is that his real name?'

'I don't remember.'

On and on the questions went and the days turned into weeks.

Meanwhile, Bertram returned to Holland, met Fauquenot and told him that he had left Marie in Liège as agreed. Fauquenot said that a month had passed and they had heard nothing. He demanded to know what had happened. Bertram flew into a rage and threatened to resign. 'If you don't trust me I'm going!' Then he calmed down and explained that he had left her in a small café in Liège. He reminded Fauquenot that he had been ordered to ask no questions and not to try to find out who she was. Then he admitted that Marie had asked to be returned to the frontier. He said he had escorted her back to a safe house on the other side of the fence in Belgium where she was now waiting. After much thought Fauquenot and Creusen agreed to accompany him to the frontier.

On 30 June 1916 they set off, deeply suspicious of Bertram but thinking that as they were on Dutch soil they would be safe. They approached the fence in the pitch dark and were suddenly attacked from behind, knocked unconscious and dragged from Holland into Belgium. By the end of the night they too were in Saint-Léonard prison. The arrest had been a breach of Dutch neutrality.

Creusen and Fauquenot were tried for spying and sabotage, found guilty and sentenced to death. Creusen was transferred to Chartreuse where the execution was to take place. From his cell he could see the coffin waiting for his body. By now, a nun who worked in the prison had told the Dutch government what had happened and they protested. With six hours to spare, Creusen was reprieved and returned to Saint-Léonard. As a result Émile Fauquenot too had his sentence commuted to life imprisonment.

In the prison Marie Birckel came into contact with a network of people working against the Germans, getting information out of the prison to the Service Michelin. One was a Belgian nun, Sister Mélanie, who was allowed to provide spiritual comfort to the female inmates. Another worked in the kitchen, a prisoner who had been convicted of theft and who was a Belgian patriot. Yet another was one of the guards, a Polish soldier who had been conscripted into the German army and who had a hatred of the Germans. Another link in the chain was an ex-prisoner, an unmarried woman who ran a Catholic bookshop with her sister. She had been arrested for distributing anti-German propaganda and sentenced to six months in the prison, where she met Sister Mélanie. These people became a network, collecting information. The cook took food around to the cells accompanied by the Polish guard. Messages were passed to the cook, who gave them to the guard, who passed them on to Sister Mélanie, who took them to the bookshop, from where they were passed on to the Service Michelin.

Arrested agents often spent time in Saint-Léonard awaiting sentence. Marie Birckel was able to talk to them, find out who had betrayed them, how and why they had been arrested. The agents could identify people who had been compromised by the arrest and what documents had been seized. This important information was transmitted to intelligence networks outside the prison, often within twenty-four hours.

Another woman who formed a link in the chain was Juliette Delrualle, the daughter of one of the Belgian directors of the prison. Juliette's father lived in the prison and she often walked in the garden at night. From her first-floor cell and under the cover of darkness, Marie was able to lower messages on a string to Juliette.

Meanwhile, in Luxembourg, Mme Lise Rischard received a letter from her son in Paris. His father, Lise's first husband, was French and Marcel was liable to be called up into the French army. He wrote wondering if there was any way his mother could come and visit him. She immediately applied to the German commander, General Richard Karl von Tessmar, for a visa to travel to Switzerland. When von Tessmar asked her to explain why she wanted to go she replied that a close relative, living in Lausanne, was ill and needed someone to nurse her. Von Tessmar accepted her explanation but did not want her to travel on to anywhere else. He told her that he would grant permission for the trip, but there was a condition: on arrival in Switzerland she must lodge her passport with the German legation in Berne.

Soon she was on her way, thinking she would be gone for only a few weeks. When she arrived in Berne she found that the German legation was closed. The police said it would be fine if she left the document with the Dutch legation. Now safely out of the control of the Germans, she asked the officials at the Dutch legation for a pass to allow her to continue on to Paris. This was granted. Mme Rischard travelled on to visit her son but did not tell either the German or Swiss authorities where she was going. At the French border she did not show the Dutch pass and it was not stamped.

When the time came for Lise to return she found that the rules had changed and that she needed a visa. She discovered that she was in a diplomatic no-man's-land. Her passport was in Berne and the Dutch document had not been stamped at the border, so there was no proof of who she was, where she had come from or where she was going. The French authorities declined her visa request. A high-ranking diplomat friend whom she had known when he was stationed in Luxembourg told her that she was in a very difficult position and advised her to apply for a new French passport, with which she stood a better chance of getting a visa. She was, after all, French by her first marriage, with a French son. For the moment she was trapped in Paris, struggling with a bureaucracy that was grinding small and slow because of the war.

On Saturday, 1 July, Lance Corporal E. J. Fisher prepared to lead his section across no-man's-land for the start of the first day of the Somme offensive. He scrambled over the parapet and began the terrifying walk across towards the enemy. He reported that, as he advanced,

> ... I saw a sight I shall never forget. A giant fountain, rising from our line of men, about 100 yards from me. Still on the move I stared

at this, not realising what it was. It rose, a great column nearly as high as Nelson's Column, then slowly toppled over. Before I could think, I saw huge slabs of earth and chalk thudding down onto the troops as they advanced, some with flames attached.

In the sky above him the British pilot of a Goshawk biplane looked down and saw that

the earth heaved and flashed, a tremendous and magnificent column rose up into the sky. There was an ear-splitting roar, drowning all the guns, flinging the machine sideways in the repercussing air. The earthly column rose, higher and higher to almost four thousand feet. There it hung, or seemed to hang, for a moment in the air, like a silhouette of some great cypress tree, then fell away in a widening cone of dust and debris. A moment later came the second mine. Again the roar, the upflung machine, the strange gaunt silhouette invading the sky. Then the dust cleared and we saw the two white eyes of the craters. The barrage had lifted to the second-line trenches, the infantry were over the top, the attack had begun.

What they had both seen was the detonation of mines, nineteen in all, that had been tunnelled and placed under the German positions.

The mines did not stop the German machine guns. The first day on the Somme was the deadliest in the history of the British Army. As darkness fell, nearly 20,000 soldiers were dead and more than 38,000 wounded.

In Roulers, Marthe Cnockaert became a trusted friend of the Germans. She picked up bits of information which were transmitted to the Allies through Canteen Ma and through a chemist's shop, the owner of which had become part of the undercover communications network.

One evening, she was invited to dinner by a pilot whom she had met when he was in hospital. As he drove her across the airfield she saw a line of small torpedo-shaped fighter biplanes – the Albatros. The young man told her that they had just arrived from the factory and he and his comrades had been test-flying them. He said they were splendid planes that climbed like rockets and were faster than any Allied plane he had come across. Marthe was surprised that he told her so much, but assumed that he trusted her because she was a nurse and a recipient of the Iron Cross. She also thought he was drunk.

They ate in his quarters and at one point he excused himself and said that he had to finish and seal up his report on the aircraft, ready for his commanding officer the next morning. He also had a request for leave that needed to go to the squadron office. He finished the report and put it in an unsealed envelope, leaving it next to the envelope containing his leave request, also unsealed. Then he said that they must have one more drink and left the room to call his batman. While he was away Marthe swapped the letters, hoping that the senior civilian clerk in the office, whom she knew and who was working with the resistance, would be able to intercept it and copy the contents.

The next day the clerk called at the café with a copy of the report. Marthe cut the report into strips, numbered them and sewed the strips into the hem of an old skirt. The following morning Canteen Ma appeared with vegetables and took the skirt. The report made its way across the border and reached GHQ. In the air raid that followed the pilot was killed.

Later, in the café, Marthe heard a burly sergeant boasting that the war would be over by Christmas. He said a big Zeppelin raid was about to take place, led by a pilot called 'Mathy', adding, 'He knows how to get them on the hop.' Marthe asked him who 'Mathy' was. 'Our great Zeppelin leader, who is showing those English what war feels like.' Heinrich Mathy was a German hero, thirty-two years old and an experienced Zeppelin raider, famous for an attack on London which had caused over a million pounds' worth of damage and killed twenty-two people.

The sergeant boasted that he had heard the air commander talking about the raid and that it was scheduled for 1 October, 'the most *kolossal* raid of the war. Eleven Zeppelins – London has had it! Home by Christmas.' Marthe duly wrote a report.

On the night of 1 October, at five o'clock in the evening, she heard the drone of Zeppelin engines over Roulers. She could not see them because of low cloud but wondered if this was the raid she had heard about and whether the legendary Mathy himself was in command.

The Zeppelins flew on over France and the Channel, heading for London. High over Potters Bar they were caught in anti-aircraft search-lights, shells from the ack-ack guns exploding near them. Mathy's Zeppelin received a hit from a fighter plane firing incendiary rounds. On the ground crowds watched as the great structure caught fire and sank slowly to the earth. Zeppelin crews used to ask themselves what they would do if on fire – stay with the flames or jump? Mathy wrapped himself in a scarf that his wife had given him and jumped from the gondola, now tilting at a strange angle like the hull of a sinking ship. The Zeppelin hit an oak tree where it burned until dawn; the flames could be seen for miles around. Mathy made a man-shaped hole in the ground; none of his crew survived. One had written:

I dream constantly of falling Zeppelins. There's something in me I can't describe. It's as if I saw a strange darkness before me, into which I must go.

While Mathy himself had written:

It is only a question of time before we join the rest. Everyone admits that they feel it. Our nerves are ruined. If anyone should say that he was not haunted by visions of burning airships, then he would be a braggart.

The Germans never mounted such ambitious raids again.

In late October Canteen Ma disappeared. No one knew what had become of her. The driver of the dray that brought wine and spirits to the café revealed himself as Marthe's new contact.

An officer staying at the café told Marthe that he was fed up because the following Sunday a bishop was coming to hold a big church parade. The whole division was to form up, with a band, in Westrozebeke, her home village. He told her that he would need his breakfast early that day and they joked together about what would happen if the parade was bombed.

'As well as blowing up our bloated staff, which would undoubtedly be the better for it, they might blow us up as well!'

Later that day Marthe sent a message about the parade. She felt guilty about the officer, knowing that he and his men might die as a result of her actions. But the chance to destroy a whole division was too good an opportunity to miss.

On the day of the parade Marthe watched the troops getting ready. They marched off towards Westrozebeke to the accompaniment of military bands and then silence returned to Roulers. As she walked back to the hospital, an orderly said that she was to report to headquarters immediately. She was told that the bishop had asked for some of the wounded to attend the parade. Twelve men had asked to go and she was to go with them. A lorry was coming to transport them.

'You have no objection?' he asked.

'None, Herr Oberatz.'

It was a warm day and the first time she had been back to Westrozebeke since she had been evacuated more than a year ago. She peered through the windscreen of the ambulance and saw nothing but ruins. A few gutted, blackened houses, blasted walls and piles of bricks were all that remained of the pretty country village that was her home. There were tents everywhere, men parading and bands playing, like a local fete among the ruins. When the service started, the lorry full of wounded men, attended by Marthe, was parked near the bishop and a group of staff officers. Marthe sat tense, waiting for the noise of approaching Allied fighter-bombers, scanning the sky for the little black dots of aeroplanes. There were none.

The service drew to a close, the bishop blessed the congregation and the band began to play the last hymn. Male voices rose in harmony as, appearing out of nowhere, aeroplanes thundered above them. Bombs fell, exploding among the singing soldiers. The parading division disintegrated into bloody chaos. A medical orderly shouted for Marthe to help him get the wounded under the protection of the lorry. As they struggled to reach safety the planes banked and came round again, machine-gunning the parade. The orderly fell, hit in the head. The planes banked again and joined each other in formation, flying west, back over the trenches to the safety of their own lines. Dead and injured lay everywhere. In the chaos Marthe was sent back to Roulers and spent the rest of the day and the night receiving the wounded. Some died in her arms, not knowing that their Angel of Mercy was also their Angel of Death.

When she finally got home she found a soldier removing the officer's things and asked him what he was doing. He told her that the lieutenant had been killed in the raid and now had no use for his room or any of his worldly possessions. He had been a good officer, the man said, and they would miss him.

To the southeast the fighting round the town of Verdun went on. The dead and wounded French and German soldiers had reached nearly half a million.

CHAPTER SIXTEEN

THE WAR DRAGS ON

Some time later Marthe was approached by a neighbour, Alphonse, with an idea for sabotage. Roulers had become an important centre for supplies of all sorts and a giant ammunition dump had been set up in the grounds of a large house that had a wall running around the acres of land in which it stood. The perimeter was protected by machine guns, searchlights and barbed wire, and was patrolled day and night. Marthe had acquired two sticks of dynamite and she knew they could do a lot of damage to the dump but had no way of getting them inside.

Alphonse remembered that during the invasion a shell had landed in the hospital grounds revealing the mouth of what looked like a tunnel, which he and a few friends had investigated. The German occupation had stopped their efforts and all the men who knew about the tunnel were now either dead or had been transferred away. A hut to store equipment for the hospital had been built over the crater.

Alphonse had found a book about medieval Roulers and in it was a description of a water conduit that had run the length of the town, across the fields and into the river. He thought that the crater had uncovered the remains of that conduit and that the hospital had been built in what had once been fields. He worked out that it was possible the tunnel passed under the land where the ammunition dump had been created. He guessed that from the hospital to the dump was around 2 miles.

They decided to inspect the tunnel. The hut was built on a slope and had been raised up to avoid the damp and as a precaution against rats. That night Alphonse brought a hammer, a chisel and a saw. They crawled under the hut and found that there were some loose planks which they prised up to discover an opening to a sort of passage. It was dry, dusty and covered in cobwebs. Alphonse had a length of string with him and had worked out a way to measure the distance they were travelling. Moving in the dark along the tunnel was a frightening experience, made worse by the presence of rats.

It took a long time but eventually he thought they had travelled 2 miles. Above their heads was a heavy-looking stone slab which would have to be propped up while they tried to free it. They had done as much as they could for one night and so, exhausted, they made their way back along the eerie subterranean passage.

After several nights' work they succeeded in propping up the roof and making a cover to hide the hole which would be caused when they released the stone. They had also made a crude ladder to help them to climb out of the sewer. Freeing the stone slab was difficult; earth and dirt poured into their faces and they were frightened that it would fall in on them. They had no idea where they would appear when they broke through to the surface. What would happen if they emerged into the barrel of a gun held by a patrolling guard?

Eventually the moment came to remove the prop holding the slab in place. Marthe crouched back in the darkness as Alphonse knocked it away. Nothing happened. He began to work at the edges, unable now to stand underneath it. Then suddenly it dropped, causing an avalanche of earth and stones. For a moment they stood silent. Above their heads they could see the sky. Alphonse worked at the hole with his crowbar, making it big enough to climb through. As they clambered up they saw that all around them were huge tarpaulin-covered piles. Through gaps in the mounds they could see sentries and hear their heavy boots as they walked up and down the metalled roads. In the distance they heard a voice call a challenge. They froze in fear; the voice called again, then nothing. They heard feet moving away, the measured tread of a guard. They made ready the camouflage lid with which they hoped to hide the tunnel entrance then crept towards one of the piles. They placed Marthe's dynamite against it and ran yards of fuse back to the hole. Marthe scrambled back down. Alphonse lit the fuses and followed Marthe into the darkness, pulled closed the camouflage lid, grabbed her hand and dragged her along the tunnel, terrified that the blast would cause a cave-in.

The noise of the explosion was huge, even though it was muffled by the roof of the tunnel and the tons of earth covering it. Rocks and dirt fell in on them but the structure held. They struggled back and crawled out from underneath the hut to see the horizon lit by an orange glow, silhouetting the town buildings and the church spire. They hugged and separated, Alphonse disappearing into the night. Marthe wrapped herself in her cloak and walked back to the centre of town, hoping that the mud and dirt on her would be hidden by the dark of the night.

The Grand-Place was lit by the flames from the burning ammunition dump. The air was full of the sound of exploding shells; hosepipes snaked across the square, leaking water. Men ran about shouting orders as the whole garrison turned out to fight the fire. Marthe hurried to the café knowing that her pass would explain why she was out after curfew but not why she was covered in grime.

Inside, she found her mother sitting in the dark watching the inferno through a bedroom window. Without taking her eyes off the blaze, her mother said, 'I am proud of you, Marthe, but I worry that one day your luck will leave you.' When dawn broke the fire was still burning.

As she got ready to go on duty at the hospital Marthe realised that, during the night, she had lost her gold wristwatch. The clasp had been loose for some days and she had kept thinking she should get it repaired, not an easy thing during a war. She wondered whether it had fallen off in the hospital but thought it more likely that it had come off while they were struggling in the tunnel. The watch had her initials engraved on the case.

In the next week eight new volunteer nurses arrived from Germany with a new matron. Neither the matron nor the nurses liked Marthe and tried to ostracise her. Matron ordered that Marthe, as a Belgian, must not talk to the German patients except when dressing their wounds. The row rumbled on and Marthe decided to leave the hospital.

In the meantime there had been an inquiry into the explosion. The authorities came to the conclusion that because the site was heavily guarded it would have been impossible for saboteurs to penetrate the dump. They concluded that the explosion and fire had been caused by mistakes in stacking the ammunition.

Marthe resigned from the hospital, promising that if they needed help she would return. She said goodbye to the doctors and the men she had nursed. Several were in tears.

Not long after the explosion Marthe saw a notice outside the town commander's office in the Grand-Place. It reported that a soldier had been arrested for theft and that he appeared to have items belonging to the civilian population. The notice ended with the invitation that 'any person thinking he recognises any of the following articles please report at this office between the hours of 10am and 12 noon'. It said that among the items was a gold wristwatch with the initials M. C. engraved inside the cover.

Marthe presented herself at the town commander's office the next morning. In his desk he had an envelope containing her watch. He gave it to her saying he was glad she had got it back. When she arrived home she found the police had called while she was out. Then a friend arrived to tell her that she and her family had been interrogated about Marthe. Towards the end of the afternoon an officer arrived with a sergeant and two armed soldiers carrying rifles with fixed bayonets. The officer told her that he had orders to search the house. He asked her to give him the keys to any locked room or piece of furniture, to 'save your property'.

Marthe could do nothing but wait and listen as the men began their search. Soon it became clear that they were ransacking the place. They started in the cellar and moved through the house, searching every room. Drawers were torn open and the contents thrown on the floor. They used their rifles to batter the walls, looking for any hollow areas, and their bayonets to slash open mattresses. Finally the officer confronted her. He had found two rolls of paper hidden under a strip of loose wallpaper behind the washstand in her bedroom. He waved the strips in the air and told her that she would face a firing squad, 'anytime we please'.

She was arrested and taken on foot to the Kommandantur, where she was charged with espionage. She was not allowed to speak but was marched, again on foot, through the town to the prison. As they passed the tram terminus a crowd of civilian labourers saw her surrounded by soldiers. A man shouted, 'Courage, little sister.'

Night fell and Marthe sat on her prison bed. She could not work out how they had discovered her. She could hear a guard pacing outside and wondered if there would be a firing squad waiting for her in the morning. She sat on the coarse straw bed and wept.

For three days nobody spoke to her. She received food, sometimes an eye peered at her through a spy-hole in the door. Once, a steel panel in the door opened to reveal the face of a detective she vaguely knew. Her breakfast was tea and black bread, at midday a thick soup and for supper a thinner soup. The time passed slowly and she was frightened. By the fourth morning she thought that death was the only way out. She was terrified of betraying the people she had worked with. She thought she could starve herself to death and began to refuse her food.

On the fourth day, in the afternoon, the detective reappeared and told her that he had arrested all her accomplices, that they knew everything about her and that she should make a statement and tell the truth. Marthe did not reply. She refused to answer his questions. Then he lost his temper, dragging her to her feet and shouting in her face that it was easy to make people talk, especially women. The interrogation went on for three weeks. Men burst into her cell during the night, intimidating her and making it impossible for her to sleep. Usually she was questioned by the same detective but sometimes he was replaced by a quieter man who hissed and wheedled in her ear. She became disorientated from lack of sleep and food. Then, for no reason and for a whole day, neither detective appeared. Instead, a pretty young Belgian woman came into her cell. She told her that she was a civilian whom the military had ordered to be Marthe's warder. She said that the detective was a terrible man and suggested that Marthe tell her enough to keep him quiet.

'I am saying nothing. I know nothing of spies who are working against the Germans in this town. They won't break me and in any case I shall soon starve to death. And unlike you I am not a traitor to my country.'

At this the woman swore at her and stormed out of the cell. The questioning resumed; there was someone with her all day and all night. She had been in the cell for three weeks without a change of clothes and without the cell being cleaned. For much of the time she was in a semi-conscious trance. A doctor came into her cell and told her that if she did not eat he would have her force-fed, with a rubber tube that would be rammed down her throat. She relented, eating small amounts of food. She was cold, hungry, filthy and growing weaker by the day. Eventually she was so ill she was taken to the hospital where she was treated as a criminal prostitute.

Her mother visited, bringing eggs and fruit. She did not recognise her daughter and when she did she wept, saying, 'My three sons have gone and now they will take my daughter too.' The old woman recovered from the initial shock and whispered that the doctors in the hospital where Marthe had worked were going to put in a good word for her at the court martial. Then a guard appeared and she had to leave; visitors were only allowed to stay for twenty minutes.

Her mother had told the staff that Marthe was herself a nurse. When the priests and nuns who worked at the hospital learned who Marthe was, the head sister came into her prison cell and apologised for the way they had treated her. As she left she said that she and her staff would do whatever they could to look after her; she had done so much for her country that it would be 'an honour'.

The weeks dragged on. Marthe was not allowed to see her mother again and was certain that soon she would be shot. Then, after more than another month had passed, she was told that the next day an ambulance was going to take her to Ghent.

By the following night Marthe was in a new cell in a military prison. It was clean but she felt cut off from the world, as if she was no longer a human being. More days passed and then an officer appeared and told her: 'By order of the General Officer Commanding Occupied Areas you will be tried by general court martial. This will take place in one week's time. In conjunction with the special decree recently issued you will be charged under Article 90 of the penal code, Sections 2 and 4, which deal respectively with the destruction of ammunition and serving as a spy to the enemy. I have been detailed to act in your interest as your defending officer, mademoiselle.'

'I do not wish a defending officer.'

The officer said that he knew she did not trust him; she was wrong to do so but he could, if she wanted, supply a civilian lawyer 'of your own nationality'. Marthe then told him that she did not want to be defended at all and that she would refuse to plead. The officer waited and told her that the work she had done for the German hospital would count very much in her favour but that, even so, the evidence held against her was damning.

'I am only partially aware what the evidence is that the prosecution holds against me. How did they come to obtain it?'

The officer told her that her watch had been found in the tunnel leading to that ammunition dump. He said that as she did not wish to use him he would go. He assured her that, should she change her mind, he would remain at her service.

'Whatever you did, I believe you did it for the good of your country. Mademoiselle, may luck be with you.' He stood and bowed, clicking his heels. He was let out of the cell and disappeared from her life. The week until the trial passed with Marthe unable to think, her brain hardly functioning.

She was taken under guard to the court. On the way she watched the rest of the world going by. Tiny details imposed on her mind, smoke from a chimney, a sparrow perched on an iron gutter, the tiles on a roof, all distant and now unreal. Stone steps led to the courtroom, where nine uniformed men sat at a long table, papers, pens and legal books piled in front of them. To one side sat two other

officers. The president stood, a white-haired general with an immaculate tunic, medals on his breast. He began to speak, his words, in
German, coming as if in a dream.

'Marthe Cnockaert ... jurisdiction of the Imperial German ...
military code ... subject to laws ... The offence is treason and pun-
ishable by death ... I will prove ... guilt of the accused.'

He went on to describe her 'diabolical role' posing as an angel of
mercy, working near the front. He described her parents' café and
what a useful place it was from which to organise a spy ring. How
she had used her charm and skills to send German soldiers to their
deaths. She was a dangerous and relentless enemy. He would call
witnesses who would testify to her 'blood guilt'. He then said that
the state was in danger, the lives of comrades in the trenches must
be protected and that 'no sentiment of sex or womanhood must be
allowed to blind our judgement'. He finished by declaring, 'There is
only one fate for the assassin who stands before this council of justice,
and that, I demand in the name of our common fatherland, is death.'

The president then began to question her. He wanted to know if
she had anything to say in her defence. Marthe said that she did not,
speaking in Flemish and refusing to use the language of the court,
which was German. He then pressed her to reveal her associates,
especially 'the known spy Lucelle Deldonck'. She again refused to
speak, shaking her head. He warned her that her silence was harming
her case. Still she refused.

Various witnesses were called, including the man who had interrogated her in Roulers prison. He said that under questioning the
accused had admitted her guilt. Marthe now spoke, still in Flemish,
her voice very low.

'It is a lie. This man tried every human means to get me to commit
myself. He invaded my privacy night and day at Roulers prison. I was
weak from hunger and loss of sleep – he manhandled me, threw me
against the walls, swore that he would drag the truth from me or kill
me. And now you take that sort of evidence on oath!'

More witnesses were called and at one point Marthe burst out that
she looked on herself as a soldier in the field with a soldier's rights

and that the Germans were invaders who had pillaged her country. She finished her tirade shouting, '*Vive la Belgique! Vive les Alliés!*'

The court then agreed to hear the evidence of the German doctor in charge of the hospital in Roulers where Marthe had worked. He said that in his opinion she had operated for humanity. He then told the president that he had come to the court specifically to inform it that 'Mademoiselle Cnockaert was awarded the highest honour that our fatherland can bestow . . . the Iron Cross'.

Two other doctors were allowed to give evidence about her character. After this the president said that he would pass sentence in four days' time; then the court adjourned. Four days later an officer came into her cell and she was marched back to the room where the hearing had taken place. She entered to find the president sitting with two senior officers. He stood and spoke: 'It is a terrible thing to condemn a fellow creature; especially when that creature is a woman; but you have been the cause of the deaths of many of my countrymen during the many months of your nefarious activities. The sentence is therefore that at an hour and a place to be appointed later, you will be taken out and shot to death.'

Marthe felt as though she was in another body watching her grey-clad prison self being marched back to her cell between uniformed guards. She lay in her cell in misery. A German priest visited her. She was not allowed to speak to anyone or have visitors. She tried to keep her mind blank and felt dead to the world, but not afraid.

The next day she was marched for a third time to the court. The same stone corridors, the same officials, the same president. All with unsmiling faces. Once more the charge was read to her and the same death sentence pronounced. Once more she blanked what was being said. Then: 'Do you understand what I am saying?'

Marthe shook her head. He told her that there were mitigating circumstances, especially the fact that she had earned the Iron Cross for her work as a nurse plus the representations made by the doctors, and that, therefore, 'the Commander-in-Chief of Areas under the Occupation has graciously consented to commute this death sentence into one of imprisonment for life'.

He asked her if she had anything to say. Unable to speak, Marthe shook her head and was once more led back to her cell. She thought of the endless days that stretched ahead of her, a prisoner for life. But then she thought of the fact that she was certain the Germans were going to be defeated; she had no idea how long it would take, but when it happened she knew she would be released, even if she had been shipped to some grim fortress in the fatherland.

She fell into a routine in which she was woken at dawn and given tea substitute, then had to clean her cell, then breakfast, more tea and sour black bread that seemed to have been made from anything except flour. Most other meals were beetroot and a thick bean soup. Marthe grew fat but was undernourished. Every day she was taken to a room with twenty-five other women, given string and straw and told to make mats. She had to sit apart and was not allowed to speak to anyone.

In the prison in Siegburg the Princess de Croÿ was amazed when, early one morning, the cell doors were opened and the prisoners herded out and assembled in the central hall before the senior wardress. She announced that soon there would be a peace. The princess was now weak and ill, and had been transferred to an invalid cell, but even so she asked in a quavering voice what the wardress meant. The reply was that the emperor had written a letter proposing peace to the world. The princess doubted that the Allies would respond, though she had no idea of the details of the emperor's letter.

In fact, the letter was the initiative of the German chancellor. The army had just captured Bucharest and it was thought that the moment of victory was the time to try to bring the war to an end. To wild applause he had read his letter to the Reichstag. It had suggested that peace negotiations be started at once to avoid further bloodshed. If the Allies declined, then the Germans and her allies were prepared 'to fight until victory has been achieved. [And therefore we will be] absolved, by humanity and history, of any guilt for the continuation of the war.' Within a week the offer had been rejected.

In the same week the princess was allowed to sit outside her cell near a fellow inmate, the only other woman held in the invalid cells. The woman was called Madame Ramet and two of her children had been condemned to death. Another two of her daughters were serving sentences of penal servitude. The princess and Mme Ramet were listening to Christmas carols being sung round a meagre Christmas tree set up in the central hall. They were not meant to talk to each other and were under the scrutiny of wardresses standing on observation platforms. Using the singing to hide their voices they whispered to each other. Mme Ramet asked if there would be peace and the princess thought she hoped her sentence would soon end. Then Ramet said, 'There mustn't be peace.'

This delighted the princess, who replied, 'I feared that being ill you were in a hurry to be released.'

Ramet whispered back, 'I don't mind being ill, I wouldn't mind dying here, but there mustn't be peace before victory.'

The carols ended and the women were once more locked in their cells where, a short time later, Mme Ramet died.

Some of the prisoners were ordered to undertake new work which involved coating small discs with a green substance and then covering them in white paper. A prisoner smuggled one of the devices to Louise Thuliez, who in turn showed it to her fellow prisoner Louise de Bettignies. The two women worked out that it was probably part of the manufacture of a grenade. De Bettignies protested, telling her fellow inmates that they should refuse to make the devices; they were part of weapons that would be used against their countrymen. Very quickly Louise was taken to a punishment cell known as a *cachot*. The room was narrower than the usual cells, a high window let in very little light, the bed was a plank of wood and the cell was freezing. During the day the bedclothes were removed and the rations were reduced from even the meagre amount enjoyed by the others. As a further punishment Louise's woollen clothes were taken away and replaced with a light cotton uniform, designed for summer. When she was finally released from her punishment she was severely underweight, had a high temperature and was suffering from pneumonia.

*

At 10am on 15 December 1916, the French began another bombardment at Verdun. Again over a million shells were fired, directed by artillery observers in aircraft high over the battlefield. Two days later the battle was over and the French had retaken all the ground lost. German officer prisoners of war complained about their conditions and were told, 'We do regret it, gentlemen, but we did not expect so many of you.'

Three-quarters of a million men had fallen. The area around Verdun was turned into a cratered wilderness. Shell holes filled with water into which men fell and drowned. Trees were reduced to matchwood and soldiers became depressed and mutinous.

The same thing had happened along the Somme, where in the carnage very few prisoners were taken. One German soldier wrote: 'No man who falls into enemy hands can reckon with a pardon. Every man here knows that he must kill or be killed and the combat is extremely bitter.'

Before the battles of the Somme and Verdun ended a French officer wrote:

Humanity is mad. It must be mad to do what it is doing. What a massacre! What scenes of horror and carnage! I cannot find words to translate my impressions. Hell cannot be so terrible. Men are mad!

1917

CHAPTER SEVENTEEN

THE ROAD TO LUXEMBOURG

On 23 February 1917, International Women's Day, Russian women began to pour onto the Nevsky Prospekt in St Petersburg. They carried banners with handwritten slogans: 'Feed the children of the defenders of the motherland' and 'Supplement the rations of soldiers' families, defenders of freedom and the people's peace'. By noon there were tens of thousands of women on the streets, peasants rubbed shoulders with 'ladies of society' and students. Later they were joined by female workers from the textile factories. The crowd was now shouting 'Down with the Tsar' and 'Bread'. As dusk fell there were nearly 100,000 demonstrators on the Nevsky Prospekt. Fighting broke out, shops were looted and the police tried to disperse the crowd. Several thousands of the demonstrators climbed down onto the frozen river Neva and crossed on foot to avoid the police who were guarding the bridge.

The next day men followed the example of the women. There was more fighting in the streets, and more looting, while vehicles and trams were overturned. Within a few days the Tsar had abdicated, the old order was vanishing, and with it the command of the Russian troops on the Eastern Front.

The Princess de Croÿ was now very ill. One Saturday night, while getting ready for bed in the pitch dark, she had begun to cough and choke. She could feel something warm running down her arms. Hearing de Croÿ's faint cries, her neighbour, Jeanne de Belleville, began to bang on her cell door, screaming for a wardress from the night watch. The woman arrived, flinging open the door to find the princess covered in blood. Nothing could be done, said the wardress, until Monday morning. They allowed another prisoner to sit with her, leaving the door open and letting her have access to a tap of ice-cold water to bathe the princess's forehead.

When at last the doctor appeared he was shocked at her appearance and said he would telephone Berlin for permission to move her to a hospital in Munster. The answer took many days to arrive. She was asked to write down the names of relations to whom her death should be announced. Even in her weak state this amused her and she wrote on the paper, 'I am not going to die.'

Eventually Berlin gave permission for her to be moved to a hospital. The princess said goodbye to her comrades, including Jeanne de Belleville, Louise de Bettignies and Louise Thuliez. She was sad and anxious to be leaving the prison which held many friends and compatriots, even if it was a filthy place in which to live. Just before she left, a group of women who worked in the section where prison clothes were manufactured presented her with a doll. They had made it with scraps of cloth used in making the prison uniforms. The doll had real hair, which one of the women had cut from her own head and plaited in the regulation fashion. In one hand it held a cardboard mug and in the other a scrap of the hard bread substitute with which they were issued every day. Even the detail of the shoes was correct; they were held together with tiny nails. The princess remembered that when her own shoes had fallen to pieces they had been mended with cardboard soles which disintegrated in the damp of the exercise yard. She had fixed them herself with some metal and wire from a tin of biscuits she had received from the Red Cross.

The move was disorientating and exhausting and on arrival the princess collapsed, weeping night and day. Later she caught dysentery, a disease from which she had already suffered.

Meanwhile, the work of espionage went on. In mid-March 1917, in a French foreign ministry building in the Quai d'Orsay in Paris, two

British officers stood behind a curtain in the office of a man who had served as a diplomat in Luxembourg. They were listening to a woman asking for help to get a visa to enter Switzerland, from where she would be able, she hoped, to return to her home in Luxembourg. The woman was Madame Lise Rischard; the two men were Captain Lewis Campbell and Major George Bruce. Bruce was a 34-year-old bachelor who ran a British intelligence organisation in Paris known as the 'Permit Office'. His colleague, Campbell, had worked undercover since the start of the war and was an expert on codes. For some time Bruce had been trying to establish a train-watching network in Luxembourg, which, like Hirson, was one of the most important junctions in occupied Europe. The two officers knew that Mme Rischard's social credentials were impeccable and that her father-in-law had high-level contacts within the Luxembourg Railway Company. They knew too that, as medical adviser to the Luxembourg Railway Company, Mme Rischard's husband had contact with railwaymen at all levels and was trusted. No one was better placed to form a train-watching network.

They knew too that to return home she needed a passport and visa to get back into Switzerland, where she could pick up the passport she had deposited with the Dutch legation and then travel on, back to Luxembourg. The French authorities were refusing to supply one. She had been marooned in Paris for months. The official she was talking to was a family friend whom she had asked for help several times. So far he had, he said, to his great regret, not been able to assist her. However, he now had a possible solution. With a theatrical flourish he stood up and swept back the curtain to reveal the two officers, whom he introduced as 'Réséda' and 'Rose'. The two men explained to the confused Mme Rischard that they were British intelligence officers and had come to ask for her help.

They produced a message written on thin paper and asked her to take it to Luxembourg; they suggested it might be possible to screw it tight and hide it in her ear. If she agreed to help with their undercover work they were sure they could solve the problem of her visa. Mme Rischard was shocked. To a woman of her class and strict bourgeois upbringing the fact that intelligence officers worked undercover was reprehensible; deceiving people was not worthy of a gentleman, they were almost as bad as spies. She refused point-blank and left, heading for the house of her cousin, where she was staying.

When she arrived the maid told her that there were two gentlemen waiting for her in the salon. She entered the room to be again confronted by Bruce and Campbell, who repeated their offer. For the second time that day Mme Rischard refused and the men left.

Mme Rischard returned several times to the Quai d'Orsay and each time Rose and Réséda were waiting to repeat their offer. Each time she refused.

In the end, exhausted by their attention, Mme Rischard went to a priest. In the confession box she asked him what she should do. He asked her if she was French and she replied that she was French by marriage. In that case, the priest said, it was her duty to work with Allied intelligence.

The next time she returned to the Quai d'Orsay the two men were, as usual, waiting. She now agreed to work with them. They told her she was to recruit her husband and together they were to set up a network of train watchers. This new request concerned her; she asked for more time to think, explaining that they were asking something which carried with it a heavy responsibility. They agreed but insisted that from now on she be known as 'Madame Léonard'.

Four days later she came back and this time said she was fully at their disposal. She immediately started a period of intense training, similar to the one Gabrielle Petit had undergone in London in 1915. An apartment was organised where she could live alone and in safety. Next, she was placed in a classroom, around the walls of which were tailor's dummies dressed in German uniforms that had been scavenged from prisoners of war and dead soldiers. They trained the genteel middle-aged woman to become an expert in the mechanics of warfare. She had to memorise lists of German regiments, the ranks used and the formations they fell into. She was shown silhouettes of trains and diagrams of weapons. She became familiar with the formation of machine-gun and mortar units. She came to understand technical terms like 'constituted unit' and the difference between field guns and howitzers, and learned to distinguish their different shapes.

While memorising this mountain of information she was taught how to translate everything into a code invented by Campbell. It was complicated and subject to regular change by its inventor. By the beginning of May, Mme Rischard had learned enough to return to Luxembourg and put her newly acquired skills to the test. It was important that she travel home with no further delay. As always the problem was how to get her there.

Bruce and Campbell had two options. As she still had no visa or even a passport, they could smuggle her into Switzerland by hiding her on board a boat crossing Lake Geneva, or they could take her over the frontier by train. The second option ran the risk of arrest but they thought it might be easier for the middle-aged woman. Strings were pulled and she was told to apply for a French passport. She obeyed but heard nothing. For the time being her training went on. After a while she was told to apply again, which she did.

Bruce had decided that Mme Rischard should enter Switzerland by train. Once there, her first task was to get her passport back from the Dutch legation. He knew that he was sending her, an inexperienced British agent, into a country that was swarming with intelligence and counter-intelligence agents. Every transaction she made – buying a tram ticket, booking a hotel, eating in a restaurant – risked the possibility of observation, not least of all by the Swiss police. In spite of his promises that she would be safe, Bruce knew that there were almost no British agents in Switzerland and that there was no one to protect her.

The strain was beginning to tell on Mme Rischard. She wrote to Bruce, in code, telling him that she was frightened, dead-tired and very unhappy. The long hours and the intensity of her training had taken it out of her. The mission itself was a frightening and daunting prospect. She told him that she was suffering 'great emotions; all the sombre thoughts and the most intolerable mental worries of the past weeks have unnerved me ...'

Bruce tried to reassure her. He told her that her passport

application had at last been approved and that she could now rest until the moment came to leave. As for the border, he promised that things would be arranged so that she would have no problems. On 11 June 1917 he met her alone in the rooms they had organised for her.

For a while they talked, then without warning the older woman rounded on the young major. She said that when she had agreed to take on the task she had done so with great enthusiasm and that he had undermined her. He was always telling her what she was doing wrong and never praised her. She hated the way he treated her and now often thought that she should abandon the work, which she was finding thankless. He had paralysed her, she said, with his constant criticism. She reminded him that her morale was important and that he had completely neglected her emotional state. 'You are cold and unfeeling,' she said. 'You are capable of great things but you have been too stiff and inflexible in your feelings with me. You should have more confidence in yourself, Major.' Bruce left, shattered by what she had said.

The next day he received a letter from her apologising for the way she had spoken to him and hoping that her words would help him. She assured him that, in spite of everything, he could rely on her complete loyalty. The letter was written on stiff paper with a black border, funeral paper which she had bought when her father died a few months before.

Bruce sat down, thinking about what she had said and the things she had accused him of. Then he too wrote a letter, saying that he was grateful to her and that her criticisms could only do him good. He tried in his letter to express his real and heartfelt admiration for her and the way she had undertaken the work. He knew that her decision had been difficult and the outcome honourable. She was doing, he added, a huge service, not just to the Allies but to humanity as they tried to wipe out evil and restore lawfulness and peace. He called her sympathetic and gracious and said that her example would inspire everyone who knew her. He asked her to believe that he had the deepest esteem and respect for her.

On 14 June she set off without saying goodbye. She said, 'I could not find the words, emotion had extinguished them all.'

CHAPTER EIGHTEEN

LA DAME BLANCHE ARRIVES

Meanwhile, in Belgium disaster had struck the newly formed Service Michelin, which had been penetrated by a German double agent codenamed 'St George'. As a result four agents were arrested. One was caught while waiting for a rendezvous with St George; another was arrested with reports hidden in his socks. The most senior to be taken was Father des Onays, who was a professor at the Collège Saint-Gervais. One day, while he was taking a lesson on Virgil, the classroom door burst open and German secret policemen crashed in to arrest him. Des Onays had incriminating documents hidden in his cassock. He blustered and became angry, demanding that the college head be called. There was an argument and in the end one of the policemen left to get the principal. Father Des Onays then demanded that the arresting party wait outside and allow him to finish the lesson.

Meekly, they filed out of the room, and watched him through the glass door. He opened his copy of the *Aeneid* and began to read from it. As he did so, and unseen by the waiting Germans, he reached inside his cassock, pulled out the folded documents, placed them on the page he was reading, snapped the book shut, walked down the lines of desks and put the now hidden evidence on the desk of one of the students. The principal came into the room, followed by the police. Des Onays was arrested and taken to Brussels. The book, and the evidence it hid, remained in the classroom.

Thanks to the double agent St George, eight Belgian agents were shot and many more arrested. St George was described as 'undoubtedly one of the best of the German counter-espionage agents'. After a year of useful activity, the Service Michelin ceased to function.

While the arrests were taking place, a Belgian railway engineer named Gustave Lemaire, also working for the Service Michelin, arrived in Rotterdam and made contact with Henry Landau, the young and newly appointed director of undercover intelligence. Lemaire had been sent to ask the Allies for money and for help getting information out of Belgium.

Landau immediately offered to provide the Service Michelin with access to any of the six frontier crossing points under the control of the British secret service. Lemaire said, 'There are two conditions, however; suitable arrangements must be made to cover their financial expenditure and they also insist on being enrolled as soldiers.' Landau had no idea how to respond. He did not know if the British government would agree to make soldiers of Belgian civilians. He did not think that even the Belgian government in exile could do such a thing. A further problem was that many of the agents were women and it was impossible to enlist them in the army.

Lemaire went on to say that if Landau did not grant his request he would go to the Belgian authorities in Le Havre. Landau was not going to let this opportunity slip through his fingers, it was too valuable to his own organisation. He told Lemaire that he had to talk to his 'Chief' in England and that he would have an answer in a couple of days.

Landau was lying; he knew that it was a waste of time trying to get permission from London. Even if the War Office were willing, it would also need the sanction of the Belgian government and that could take months, by which time much vital intelligence would be lost, and possibly the war itself. He took a deep breath and assumed responsibility, granting both the requests. The agents would be given the status of soldiers and funds would be arranged. Any money already paid out would be refunded after the war. He asked Lemaire to write a letter to the organisers of the Service Michelin and he, Landau, would see to it that the letter was sent through a secure agent, a 'letter box' who was known and trusted.

Three days later, on 16 July 1917, word came that the 'letter box' had been arrested. Landau immediately got in touch with Lemaire to find out what had happened; neither man knew about the betrayals of St George. There followed days of confusion. The German counter-intelligence net was tightening and in Belgium more agents were arrested.

Landau realised that the Service Michelin must have been too heavily compromised to go on. It suited him to let the Germans think they had destroyed it.

He then set about creating an entirely new network. First he called it 'B.149', and then changed the name to 'La Dame Blanche' – The White Lady – a legendary figure whose appearance would herald the fall of the House of Hohenzollern, the German imperial family. The new organisation was divided into three battalions. Each battalion was subdivided into companies and platoons. The battalions were based at Namur, Charleroi and Liège. Letter boxes were established for the collection of reports, and the existence and identity of each letter box was kept isolated.

Once collected, the letters were taken to the frontier for transmission to GHQ. Arrangements were made to spirit compromised agents out of Belgium by hiding them and then helping them cross the border into Holland.

Finally, as part of the militarisation of La Dame Blanche every 'soldier' was required to take an oath of allegiance. It started with the words 'I declare I have engaged myself as a soldier in the Military Observation Corps of the Allies ...' and contained the undertaking 'not to reveal to anyone whomsoever, without formal permission, anything concerning the Service, not even if this should entail for me or mine the penalty of death ...'

All the soldiers so sworn in were given lead identity discs with name, date of birth, place of birth and an identification number. Each soldier then buried the disc in a place where it was to stay until the end of the war. These 'soldiers without uniform' were now subject to much greater discipline, an essential part of running an underground organisation. In the interests of strict security they were to do only as ordered and were forbidden to help with the distribution of *La Libre Belgique,* or to help men of military age get out of the country to join the Allies.

Other measures included the use of false identities. Buildings used as headquarters were modified to make them as safe as possible. They became rabbit warrens, with many exits and false doors into the adjoining houses. Showing lights after curfew was illegal, so several houses were fitted out with windowless 'blind rooms', where meetings could be held late into the night without fear of light spilling onto the road. Only Landau, in Holland, had direct access to the leaders of the White Lady.

One of the early recruits to the White Lady was Jeanne Delwaide, who, with her sister, had been helping young men into Holland where they could enlist in the Belgian army. Delwaide's soldier number was 20. After making her oath of allegiance she was ordered to break off all contact with her former comrades.

Jeanne Delwaide lived at Pepinster near Verviers which was on the Aix-la-Chapelle–Herbesthal–Liège line, the main railway line between Germany and Belgium. It was to cover this line that she set up her organisation. In the same town, the owner of a small inn, a Monsieur Siquet, had set up a parallel watching post, the one backing up the other and able to take over if either one was discovered and destroyed.

In spite of the orders not to get involved with other underground networks, Jeanne Delwaide knew about M. Siquet. She had been approached by representatives of a separate network in Namur that had lost its couriers and had agreed to help them. She revealed Siquet's password and so he began to act as courier to the other service. Later, Jeanne Delwaide was discovered and forced to flee. She asked Siquet for help and he put her in touch with a guide who was about to take a group across the border.

The group assembled, about thirty people including Belgian

civilian men and women, a Frenchman, some prisoners of war and a Russian. They moved by night across country until they were close to the German border. Here they found their guide, a man of about thirty who spoke fluent French and German. He told them that they must wait while he went ahead to identify the exact point of the sentries. It was a long time before he returned and they could set off along the fence.

After moving quietly for about 50 yards they were pounced on by five members of the secret police holding revolvers. The group was paralysed with shock and meekly obeyed as they were rounded up and marched off. By midnight they were on a train to Namur, where they were separated and put into solitary confinement.

Some time after her arrest, the prison chaplain visited her. When he was alone with her he reached into his robes and pulled out a message which contained a sentence that she was to learn by heart. It was a code with which the White Lady could communicate with her.

Later she received another message. It read:

Remember you are a soldier. Remember your oath. Deny everything. Refuse to use the German language; you can defend yourself better in French. I congratulate you on your heroic attitude. Be calm. No bravado. We have taken precautions here; none of us has been arrested. I am with you with all my heart. I will pray for you. I have advised your parents. 'Theo'.

These messages reached her before the secret police began their interrogation. By now three weeks had passed; the Germans thought she was a refugee and had no idea about her undercover activities. When they questioned her she denied everything. She said she did not belong to any spy network, and had not been trying to escape from Belgium. What had happened, she claimed, was that she had set off to buy butter at a nearby farm and had got lost. She had then fallen in with a group of young men whom she did not know and had followed them thinking they were heading for Verviers, where she lived. She was amazed, she said, when they had all been arrested.

After she finished giving her alibi, her interrogator called for someone to be brought in. It was the 30-year-old French- and German-speaking guide, himself a member of the German secret police. Later, she was confronted by a woman who had been part of the group that was arrested. Jeanne had thought she was a fugitive like herself; in fact, she was the mistress of the guide, and she too was working with the German secret police. Part of her role was to share a cell with other prisoners and get them to tell their stories, thereby unwittingly betraying their comrades. One of the men arrested with Jeanne was tricked into revealing the name of Siquet. He shared a cell with a priest who tried to comfort him. The man trusted him and revealed all. The priest was working for the secret police.

When the police arrested the innkeeper Siquet they discovered that he had a lot of compromising material on him waiting to be picked up by a courier. Next, they waited at his inn for the courier to arrive, a woman. She walked in, asked for Siquet and was arrested. More incriminating material was found sewn into the hem of her skirt.

The police finally realised that in Jeanne Delwaide they had an important agent and began to interrogate her in earnest. They believed that she knew the identities of men who would lead them to the centre of a major espionage network. Jeanne knew the names of the senior commanders of the White Lady. She was questioned for seven months and kept in solitary confinement. She looked like a broken, filthy wreck, her face thin, her expression worn, still in the dress in which she had been arrested. In the end the police gave up and brought her to trial, where the death sentence was demanded. She was sentenced to life imprisonment and fined 1,000 marks. She managed to send a coded message which read:

Tell my parents, I am of age, and am amply responsible for my actions. Not one sou for the Germans, if they inflict a fine on me.

Siquet was tried and shot.

*

Mme Rischard was now on her way into Switzerland. On Sunday, 17 June she arrived at the Swiss border, trusting Bruce's promise that she would have nothing to fear and that there would be friends to look after her. A customs officer looked at her new French passport and asked, 'Where are you from?' She replied that she had come from France. He then asked, 'Where are you going to?' She gave an address in Lausanne and the passport was stamped. Waiting for her on the Swiss side was her old friend Captain Lewis Campbell, whom she had first met when he emerged from behind the curtain with Bruce. He thought she looked pale, tense and 'awfully tired'. When she saw him her face lit up. Mme Rischard was the last person through and it was now eight o'clock in the evening. Campbell just had time to see her on her way before himself leaving for Evian. Mme Rischard spent the next week alone and wrote four letters.

She had been told that any letter she wrote was to be placed inside an envelope which she was to address to one of three intermediaries living in Geneva, who would send it on to Paris. She was to write using Campbell's code unless she was referring to non-sensitive things like the weather or how she was feeling. Nevertheless, Mme Rischard wrote uncoded sentences referring to her husband and how she hoped to 'win him over'. And in one letter wrote critically about the German occupation, saying, 'I don't know what I'd give to be rid of these swaggering figures with all the trappings of their stupid and ridiculous arrogance.' Two of the letters she wrote never arrived.

In Paris the letters that did arrive caused alarm, especially when she asked, explicitly, for an address she could use in an emergency and whether she was to burn her papers when she left on the last leg of her journey to Luxembourg.

Mme Rischard asked for an urgent interview with Campbell and wanted him to come to a boat by the lake the following day or the day after. She insisted that it was imperative she see him face to face. He let her know that he could not come 'just like that', it would be too risky, could arouse suspicion and lead to them both being arrested by the Swiss. Dismayed by the delay Mme Rischard wrote, 'For God's sake ... I despair!' Later, she wrote another letter saying that if she was prepared to place herself in danger then Campbell should be prepared to do the same.

While waiting for Campbell to arrive she began to extricate herself from the bureaucratic net in which she had been trapped for months. She went to the Dutch legation to try to get her original passport back. The Dutch demanded that she return the permit they had issued allowing her to get into France. She persuaded them that she had destroyed it. Reluctantly, they returned her passport. Then a doctor in Lausanne gave her a certificate confirming that she had been under his care for the past six months; this, with other papers that she had, made it appear to the Germans that she had never left Switzerland. She also had a *permis de séjour*, which a friend had renewed for her.

When Campbell eventually got to Lausanne he reported that he found Mme Rischard 'very much in the depths'; that she had been alone for nearly three weeks and had become paranoid that her letters were being intercepted and that she had inadvertently betrayed everybody. Campbell spent the morning with her, calming her down. They talked for a long time about things in general and after a while she relaxed. There was another bureaucratic problem, as since her departure from Luxembourg the rules had changed – in order to go home she now had to travel via Germany and for that she needed a visa that could only be obtained from Berlin. This would take at least three and possibly six weeks, assuming that there were no problems. She was by now very frightened and wrote to Campbell asking for reassurance and a guarantee that, if she were captured and interned, the British would make sure she was repatriated at the end of the war. This was an impossible request – what if the British lost the war? Later, she learned that her request for a visa had been refused. There was always the problem that if she did get into Germany she might be arrested. She wrote: 'Better death than captivity ... the worst tortures will not make me abandon my duty ...'

As dawn broke on the morning of 7 June 1917 the professor of geology at Lille University woke to a strange trembling that rattled the windows of his house and shook the china in his cupboards. He assumed that what he was experiencing was an earthquake and began to ponder on the geological conditions that had caused it.

At the same time in London, in Downing Street, the prime minister, David Lloyd George, woke to the sound of a deep, rumbling boom that had evil at its heart. He knew that this was the start of the battle for the Messines Ridge and that the noise signalled the detonation of mines dug below the German lines.

The detonations were greater even than those that had erupted on the Somme just under a year before. On the front line, mining engineers watched as along the ridge the ground erupted into huge thundering towers, hundreds of feet high. At the centre of each tower, fire billowed white and red, throbbing in the cool light of the rising sun. Caught in the blast were the shattered bodies of nearly 10,000 German soldiers, torn apart as they rose into the air, bloodying the earth and stone as they fell back to the ground.

British soldiers, waiting for the battle to start, watched in awe, some of them knocked over by the shock of the explosion. For two years the miners had laboured underground, digging nineteen mines and packing them with 450 tons of ammonal, a highly explosive mixture of ammonium nitrate and aluminium powder. Their work would scar the minds of all who witnessed it and the land itself for years. There had never been, in all of history, such a loud detonation and it would not be until atomic bombs were dropped on Nagasaki and Hiroshima that such force would be unleashed at a single stroke.

Seven days later the battle of Messines was over and the ridge was in Allied hands, at the cost of over 24,000 casualties. The attack was just the prelude to a much larger offensive, Ypres, where fighting had continued since 1914.

In Paris, Bruce dealt with the problem of getting Mme Rischard's reports out of Luxembourg, should she ever get there. He had made contact with the publisher of a local newspaper in Luxembourg called *Die Landwirt*. Earlier in the war the man had faced arrest by the Germans and had fled to Switzerland. He was now living in

Paris. He explained to Bruce that while he was in exile his business was being run by his wife and extended family. He communicated with them through a trusted friend in Switzerland.

Although *Die Landwirt* was a local paper it had subscribers in Switzerland, who received it on a regular basis. It was agreed that coded messages be inserted into the paper which, when the copies arrived in Switzerland, would be sent straight on to Bruce.

CHAPTER NINETEEN

YOUNG WOMEN SPIES

While Mme Rischard struggled to return home and start her mission, the train-watching networks across Belgium were growing and recruiting people from all elements of society. Two 25-year-old women, the Baroness Clémie de l'Épine and Thérèse de Radiguès de Chennevière, whose father was a marquis, had been ordered to cross the border into France, travel to Charleville, about 30 miles away, and find a person who could be chief of a new platoon responsible for watching the railway there.

Charleville, the headquarters of the German crown prince, was another important railway junction on the line linking Trier in Germany with Hirson in France. The line went through Luxembourg.

Clémie's family had an estate at Gedinne, on the border with France; she had friends in Charleville, and knew the area. Now, dressed in filthy, threadbare, hooded cloaks the two aristocratic young women pushed through a thick wood following a 'big strapping fellow' carrying half a sack of potatoes on his back. His name was Georges; he had been found by one of the foresters on the estate and had undertaken to guide them for a charge of one hundred francs.

As they approached a small farm a voice, in German, ordered them to halt. They froze and two members of the secret police emerged from the undergrowth and demanded their identity cards. These were produced; they were still in Belgium and for the women all was well. Georges was taken off. He was away for an hour and, to their relief, when he returned all that had happened was that his potatoes had been confiscated by the hungry soldiers. They carried on through the forest, climbing a steep slope until they came to a 10-foot-high barbed wire fence which in this area was the only barrier between France and Belgium and had been there since before the war. They followed it for several hundred yards and came to a hole that had been cut by smugglers. They scrambled through and were in France. In the failing light they reached the village of Monthermé, where Georges had friends and where they were to spend the night. They were given a cup of brown ersatz coffee and then went to bed; there were no sheets and they slept in their clothes.

At four in the morning Georges woke them and they continued on their way. The area was heavily wooded and the going was steep until they descended into the valley of the Meuse. By the river's edge there was a cottage, the owner of which was another friend of Georges. He lent them a boat. Georges rowed them across. On the other side they hid the boat ready for the return journey and pushed on through the woods. It had rained in the night and they were soaked through. At one point they heard voices and had to hide, thinking they were about to run into an enemy patrol; instead it was woodcutters.

Finally, they reached the outskirts of Charleville but they were now so bedraggled they worried they would arouse suspicion. The young women tried to tidy each other's hair while Georges cleaned their shoes with clumps of grass. As they walked into the town they saw hundreds of German soldiers milling on the roads ahead. They had not realised that this was a garrison town. They darted into a doorway, barging into the house and colliding with a woman holding a baby who did not seem in the least surprised. The only chance they had to escape suspicion was to walk about the town as though they were natives and to pray that they were not stopped and asked for their identity papers. The woman with the baby sent her small daughter to accompany them. The child walked innocently between her new friends, holding their hands. It was nine o'clock in the morning.

They were looking for an old family acquaintance, a priest whom they hoped to persuade to set up and run the train-watching platoon. The priest had not seen them or their families since the war had disrupted everything. They told him their mission and asked him if he would help. He said he was sorry but he could not help because of his religious duties but he knew that the editor of the local paper would be sympathetic. An hour later he appeared with the editor, who said they should have contacted him earlier. He had friends who ran a pharmacy and he was sure they too would help. They set off for the pharmacy and soon were sitting in the back room talking about what exactly needed to be done. The pharmacist's wife fed them and gave the two women fresh clothes to replace their filthy, torn wet ones. After several hours of discussion it was decided that the editor would be the chief of the Charleville platoon and his wife his assistant. They undertook to recruit agents to mount a comprehensive train-watching agency and also others who would monitor troop movements in and out of the area. They had even identified a courier to carry the intelligence first to the women's woodman, from where it could start its journey to GHQ. There would also be a hiding place in the woods where reports could be left.

By the time they finished it was six o'clock in the evening. The women were given a big dinner and then taken back to the priest's house where they rendezvoused with Georges to begin the journey back. After evading German patrols by wading into the Meuse and spending hours in the dark looking for the boat, they arrived home. The 60-mile round trip had taken forty-eight hours, almost all in the dark. After some weeks reports began to come through and were transmitted to Landau in Holland. Shortly after that he received a telegram from GHQ congratulating him on the establishment of a new spy network.

A few weeks later, the two young women heard that the courier element of the network had broken down. They immediately volunteered to go back to Charleville to find out what had happened and successfully got it going again.

*

Nuns proved to be very useful recruits to the White Lady organisation. The Congrégation Nancéienne de la Doctrine Chrétienne was a French order that the invaders had expelled from France and sent into Belgium, to the town of Chimay. Here a German military hospital had been forced on them, equipped with all its own staff of doctors, nurses, surgeons and orderlies. The nuns knew that, as they comforted the sick and helped the doctors, they could pick up priceless pieces of intelligence.

In due course, and with the approval of the mother superior, two of the nuns were formally enrolled as soldiers in the White Lady. They took the oath and received their identity tags, which they buried in the convent grounds. Their names were Sister Marie-Mélanie and Sister Marie-Caroline. These two women were not asked to nurse the wounded but instead ran a small shop where they sold postcards, tobacco and other small things to the staff and patients. Over time the customers got to know them and talked. Lonely men, far from home and who had lived in the grip of death, found it a comfort to befriend the two religious sisters.

The women were meticulous in their observation of where the men had come from, what their units were, what divisions they belonged to and what their morale was like. Bit by bit, and on a daily basis, these fragments were gathered and sent by White Lady courier across the electric fence into Holland where they were examined by Major Oppenheim and collated for transmission to GHQ in Montreuil.

Danger was everywhere for the underground armies but it was the couriers who ran the greatest risks. One of the White Lady's couriers was codenamed 'Juliette', a young girl working between Liège and Namur. She regularly arrived at Namur station by train and had to present her identity cards at the platform barrier. Concealed in her clothes was a tiny roll of black cloth in which were wrapped the incriminating reports. Sometimes she was waved through but at others she was ordered to 'get over here'. After that frightening command she was interrogated and asked who she was, where she was going and what the purpose of her journey was. Once, she was taken into a waiting room where she managed to slip the black cloth behind a radiator. She was then interrogated by a woman who made her strip naked. All her clothes were searched and the seams opened with a razor blade. She explained that she was visiting a sick relative. Eventually, when nothing incriminating was found, she was let go. Slowly she dressed. By now the police had left and, as she walked back through the waiting room, she recovered the roll of cloth from behind the radiator and disappeared into the anonymous streets.

In late June 1917, General John J. Pershing, the commander of the American Expeditionary Forces (AEF), watched as the first US soldiers disembarked in France. They were mainly engineers and infantrymen. 'They are sturdy rookies,' he is reported to have said, 'we shall make great soldiers of them.'

On the other side of the Atlantic men were joining the army and starting their training. The trickle of troops arriving from the United States would soon turn into a torrent of millions.

In 1914 the Vale of Ypres had been the home of prosperous market gardens; its heavy clay soil was well drained and carefully tended. By 1917 high-explosive bombardment of every sort had reduced it to a wilderness.

At 3:50am on 31 July, in the gloom before dawn, yet another Allied campaign began at Ypres. Once more the men of the Allied armies hauled themselves out of their trenches and began the slow advance across no-man's-land, sliding and slipping in the greasy clay as they walked, torn apart by artillery fire and sliced open by machine guns or simply dropping exhausted into water-filled shell craters where they drowned. At the start of the battle the Allies had recaptured 7,000 yards of land. Then the Germans counter-attacked and took back the lost ground, after which the battle ended. Both sides lost nearly 40,000 men. It became known as the battle of Passchendaele.

*

In Luxembourg, Lise's husband, Dr Rischard, was attending an aristocratic patient, Princess Charlotte. She asked after his wife and he told her that she was stranded in Lausanne. Charlotte reported this to her sister, the grand duchess, who instructed that a letter be sent immediately to Berlin demanding that Mme Rischard be repatriated. In spite of this there was no news and the weeks dragged on. Bruce and Campbell feared that Mme Rischard's mission might soon become useless.

At the end of November Mme Rischard received a letter from her husband telling her that a neighbour, Pierre Huss, was in Lausanne and that she might want to meet him. Mme Rischard agreed and a rendezvous was set up. M. Huss told her that French Intelligence had arrested his son. The young man had been tried and found guilty of espionage and sentenced to life imprisonment. Huss was desperate to clear his son's name and had a plan to destroy a viaduct, part of the railway junction in Luxembourg, and hoped that by so aiding the French cause he could help have his son's sentence commuted.

They met several more times and, as a result of their conversations, Mme Rischard wrote in code to Bruce saying that she had vital intelligence for him and that he must come and see her as soon as possible. Later she sent another message, this time written by Huss himself and coded by her. It read:

Reprovisioning, coal and work stopped metallurgical factory by demolition of viaduct. Reply if you approve: instructions and terms. Huss.

This scheme, conceived and presented by amateurs to British Intelligence, could endanger the whole plan to put the railway junction under surveillance. Blowing up any part of the junction would put the Germans on their guard and make further espionage work very difficult. This danger was compounded by the equally amateur nature of elements of the British and French secret service organisations.

At the beginning of December 1917, Bruce again travelled to

Lausanne to meet Mme Rischard. On arrival he thought he was being followed and spent some time shaking off his pursuer. Then he went to Mme Rischard's lodgings. They had not met for six months. They discussed the question of Pierre Huss and his son. They decided to test him by asking him to supply information about the shunting yards. If he supplied what they asked for they would have a fairly good idea that he was genuine.

Next, Bruce told her that he had found a man who could work with her when she got to Luxembourg. He told her only that the man's codename was 'Conrad Bartels'. He asked her whether, if they got him into Luxembourg, she would be able to arrange cover and living quarters for him. She thought she could. She said she would send examples of identity cards and food coupons to Paris where they could be copied and issued to Bartels. Then Bruce left, promising to return the next day.

What Bruce did not tell Mme Rischard was that Conrad Bartels was an escaped prisoner of war and that for the last few months a plan had been developed to insert an agent deep into enemy territory by balloon. The idea was under the control of William 'Pink Tights' Pollock, an expert balloonist and commander of the Naval Ballooning School at the Hurlingham Sports Club on the river Thames. He had acquired his nickname when his trousers had become entangled in the rigging of a balloon and been torn off to reveal that he was wearing pink combinations. Pigeons had already proved a successful way of getting information to the Allies and tethered balloons were used on the front line to observe enemy troop movements and to control artillery fire. With the co-operation of 'C', Wallinger and Sigismund Best, Pollock had come up with a plan to combine the mobility of the pigeon with the flying potential and silence of the balloon. Tests were about to be carried out with three French volunteer agents.

On a dark night, when the wind and the moon were thought to be right, the first two volunteers shook hands with Pollock, climbed into a balloon and ascended, shouting '*Vive la France!*' while a wind-up gramophone played the 'Marseillaise'. With them were pigeons in a basket that would be used to send back messages. The next night the third volunteer took off. One pigeon message was received, the first pair of agents vanished, the third volunteer broke his leg on landing and was shot. More attempts were made; very little information was gained and several more volunteers were captured and shot. None of this put off the agent known as Conrad Bartels and plans were well advanced. His balloon was to be launched somewhere near Verdun. The balloon trip to Luxembourg was nearly 80 miles. 'Pink Tights' himself declared that they would be lucky to hit 'the Province of Luxembourg', let alone a specific target. Nevertheless there was great enthusiasm for the project among some of the higher echelons of the intelligence organisations.

Of all this excitement Mme Rischard was blissfully ignorant. On leaving her house Bruce once more thought that he was being followed. When he got to his hotel he found a letter from 'Jim' containing a coded warning that he should leave at once. He wrote a coded message to Mme Rischard, telling her that he had to go back to England immediately and would not be able to meet her the following day. By mistake he put the letter from Jim in the envelope too. When she received it Mme Rischard was baffled. She had no idea who Jim was but she recognised the handwriting of the other letter to be Bruce's. In his letter Jim referred to a woman and began, 'My Dear Old Boy . . .'

The writer went on to say how he had met an attractive woman who asked him whether he had met a tall Englishman who was to escort her. He replied that he had not but volunteered to step into the breach and escort her himself. Sadly the offer had been refused. The writer ended the letter describing how people in Luxembourg who had been hostile to the Allies were now changing their minds and becoming sympathetic. The writer signed off by saying how he looked forward to being told how to proceed 'on my return'.

'Yours as ever, Jim.'

Mme Rischard wrote to Bruce, one of whose codenames was 'Georgette'. She complained:

I have fallen once more into the deepest despair. I have lost confidence in Georgette and therefore in myself and in that state can I really do what you wish me to do? Would it not be better to give me up?

Bruce wrote back, telling her not to worry and to ignore the letter from Jim. This made Mme Rischard even more confused and upset.

Another of Bruce's aliases was 'Nicole'. In order to clear up the confusion and settle Mme Rischard he now wrote to her as Nicole, using a previously agreed code – 'just a line to say that Mummy posted a letter, she thinks to you, yesterday, which she says was not for you ...'

Mme Rischard was completely unnerved. She wrote back that she was resigning and asked Bruce to 'insist to Mummy that she set me free once and for all ...'

This letter crossed with another from Bruce trying to calm her down and reassuring her that there really was nothing to worry about in the 'Jim' letter.

In August a young man called Edmond Amiable appeared in Landau's office. He had intended to become a priest but after a year as a noviciate had decided to escape Belgium and join the army. He had come from the Hirson region, with its big railway junction and marshalling yards, which for two years the Allies had been trying unsuccessfully to penetrate. Landau thought that the attractive young man in front of him would be much better employed working as an agent for the White Lady and, after some discussion, recruited him, giving him the number A91.

A91 contacted his father, an old soldier, who in turn contacted a friend, Félix Latouche, who loathed the Germans because they had threatened his family with deportation. Both men lived in Hirson, where Latouche's cottage overlooked the important railway. He agreed to help and keep the line under constant observation. With his wife and two young sisters aged fourteen and thirteen he organised a roster, the girls watching by day and Latouche and his wife watching during the night. They monitored the line through a slit in the heavy curtains that covered the windows. Accounts were kept using food from the kitchen. Dried beans for soldiers, chicory for horses, ersatz coffee for cannons and so on. Their reports were hidden in the handle of a broom. The post was given the codename No. 201 and the line was kept under surveillance for the next fifteen months, until the war ended.

Amiable's father recruited other agents but became worried that one of his volunteers, a courier with whom he was in constant touch, was under suspicion. The courier's wife took over his duties. Her profession was that of midwife and she had permission to travel about the area. She delivered babies and deadly spy reports cleverly hidden in the whalebone of her corsets.

One place where even the midwife could not safely travel was the area around the Château de Mérode near Trélon. The chateau was often used by the Kaiser and as a result the whole area was heavily guarded and patrolled. Spying near Trélon was undertaken by a woman called Eglantine Lefèvre, who used the nights to carry reports, crossing fields and woods, travelling in all weathers. One day she went down with Spanish flu, an epidemic that was sweeping Europe. She insisted on carrying out that night's mission and arrived in Trélon with a high fever. After delivering the reports she collapsed, complaining of a terrible ache in her limbs. By the morning she was dead.

In spite of her sad end the Hirson platoon grew to fifty people, an invisible network of civilian soldiers watching and reporting on the Germans' every move. The Hirson platoon, like all White Lady networks, was a family-run operation. Husbands, wives and children working together. Household furniture was often used to conceal reports, and in Liège there was a man manufacturing hollowed-out canes that were a favourite device of the couriers. The bent end unscrewed to reveal a cavity in which could be hidden twenty-five sheets of rolled-up fine tissue paper on which were typed the daily reports.

*

Marthe Cnockaert continued to endure the months of dreary imprisonment. She tried to judge the passage of time by the length of the days and the changing seasons. She received a visit from one of the doctors at the hospital in Roulers, who had managed to get a special pass to see her. He was upset and shocked by her appearance. She looked worn out and malnourished, very pale from the lack of exercise and fresh air, almost never being allowed to leave her cell. He brought her some food and chocolate. He said that he was going to see the governor to try to get her moved to a hospital.

Meanwhile, Mme Rischard was still marooned in Lausanne. To pass the time and to alleviate her growing feelings of loneliness and isolation she took a course of English lessons. She tried yet again to get permission to travel to Luxembourg via Germany but her application was disallowed. This time it was Campbell who was sent to talk to her. She told him that she planned to communicate with her husband by wrapping a coded message in a ball of silk which she would wrap inside her crochet work. One of Dr Rischard's patients was convalescing in Switzerland and she felt sure he would agree to carry the message for her. Campbell was furious and told her that the plan was mad. If the unofficial courier was stopped and the message discovered her whole mission could be destroyed. Disappointed, she acquiesced. Campbell left and she was once more alone, with only her English lessons and the crochet to pass the long winter hours.

Bruce, the young restrained British officer, the man she had described as cold and unfeeling, assumed more and more the character of one of his several codenames, 'Madame Garland'. He wrote that what he wanted to say to her was: '... how can I chase away the black serpent that slithers in your thoughts and eats away our friendship ...'

For her part, she wondered whether she would get home before the war ended and whether the anxiety, fear and tension she had felt since she was first approached, plus the endless hours of instruction in coding, would all have been in vain.

By the end of November, and to her great relief, Mme Rischard heard that General von Tessmar, the commander in Luxembourg, had personally written to the authorities in Berlin asking them to allow her to return home. At last things might start to happen.

A few days earlier, on 11 November 1917, General Erich Ludendorff held a conference at Mons, the place where the British Army had experienced its first, bloody battle of the war. General Friedrich Graf von der Schulenburg argued that the only way to win the war now was to break the French army and he proposed to do that at Verdun. He asserted that if his plan succeeded, the British would be alone. Other officers agreed with him. However, their commander, Ludendorff, did not. He argued that the German army had only one chance to beat the British and said that an attack must be mounted near Saint-Quentin. This was the site of the Somme battlefields, now turned into yet another apocalyptic landscape of abandoned trenches, mud, and fields blackened and ruined by shell holes. At Saint-Quentin, Ludendorff argued, the British Army could be driven into the sea and the alliance between the French and the British fatally weakened. He gave the operation the codename 'Michael'.

On 7 December, the head of British Intelligence, Brigadier General John Charteris, usually a brash, over-optimistic man, promoted so fast that he was nicknamed 'The Principal Boy' and who liked to start his day with a whisky and soda, was downcast. He wrote: 'The hard facts are that we face the new year without Russia, with Italy almost on her knees, with France exhausted, with America of little help until June and with the initiative again with Germany.' During his career Charteris was described as a man whose 'vitality and loud-mouthed exuberance' made him unpopular. He was also seen as Field Marshal Haig's 'evil counsellor' and was blamed for being over-optimistic about the poor state of German morale. Criticism against him grew and he was replaced by General Sir Herbert Lawrence. Charteris became deputy director of Transportation at GHQ.

1918

CHAPTER TWENTY

HOME RUN FOR MME RISCHARD

On 18 January 1918, Mme Rischard was called to the German consulate in Lausanne, where she was told that a request for her repatriation had come from the highest levels of the Luxembourg government. As a result the authorities had agreed that she could go home. The grand duchess's string-pulling had worked. Mme Rischard could leave in two or three weeks.

By now La Dame Blanche had grown under Landau and had 919 agents reporting from ninety observation stations. Most of the intelligence came from the train-watching posts. Landau wrote to the leaders of the network: 'There is no doubt that at this critical moment you represent by far the most abundant intelligence source and that the results you are achieving are of inestimable value.'

On 21 January Ludendorff respectfully informed the Kaiser that Operation Michael was set to take place in the spring. Ludendorff told his master, 'It will be an immense struggle that will begin at one point, continue at another and take a long time ... it will be successful.' He christened the offensive '*Die Kaiserschlacht*' – The Kaiser's Battle.

By 6 February Mme Rischard was ready to go home. Her ticket was booked, her bags were packed and, to her great delight, she received a farewell visit from Bruce. He had arrived two days before, in the guise of a lawyer advising her on her late father's estate. He gave her a cigarette case, saying, mysteriously, that it contained things that would bring her comfort. He also gave her a supply of addressed envelopes. Finally, he told her that his family motto was '*Omne Solum Forti Patria*' – Every Country Is a Brave Man's Land – and asked her, with great affection, to use it as her watchword. Then he left; the two of them had at last made their peace. By 7 February, Mme Rischard was on her way home.

The first part of the journey passed without mishap and by the evening she was in an hotel in Offenburg where she spent the night. She set off early the next day, changed trains at Strasbourg and started the final leg. The nearer to her destination she got, the slower the journey became. There were many stops, and hours of delay. Luggage was regularly searched for food that could be confiscated – especially butter, eggs and chocolate. It so angered her that she considered starting the journey again to try her luck with a different train and guards.

By ten in the evening the train pulled into Luxembourg. A short time later, after a walk through the dark streets, she stood in her own front hall and was reunited with her husband, Camille. They had been apart for nearly two years. He was recovering from a bout of the flu and looked thin, tired and drawn. He knew some of what her mission entailed but not all the details. He knew that there was special interest in the railway junction. She told him all that had happened to her from her recruitment by Rose and Réséda, to her training and the proposal to use *Die Landwirt*.

In Paris, at the Permit Office, Bruce and Campbell waited for news from their protégée. On 26 February a copy of *Die Landwirt* arrived in the diplomatic bag from Switzerland. It had been published on 22 February. They scanned the pages. In the middle of the second column on the back page was a passage of local news. It told of three piglets for sale, air raids in which a barber was injured and a café's windows blown in, horses requisitioned and a report of a request to the authorities to allow oats destined for animals to be sold to human beings. They realised this was genuine local news and not a coded message. They went on searching, looking for another clue.

Eventually they came across an article titled 'From the library table' – this was what they were looking for. Decoded it read: 'We are all ready in 46, 34 and 68, and have agreed.' The numbers stood for people and places; 68 was *Die Landwirt* itself. Another part read: 'Until today nothing to report, no constituted units have gone through. No movement of constituted units has taken place in either direction through LUXEMBOURG station during the period February 10–20.' The message had taken five days to transmit from inside occupied territory. It was immediately transmitted to GHQ as 'B.P. No. 1. 26/2/1918'.

Mme Rischard's mission had begun with a flourish.

Later that month, near the front, an officer from the staff of Prince Eitel Friedrich was thrown from his horse. An ambulance took him to the hospital where the two nuns Sister Marie-Mélanie and Sister Marie-Caroline worked and ran their shop. He spent weeks convalescing, hobbling around with his leg in a heavy plaster cast and using a wooden crutch. He was an unhappy man and was forever complaining that his fall had caused him to miss the 'big push'. As the days passed, the sisters worked out that he was talking about the 'Albert Sector' of the front. This was cross-checked with train-watching reports from the Hirson platoon, especially from the 24-hour surveillance schedule being carried out by the wife and two children of Félix Latouche. The officer was talking about Operation Michael.

While the young man with the broken leg was lamenting his absence from the coming fight, a gunner arrived at the hospital. He had been wounded in the hand on the Laon sector and boasted that he had seen an enormous gun there that could fire shells as far as Paris. Sister Marie-Mélanie teased him and said that she did not believe any gun could fire so far. The gunner replied that he had seen the artillery piece with his own eyes and speculated that soon hundreds of such weapons would be in place.

The soldier did not say where the gun was, only that he had seen it on the Laon sector. Sister Marie-Mélanie remembered that a few weeks earlier a refugee from the Laon area had been sheltered at the convent for a few nights. He had told them that his village had been requisitioned and the inhabitants driven out. The refugee said that he thought the reason was that the Germans were going to install artillery to bombard the front. When Sister Marie-Mélanie asked him why he thought this he answered that they had been laying heavy concrete emplacements and what looked like huge ammunition pits at a place called Dandry's Farm.

The commanders of the nuns' White Lady company sent a spy to the village. The agent travelled at night and hid by day; the round trip took him three days. At the village he saw the gun for himself. Three days later the information was in Landau's hands in Holland and soon after that was with GHQ. The two nuns were never told what happened to the information about the guns or whether they were destroyed.

By now Mme Rischard and her husband Camille had recruited some senior railway officials, and through *Die Landwirt* useful intelligence was reaching GHQ indicating a big German build-up. The British commander-in-chief, Haig, noted that, in part thanks to Mme Rischard's intelligence, his command knew that five divisions had been moved into France along the Hirson–Valenciennes line. This was as much as the line could carry. Field Marshal Haig wrote in his diaries of exciting documents captured from German soldiers, of information gleaned from POWs and from aerial reconnaissance. He also mentioned the information being sent by the train watchers, men and women who put their lives at risk to gather it. Even so, when he was told that an attack was imminent his response was: '. . . the enemy would find our front so strong that he will hesitate to commit his Army to the attack with the almost certainty of losing very heavily.'

In Liège the lieutenant in charge of the secret police received an anonymous letter saying that a woman called Marcelle had left occupied

France without a passport and was working as a domestic in the town. Further, she was walking out with a rich man. The lieutenant regularly received letters like this and thought that this one was of no importance. Nevertheless, to be on the safe side, on 8 March 1918 he sent two of his men to bring Marcelle in for questioning. Marcelle's employer owned the Villa des Hirondelles, which was a secret headquarters for the White Lady, the place where hundreds of reports were collated and typed up.

Suspecting nothing, the two German agents arrived at the villa, set in its own grounds by the banks of a river. Coming out of the house were two men. The policemen did not know that they were couriers. One of the Germans asked, 'Who lives here?' The agents were thrown and did not reply. The German, whose name was Müller, pulled a gun and ordered the men back to the house.

They rapped on the door and after a short pause a voice demanded to know who it was. Müller stuck his gun into the ribs of one of the agents and told him to reply. The door opened to reveal Madame Goessels, who was in charge of the secretariat. She knew that in the back room of the house there were two more agents who were copying reports they had just brought back. There were incriminating documents all over the table in the room.

Müller asked whether a Monsieur Reyman lived in the house. Mme Goessels said he did not and that it was her establishment. Müller then asked her if she had ever been arrested and she replied that she had not.

'You are French?'

'No, I am Belgian.'

Müller pushed past her into the house. In the sitting room were two brothers, Louis and Anthony Collard, both in their early twenties. They were part of a family of seven children and had come to Liège to try to get into Allied-occupied France and join the Belgian army. Before they could do this they were contacted by the White Lady and persuaded to become agents instead.

The raid took the two brothers completely by surprise. They both had notebooks in which was written incriminating evidence.

In desperation Anthony threw his out of the window. The Germans arrested them both and began to gather up the papers. Müller saw Mme Goessels on the stairs, dashed after her and followed her into her bedroom shouting, 'Trying to hide something?' Mme Goessels tried to lock him in the room but he wrenched the door open.

Soon everyone in the villa had been handcuffed and tied with rope. The building was searched and twenty-four handguns and 10,000 rounds of ammunition were found. The prisoners were taken to Liège police station and crammed under guard in one room. Mme Goessels quickly organised a plan. She said to one of the agents that she was his mistress and that he often visited her at the villa. The other was to say that he was a friend and often visited her at the house. The two Collard brothers were her lodgers; she did not know anything about them, who they were or what they were doing. She whispered, 'Remember your oath as a soldier. Reveal nothing.'

Then the interrogations began. Mme Goessels said that the guns and ammunition were for the refugees that she was helping to cross the frontier. The Collard brothers said that they intended to cross the frontier into Holland and had written the reports so that they could sell them to Dutch Intelligence. They did not mention the White Lady. They also knew that under German law, spies were not executed unless they had been in direct communication with the enemy; intending to communicate was not a capital offence. At the end of the preliminary interrogation they were all taken to Saint-Léonard prison. For the Collard brothers the situation was much more serious. The reports they had been working on were in code and the notebook found on Louis contained the names of some agents, including their father, who was also arrested along with three others. The secret police now had nine prisoners. Their interrogation went on for weeks. The four whose names were in Louis' notebook knew nothing about the White Lady. Mme Goessels stuck to her story. As far as the Germans were concerned, she had committed a criminal offence but was not a spy.

The Collard brothers' sister, Marie-Thérèse, tried to find out what had happened to her brothers and father. The police refused to tell her. She was eventually contacted by a member of the White Lady. The organisation undertook to take care of the children and at the same time enrolled Marie-Thérèse and her cousin Irene as agents, thinking that they knew enough to rebuild the network that had just been destroyed. This the two women succeeded in doing and even sent a message saying, 'If you have orders to give us send them along, we are entirely at your disposal ... We are happier every day that you chose us to continue the work of our dear parents. Please accept our sincere thanks and respectful mark of friendship.'

They signed the letter with their codenames. The police became suspicious and arrested them. Two weeks later they were released for lack of evidence.

Meanwhile, the White Lady directorate was trying to find out what was going on in the prison. The Collard brothers were in solitary confinement and could not be contacted. Contact was made with one of the other men who had been arrested. He said he had been accused of espionage and that false identity papers had been discovered. The Germans wanted to know where they had come from. While this was going on the Collard brothers were taken from solitary confinement, stripped naked and thrashed with a cane by their interrogators.

The owner of the Villa des Hirondelles managed to get back into the house. He found the documents hidden in the sofa and also Anthony Collard's notebook lying in the grass outside the window.

Now all the prisoners were put on trial. On 18 July 1918 Mme Goessels and the Collard brothers were sentenced to death, the others to various terms of hard labour. In the end Mme Goessels' sentence was commuted to hard labour for life.

The Collard brothers were allowed to see their father to say farewell. They met in a long room in which the director of the prison sat with other officers at a long table. Outside stood immobile and respectful soldiers. The doors opened to signal that the farewell was over. The brothers fell to their knees saying, 'Father, give us your last blessing.' He blessed them and then himself sank to his knees, saying, 'You also, my children, before you die, bless your old father.'

The young men were led away, no tears and their heads held high. Their father, realising he would never see them again, rushed after them, pushing past the soldiers guarding the door. He was in time to see them at the end of the corridor; they turned and shouted, 'We'll meet in heaven' and disappeared from his sight.

CHAPTER TWENTY-ONE

BATTLES AND BALLOONS

By 10 March the detailed plans for the 'big push' – Operation Michael – were in place: 'The Michael attack will take place on 21 March ... [we will] break into the first enemy position at 9:40am.' By chance Ludendorff had chosen to attack in the weakest sector of the British front, which was held by troops who had never properly recovered from the earlier fighting at Passchendaele. Their commander was General Hubert Gough, a cavalryman and a poor administrator. Gough's officers felt that his failure to co-ordinate the artillery and the infantry had cost lives and that he had insisted on unattainable objectives. Lloyd George had tried to have him removed but without success.

On 21 March at 4:40am the British Army was blasted by the first salvo of the Michael operation. It lasted for five hours; more than a million shells landed in an area of 150 square miles, larger than any other bombardment of the war. The bombardment included tear-gas shells, which were designed to make the British rip off their respirators, forcing them to breathe in the lethal gas released by phosgene shells and to have their skins tormented by blistering mustard gas.

By the end of the month the Germans had advanced 40 miles. The French commander-in-chief told his prime minister that the 'Germans will beat the English in the open field, after which they will beat us too'.

In spite of his earlier confidence that the Germans would find his front so strong that they would hesitate to attack, Field Marshal Haig issued an order that 'every position must be held to the last man: there must be no retirement. With our backs to the wall, and believing in the justice of our cause, each one of us must fight to the end. The safety of our homes and the freedom of mankind alike depend on the conduct of each one of us at this critical moment.'

On the night of 28 March in Saint-Léonard prison in Liège, Émile Fauquenot was tearing his sheets into strips and tying them into a rope. Outside the long, high wall of the prison Juliette Delrualle and two White Lady officers waited in the shadows. They knew that, inside, the Polish guard who hated the Germans was going to unlock Fauquenot's and Creusen's cell doors. The group stared up at the high walls, wondering whether the escape plan was under way. Inside, Émile's cell door swung open, the Polish guard motioned for him to follow. The two men crept along the corridor until they came to cell 156, where there was a store cupboard holding mattresses and sheets. Waiting by the cupboard was Creusen, a pile of sheets in his arms. Minutes later they were on the roof, having dodged the guards and their fierce dogs. Below them they could see the glowing cigarettes of the two White Lady officers. Using the sheets to lengthen the rope they lowered themselves from the roof. They could see the window of Marie Birckel's cell. They had planned to take her with them but she had refused, thinking her presence would make the plan too complicated. They reached the ground and were rushed away to board a tram.

Inside her cell Marie Birckel wondered how the escape had gone and if her two friends had been successful. About an hour later there was uproar in the prison. Guards running up and down the corridors, men shouting, doors banging. Marie could hear cars revving in the prison courtyard, then accelerating away. Silence returned and she slept.

The next morning she was taken to an interrogation room and told that the two men had been shot while escaping. Fauquenot was dead and Creusen badly wounded. Her interrogators told her that

Creusen had confessed all, so she might as well tell them everything she knew. Marie just sat silent, not believing anything her interrogators said. After being told that she would face another trial for treason she was taken back to her cell.

From then on she was watched round the clock; the light was kept on in her cell and every five minutes a guard peered at her through the spy-hole. She complained to the governor that it was intolerable to have to wash under the eyes of the guards. He replied by asking her why she took two hours to wash herself; she replied that she had all the time in the world so why should she hurry.

In Luxembourg on 5 April aeroplanes of the RAF appeared over Luxembourg and dropped twenty bombs on the station. Houses were hit, four people were killed and three badly injured. Over the next few days there were more raids. The marshalling yards were undamaged and the station remained open; between 8 and 15 April a German division passed through Luxembourg on its way to Mons. Mme Rischard sent a message to the Permit Office in Paris saying that the attacks were useless and had made the situation singularly complicated. She suggested that in future the aircraft should fly low enough to be certain that they would hit their targets.

Operation Michael and the German advance looked unstoppable. At GHQ a lorry was on permanent standby, ready to leave at an hour's notice. Its task was to take maps and documents to the coast. Plans were in hand to evacuate the army from the Somme and northern France. Rumour had it that if this were to happen, there would be no ports left in France and the Americans would not be able to disembark. As a result the war might go on for ten years, or might just be lost altogether.

As the situation worsened, on the night of 18 June a small convoy of British lorries, under the command of Bruce, drew into a village a few miles to the south of Verdun and only a few miles from the German front line. The vehicles were carrying a balloon and all the equipment needed to launch it. This included a huge wicker basket,

200 feet of rope, sandbags, ninety gas cylinders, electric torches and equipment to repair the balloon if necessary, including glue and scissors. The mission was to send the balloonist Conrad Bartels, real name Baschwitz Meau, into Luxembourg to rendezvous with Mme Rischard.

Months of work had gone into preparing for the launch, which itself had been postponed several times. That night the moon and wind conditions were thought to be as good as they would ever be. If the trip was again cancelled it could not be remounted for another month, and in even a month the war could be lost.

As night fell the balloon was inflated. It was high summer, the days were long and the launch was timed to take advantage of the maximum amount of darkness. Landing would be at 3:45am, when the dawn would give just enough light to land. Meau carried money and maps tied in a bundle, to be hidden if he was in danger of capture. In the basket was a flask of coffee, some bars of chocolate and Meau's leather travelling case. It also contained an elaborate system of water tanks, which could be drained to lighten and help manoeuvre the craft. When the balloon was fully inflated and straining against the ropes tying it down, Bruce gave the order to launch. The balloon rose gently into the sky, soaring above the heads of the ground crew and disappearing into the darkness. It settled at just over 3,000 feet and the wind took it on towards Luxembourg. Light crept into the east and Meau saw ahead somewhere he could land. He estimated that he was about 40 miles to the northwest of his destination. He gathered his kit together and released hot air from the canopy. The craft sank to the ground, bumped along the grass of a field, the gas cylinders clanking against each other. He released water from the tanks, the basket tipped, Meau jumped out and, relieved of his weight and the water, the balloon rose again into the air, heading for oblivion and leaving no trace that it had touched earth.

Meau set off for the nearest main railway station at Mersch, where he hoped to pick up a train to Luxembourg. After a 12-mile walk he entered the town, found the station, bought a ticket and, by late morning, was standing in the grounds of Mme Rischard's house, hidden by trees and foliage. When he was satisfied that the coast was clear, he climbed the wide steps to the front door, asked for Mme Rischard and said that he was expected. When the two eventually met he announced himself as Conrad Bartels. At first she said she had no idea who Bartels was, worried that he might be a German double agent. Eventually he persuaded her that he was genuine and their collaboration began.

Among their priorities was to set up a system that would go on operating if either of them or Mme Rischard's husband were arrested. At the same time Meau made a thorough reconnaissance of the area and began to search for more recruits for the fledgling organisation. Very quickly a lot more information began to pour in. Mme Rischard often worked far into the night, coding it ready to be placed in *Die Landwirt*.

CHAPTER TWENTY-TWO

THE LONG DAY'S DYING

In Liège, on 7 June, Marie Birckel once more climbed into a police wagon, taking her to stand trial in front of a military court in the Palais de Justice. As usual she had no lawyer to represent her. She was asked her name and age and then told she was accused of treason against Germany, for which the punishment was death. Marie replied that as she was French and working for her country she could not commit treason against Germany. Her accuser began to argue with Marie, who had been nicknamed the 'Little French Girl' by her fellow prisoners.

The judge interrupted and asked her if, when she had returned to Belgium, she was aware of the danger she was running. She replied that she was and that she had no regrets because she was working for her country, for France. Then she said, 'If you condemn me to death you will cause an international outcry.' For a moment the judge smiled, appearing to be impressed by the unflinching bravery of the small, pretty, young woman in front of him.

After further cross-examination the judge called the proceedings to a halt, saying he would sentence her in a few days. She was led out, put back into the van and driven back to her cell. To her amazement the restrictions on her were lifted. She was no longer watched, her cell door was left open and she could walk in the prison garden. By 26 July she was condemned not to death but to penal servitude for life. Very shortly after this she was transferred, with only twenty hours' warning, to a women's prison, Siegburg, in Germany. She was just able to say goodbye to Juliette Delrualle. She was now feeling very ill and feverish. At the station she saw a huge heap of coal piled up against a wall. For an instant she considered scrambling up, jumping over the wall and escaping. It was getting dark and streets round the station were deserted. She knew she was too ill and weak and abandoned the idea.

She travelled the same route that the Princess de Croÿ and Louise Thuliez had taken months before. The journey was long, the stops frequent and tedious. Very little food was provided along with the gritty, insipid ersatz coffee. Marie could not believe it when at Bonn they stopped for the night in a small hotel and she was given a single room to herself. The guard locked her in and once more she thought of escaping, and once more she abandoned the idea; she felt too ill and did not have the strength to run for it. The next day she completed the journey, left the train and walked the last few miles, under guard, to the prison. As she walked through the high, bleak arch a voice shouted from within a cell, '*La petite Française!*' It was a wonderful salute, to be acknowledged by a fellow prisoner who must have recognised her from her time at Saint-Léonard prison.

She spent the next day and night in her cell, shivering and with a temperature, coughing all the time. Then she was made to get up and taken to the washhouse. There she was strip-searched, washed, given brown prison clothes and sent back to her cell where, once more, teeth chattering and aching all over, she lay on her prison bed. She shared her cell with a young woman called Victoire Kerf, who had also been sent from Saint-Léonard. Victoire was fifteen years old and for the next five days did her best to nurse Marie back to health. As the fever broke and she began to feel better a doctor arrived, examined her very briefly and told her that she had bronchitis. He then declared her fit for work and her life of penal servitude began.

By 17 July 1918 the enemy had at last been halted. The railway system that the Germans had used with such success now began to fail them. Mme Rischard reported that troop movement patterns had changed. It became difficult to tell whether the Germans were regrouping or in disarray.

Many German troops were demoralised or exhausted. Since the start of Operation Michael nearly a million men had been killed or wounded. As well as these casualties the army was short of 300,000 men. Their commander, Ludendorff, was in the throes of a nervous breakdown.

On the other side of the front, the British were about to send in hundreds of tanks at Amiens, weapons that had first seen action on the Somme, two years before. American troops and equipment were pouring across the Atlantic. By the end of July there were more than 1,200,000 fresh US troops already in the battle or about to engage.

The British attacked at Amiens on 8 August 1918. Nearly 17,000 German soldiers were taken prisoner, hundreds of artillery pieces were captured and Ludendorff called it 'a black day for the German army'. The chief of the German general staff, Paul von Hindenburg, described the army's position as 'promising and satisfactory despite the recent mishaps.' The Kaiser said: 'I see that we must take stock of the situation. We are at the limit of our capacities. The war must be brought to an end.'

In the prison at Siegburg Marie Birckel's day passed in forced labour, sewing rough sacks. She had no idea what they were for. The supervisor was a pinched-thin being whose uniform hat reminded Marie of a cauliflower. The governor of the prison, who oversaw both the men and the women, had lost an arm at the front and it seemed to Marie that he wanted every prisoner to pay for that arm. There was, though, an atmosphere of revolution among the prisoners, who sang patriotic songs to keep their spirits up.

Food was short in Germany, and even shorter in the prison. They were mostly served a disgusting gruel that they called 'insect soup'.

Then, without warning, Marie and thirty other prisoners were marched out of Siegburg and sent to another prison at Delitzsch. Although it was situated in a magnificent chateau, the treatment of the prisoners made Siegburg and Saint-Léonard seem like pleasant memories. They were kept in tiny wire cages. Washing was communal and relied on a thin trickle of cold water. Marie's prison underwear was too tight, while the rough outer garments were grotesquely too large and had a large blue and white cross sewn on, making it clear that they were prisoners. Marie had to share her cell and her prison cot with a huge Russian peasant woman.

Meanwhile, back at Siegburg, Louise de Bettignies had developed an abscess under her breast which rapidly grew in size and pain. Léonie Vanhoutte, the Countess de Belleville, Louise Thuliez, the Princess de Croÿ and others rallied round their young comrade. They tried to keep her warm, draping their own blankets round her thin shoulders. They wrote letters to people of influence in the outside world and demanded that the prison authorities allow Louise de Bettignies to be taken to Bonn or Cologne to have the abscess treated in a proper hospital. This last request was refused, the prison doctor offering to treat it by rubbing Vaseline on it.

Finally, at four in the afternoon, in a freezing room with almost no lighting, the operation was performed by a young surgeon from Bonn, assisted by the prison doctor and two nuns. When Louise awoke from the chloroform she said, 'I am cold.' The wound did not heal, the surgeon did not return to see the results of his work and the prison doctor ignored her. Flowers were brought to her bedside, lilac, broom and forget-me-nots. Even the woman who was the prison governor brought her apple blossom. But as spring turned into summer, Louise de Bettignies lay dying. It was eventually agreed that she should be taken to a hospital in Cologne.

She arrived at the hospital Sainte Marie on 24 July. The authorities had been informed that she was a dangerous person who had done great damage to the German cause. Louise was wearing a white cotton blouse and a dark skirt, with her hair which had once been so beautiful wrapped round her head in two plaits. She brought with her a faded photograph of her mother, a tiny French flag and a rosary. She talked for a while with a priest, telling him about her life and her hope that when she was better she might be allowed to travel to Switzerland to see her mother. The priest visited her every Thursday until, in the middle of September, he got an urgent call saying she was dying. He rushed to the hospital and found her lying in bed, having trouble breathing. He took her outstretched hand and leaned over her pale face. She whispered, 'I am going to die, Father.'

'Yes, I feel it is all over.'

He took out his crucifix and pressed it to her lips, making the prayer of absolution and anointing her with oil. She lay quiet for a day, breathing slowly and regularly; when she breathed out she did so with a small shudder. A day later, on 27 September, holding the priest's hand in her own but lost to the world of the hospital, she died.

On 28 September Ludendorff suggested to Hindenburg that he ask the American president, Woodrow Wilson, for an armistice. Later, he informed his staff that both Hindenburg and the Kaiser had agreed to approach Wilson. As he spoke in his high-pitched, strained voice several of his officers broke down and most men present had tears running down their faces.

In Kiel, on 3 November, the sailors of the German navy mutinied rather than continue with the war. Twenty thousand sailors refused to go to sea.

The German High Command fell apart. Ludendorff was summoned to the Kaiser for what would be their last meeting. The Kaiser told him he was to be dismissed, at which point the general began to shout and wave his arms about, being very disrespectful to his monarch. He was offered the command of an army group, which he refused and instead fled to Switzerland, disguised as a diplomat.

As for the Kaiser, who had once bragged about a 'fight to the death', there was much plotting about his future. One idea was that he should abdicate, another that he die fighting a last, carefully staged, battle at the front. He did neither and fled to Holland.

An armistice was signed and came into force on 11 November 1918. One of the conditions was that the German army relinquish all the occupied territories in the west within a fortnight. Further destruction was forbidden. The army marched home, abandoning huge amounts of materiel and stores. As quickly as it had arrived in the summer of 1914, the German steamroller vanished.

Nearly 2 million German soldiers began to retreat, sometimes in good order, sometimes in chaos, desperate to get home and clogging the railways and roads along which they had once stormed to victory. Along the Dutch border the high-voltage fence was pulled down.

In Siegburg prison Louise Thuliez saw soldiers wearing red cockades in their caps passing their officers without saluting. They had lightened their baggage of all that could be sold or exchanged. At their departure they sold their rifles for one mark and offered their gas masks to anyone who wanted to buy them.

In her prison cell in Ghent, Marthe Cnockaert could hear bells ringing, footsteps running along the corridors, the crash and bang of bolts being flung back. Her door swung open to reveal a group of wild-eyed soldiers shouting, 'You are free! Free!' then they ran off, slamming the door behind them. Marthe could not open it and slumped, weeping, onto her bed. An hour later the men returned, opening all the doors in the prison. She wandered into the streets, jostled by disorientated German soldiers. Belgian civilians looted cafés, dragging barrels of wine into the streets. Then she heard a strange language, English, spoken by an advance guard of British soldiers. She realised then that the war had ended and that the Allies had won. She grabbed a British officer and gabbled, 'I belong to the British secret service ... I have been a prisoner for two years ... I live in Roulers ... my parents are there, please help me get home.' Then she collapsed.

In Delitzsch, the same night, Marie Birckel had no idea what was happening. She and her cellmate, Laure Chevery, could hear shouting and banging in the courtyard below their cell. They dragged the table under the window and placed the only chair on it. Marie climbed up and tried to peer through the window to see what was happening. It was too dark. The shouting and confusion went on. Later, when dawn was breaking, she tried again. This time she could see men milling about wearing red armbands. They thought the long-rumoured German revolution must have started, but what did it mean? Who had won, the French or the Germans? Later they heard running feet and the cell doors on the corridor being opened and slammed shut. Then their own door opened and a panting soldier carrying a revolver and wearing one of the red armbands burst in on them. For a moment he stared at them, catching his breath. Then he demanded, 'Are you French or Belgian?'

'French.'

'Good, then you will leave for Switzerland in six days. The Belgians leave today!'

The door slammed shut and Marie and Laure were alone, still with no idea what was happening. They settled down to wait out the next six days. Two hours later the door burst open again. Another German soldier with a red armband stood in front of them.

'You are leaving at once with the Belgians. Get ready.'

He disappeared, leaving the door open. The two women had nothing to pack. On the way out they passed the open door of the supervisor in charge of the female section of the prison. She looked up at them, her eyes swollen and red with tears, despair on her face. She had always treated the inmates well and for an instant Marie felt a flicker of sympathy for her.

A bedraggled column of eighty prisoners, all in poor health, crept out of the prison and made their way to the station where a train was waiting for them. It was manned by women and had red banners attached to it. Marie wondered whether it was under the command of revolutionaries.

For the next four days they travelled towards Liège. From time to time they ate a slimy macaroni-like substance with their bare hands. Rumours were everywhere, even that the king of Belgium had been assassinated along with the president of France. Once or twice the train was fired upon. The women lay on the floor, bullets splintering the wood above their heads.

On 12 November some British prisoners of war climbed aboard. They seemed to know about the armistice and what was really happening. At Aix-la-Chapelle the train stopped. There was chaos on the platforms, which were choked with German soldiers trying to get home. German military police tried to keep order among the angry, shouting, pushing men. Later the train steamed into the night, heading for Belgium and Liège.

When they arrived they found more chaos, equipment abandoned in the streets, German soldiers insulting their officers, machine guns being fired in the night. Slowly, order returned. The last troops left in quiet, sullen humiliation. Marie Birckel was reunited with Émile Fauquenot, the man she had been told was dead. He looked so thin and tired that Marie wondered whether he would ever recover. The work of the White Lady went on, monitoring the departure of the Germans.

Then, at last, the French victors appeared to a joyful welcome. The streets filled with the liberated citizens, flowers in the colours of France and Belgium lay in the roads, the national flags hung from the buildings and everywhere people were singing the 'Marseillaise' and the 'Brabançonne'. Amid the celebrations Marie and Émile became engaged, their work of resistance and the days of danger at last ended. Marie was made a Chevalier of the Légion d'Honneur and was awarded the Croix de Guerre. The British gave her an OBE. Soon she and Émile were happily married.

Marthe Cnockaert returned to her village where she stood on a wrecked road in front of a bullet-riddled sign that read 'This Is Westrozebeke'. The village that five years before had been surrounded by fields, lanes and glades now stood in a blasted wilderness in which not a house remained standing, the countryside reduced to an ocean of grey mud. By the side of the road a group of British soldiers sat smoking and drinking tea. Their officer walked over to her and asked if she had once lived here. Within the year they were married.

In Cologne, Marie de Croÿ saw banners on which was written the legend: 'Welcome to our unconquered armies'. She noted that immediately after the armistice, 'alongside the railway, the German army was marching and I watched it curiously. The men marched steadily in silence with set faces and covered in dust.' She returned to Brussels and watched the triumphant return of the Belgian king and queen.

'We heard distant cheering which turned into a roar as it spread up to us ... at last a little pause and, amidst breathless silence, a group of six on horseback came slowly through the waiting streets. Leading was our soldier King with the Queen on a white horse by his side, both wearing simple khaki.'

By the end of the war, La Dame Blanche had been responsible for nearly 70 per cent of all Allied intelligence coming out of Belgium. The head of MI6, Captain Mansfield Smith-Cumming, wrote to them: 'It is on you alone that we depend to obtain intelligence on enemy movements ... The intelligence obtained by you is worth thousands of lives to the Allied Armies.'

One of the women later said, 'The feeling of danger hanging over our heads night and day did not dishearten us – far from it. It seemed that the greater the danger became, the more enchanting was our work.'

Another female agent, describing the experience, said, 'There is nothing more horrible than long winter nights in a room without light ... fighting drowsiness and fearing to fail in one's duty ... with nothing to break up the sombre monotony of this existence.'

One agent summed up what almost all of them felt: 'We were soldiers without uniforms. We have done our duty ... and we have done it with joy.'

EPILOGUE

Louise de Bettignies' body was repatriated on 21 February 1920. Her journey home started at Cologne, where generals from the French and British forces made speeches in her honour. On 16 March she was buried in Lille. Her coffin was draped in the French flag. On the flag were placed the medals of the Croix de Guerre and the Légion d'Honneur, plus two medals from the British. The citation for her Croix de Guerre recounted that she had been 'impelled solely by the highest patriotism, to the service of her country'. That she had braved the dangers of her work with 'inflexible courage ... risking her life continually ... displaying a heroism which has rarely been surpassed'.

The year before, on 17 March 1919, Edith Cavell's body had been disinterred. A post-mortem revealed that she had been killed by four shots, three to the heart and one to the forehead. Her remains were carried on the destroyer HMS *Rowena* to England, where a memorial service was held in Westminster Abbey. Huge crowds watched the procession and the *Times* correspondent wrote:

> There was no motion in the multitude and no sound came from them. But for the roll of drums, the beautiful melody of a funeral march and the slow, stately tread of the escorting guards, the silence would have been unbroken. Overhead there was a cloudless sky. Sunshine lit up the crowd and made a golden way for the passage of the gun carriage and its honoured burden. From the

buildings scores of flags flew at half mast ... the coffin, swathed
with the Union Jack, was almost covered by an immense cross of
red and white carnations.

Inside the abbey the service concluded with 'Abide with Me'. Sister
Wilkins said, 'To know her was to love her. She was indeed loved
and respected not only by her English sisters but by her cosmopolitan pupils.'

She was finally laid to rest in Life's Green outside the south tran-
sept of Norwich Cathedral.

In the early morning of 27 May 1919, a small group of people stood
in the cemetery of the military execution field on the rifle range at Tir
National on the outskirts of Brussels, where German firing squads
had executed Belgians condemned as traitors and terrorists. The
group watched in silence as gravediggers opened an unmarked burial
plot. From it they pulled a rotting pine coffin. The lid was prised off
to reveal the decaying corpse of a young woman. She was wearing
a long blue coat. There were holes torn into it around the heart. A
priest prayed in a clear voice. The onlookers crossed themselves and
bowed their heads as the body was transferred to a polished solid
oak casket with brass handles, placed in a hearse and driven out of
the cemetery. Gabrielle Petit, executed for war treason and sabotage,
had begun her last journey.

Two days later, just before noon on 29 May, Ascension Day,
three gun carriages pulled by horses processed through the streets
of Schaarbeek, one of the largest and wealthiest suburbs of Brussels
and through which Gabrielle Petit had been driven to her execution.
Each carriage carried a coffin draped in the Belgian flag. In front
and in place of honour was Gabrielle's coffin; those behind carried
two of her executed comrades. The crowds that lined the streets to
see them pass had been waiting since dawn. The procession stopped
outside the wide steps of the town hall and the coffins were carried
inside. For the next three hours, hundreds of people came to pay
their respects, many weeping, as a military band played solemn

music. Then all fell silent as the prime minister read an address. At four o'clock a majestic figure in white made a dramatic appearance. That person was Queen Elisabeth of the Belgians, revered as the 'Queen Nurse' for her war work with wounded soldiers. The regal figure bowed to the coffins, pinned awards on the flags, spoke quietly to the relatives, bowed again and disappeared. The coffins were carried outside and placed on the gun carriages. The final part of the procession took the cortège to Schaarbeek cemetery where the coffins were lowered into the ground.

Gabrielle Petit's journey from the grim obscurity of her childhood to national heroine was over.

WHEN ALL WAS SAID
AND DONE: 1919–1968

At the end of the war Mme Rischard received a letter from Bruce saying in French that her work and the reports she had sent back had proved to be of 'incalculable value'. For her work she was awarded a CBE and her husband an OBE. She was also made a Chevalier of the Légion d'Honneur and was awarded the Croix de Guerre. She and some of her comrades arranged a small celebration lunch in Prunier restaurant in Paris, where they enjoyed roast chicken and oysters, and drank Château Lafite 1907. Perhaps her greatest happiness was that her son Marcel had survived the trenches. In 1940 the Germans once more marched into Luxembourg and Mme Rischard, now a widow, destroyed the records of the work she had done as an agent. Knowing that she had worked undercover in 1918 the Germans came to raid her flat. It was May 1940 and they were three months too late, the files were burned; Lise herself had died on 29 February.

After the war the Princess Marie de Croÿ became a member of the Légion d'Honneur. She went back to Bellignies, where she lived in peace until the Germans invaded her country in 1940. Once more she joined the resistance movement, working with Louise Thuliez who had resumed her life as a teacher. Bellignies again became a hiding place for Allied soldiers. The princess was arrested with her chauffeur, who was beaten unconscious. She was released for lack of evidence against her. Of the Second World War she said: 'Of course we had many of the same experiences as in the last war.' She never married and died in 1968 at the age of ninety-two. Both the princess and Louise Thuliez wrote books about their experiences in the First World War. The princess's was called *War Memories* and Thuliez's *Condemned to Death*, which in 1935 won the Montyon Prize.

Marthe Cnockaert was mentioned in despatches and made a member of both the French and the Belgian Legions of Honour. The officer she married was John McKenna, who helped her write a memoir, *I Was a Spy!* The book was a success and described by Winston Churchill as 'the greatest war story of all ... Dwelling behind the German line within the sound of cannon, she continually obtained and sent information of the highest importance to the British Intelligence Authorities. Her tale is a thrilling one ...' She went on to write a string of spy stories. By the outbreak of the Second World War she was living in Manchester and her name appeared on a list of prominent people the Nazis were going to arrest when they invaded Britain. She returned to Belgium after the war and died in 1966.

Herman Capiau returned to his career as a mining engineer. Elizabeth Wilkins stayed in nursing and became matron of the cottage hospital in Chard, Somerset. Later she said, 'We *had* to get our men away.'

In 1928 a fictional version of Edith Cavell's life, *Dawn*, was made. It starred Dame Sybil Thorndike as Edith. Ada Bodart, a nurse from Northern Ireland who had worked with Cavell hiding the fugitives, played herself in the film. The film led to a row with the German embassy and the Foreign Office banned it, hoping not to upset the Germans. In protest Bodart returned her OBE and refused a pension from the British government. She died penniless.

Of the Germans the two policemen, Lieutenant Bergan and Sergeant Pinkhoff, received the Iron Cross 2nd Class. Lieutenant General Traugott Martin von Sauberzweig, who had ordered the immediate execution of Edith Cavell, was always thereafter linked with the controversy, which blighted his career. He died on 14 April 1920. Dr Eduard Stoeber, the prosecutor who had brought the death penalty to so many, remained a military prosecutor, and during the Second World War worked in that capacity for Hitler and the Third Reich. Death came to him in 1960; he was eighty-eight.

'Dear old Jack', Edith Cavell's dog, found life without his mistress difficult. Chained to his kennel and not exercised, he howled all the time. Eventually he was taken in by the Princess de Croÿ's mother, the Dowager Duchess of Croÿ. She too found him a challenge; he would bite anyone who came too close. However, the dowager duchess reported that in the end 'he became as good and gentle as any other dog. He was most attached and loving. But he remained dangerous to strangers.' He died in 1923. The dowager duchess said, 'He had always been good and gentle to other dogs ... He did not suffer ... I was extremely sorry to lose him.' After his death, Jack was stuffed and sent to the Imperial War Museum in London, where he remains on display to this day.

ACKNOWLEDGEMENTS

On 24 January 2020 Simon and Schuster made their offer for *I Am Not Afraid of Looking into the Rifles*. That day would have been the forty-sixth birthday of my daughter Nell Gifford, who had died a month earlier. My last book, *Lonely Courage*, is dedicated to her and this book is dedicated to her sister Clover. They are brave women and have been an inspiration. I love them both for that.

Next I must thank the writer and journalist Sally McGrane for sending me the cutting about Louise de Bettignies, which got me thinking.

I must thank everybody at Simon & Schuster. First Ian Marshall for commissioning the book and CEO Ian Chapman for his enthusiasm for the project and his kindness and care in the early stages. Kris Doyle has been a brilliant editor. His many suggestions have made the book better. Alex Eccles, the project editor, has been a model of patience and concern, as has copy editor Lorraine Jerram. I am grateful for the meticulous work of proofreader Jonathan Wadman. I love the cover designed by the gifted India Minter. Thank you to Zoe Maple for her help with the images, and to publicist Sabah Khan and Hayley McMullan in marketing. I would like to thank Suzanne Baboneau, Rhiannon Carroll and Polly Osborn for their warm welcome to the company.

I thank everybody at PEW Literary. They include my agent, Patrick Walsh – who slaved over the proposal – Margaret Halton and Cora MacGregor. I would like to thank their sometime colleague John Ash for his help in the early days.

I thank Lynn Knight who wrote to me at the beginning of the project with some very good ideas about background research; Frances Wilson for sharing her generous thoughts on writing biography; Charles Goodson-Wickes for pointing me towards material about the working of GHQ; and Barbara Trapido for her very welcome thoughts and enthusiasm.

I thank Clemence Billoud for her help translating some of the French texts.

Bart Brosius from the Belgian embassy and Stephen Lodewyck, curator of the In Flanders Fields Museum, have both taken a keen and helpful interest in the book.

In writing the book I have found Sophie de Schaepdrijver's meticulously researched account of Gabrielle Petit's life and legacy both fascinating and useful, as was Diana Souhami's comprehensive life of Edith Cavell. Janet Morgan's invaluable unravelling of the part played by Mme Lise Rischard in helping the cause of Allied intelligence was also an important reference.

I have several friends who are no longer with us but who have contributed to my understanding of the world of the undercover agent. They are Vic Gregg, who was a British double agent in the Cold War; Jock Hamilton Baillie, who spent much of the Second World War as a prisoner of war in Colditz and was an experienced escaper; the historians Alastair Horne and John Keegan for many hours of talk on all things military; Marie-France MacCarthy, who worked in the French Resistance during the Second World War and told me what it was like, as a young woman, to bicycle through occupied France with hand grenades concealed in her blouse.

Alan Ogden, Geoffrey Matthews and Simon Mayall are three soldiers and also good friends of mine who have been very helpful and generous with their time.

I thank the brilliant librarians and staff of the London Library, where much of this book was written. I am a trustee there and it is a haven for writers of all genres. Also the British Library, the Imperial

War Museum, the National Army Museum and the National Archives at Kew.

I have other friends who have been a source of encouragement and moral support in what proved quite a long haul after the death of Nell and through the pandemic. They are the musician Frank Brown, the writer Kerry Crabbe, the film maker John Irvin, the musician Mark Knopfler, Wendy and Roger Lambert, my oldest friends, the artist Jim Latter, the writer Matthew Faulk, my marathon running companion Rupert Lycett Green, the economist Jeremy Hardie and the theatre director Giles Havergal.

And, of course, my wife, Alexandra Pringle, sometime editor-in-chief of Bloomsbury. She has been described as a publishing legend, but is always my *sine qua non* and commander-in-chief.

Rick Stroud, London, 2023

PICTURE CREDITS

1. Gabrielle Petit: Sophie de Schaepdrijver, *Gabrielle Petit: The Death and Life of a Female Spy in the First World War* (Bloomsbury, 2015); Edith Cavell: Print Collector/Getty
2. Princess de Croÿ: © National Portrait Gallery, London; Château de Bellignies: Princess Marie de Croÿ, *War Memories* (Macmillan and Co., 1932)
3. German troops and fleeing women: Marthe McKenna, *I Was a Spy!* (Casemate Publishing, 2015); British soldiers: Three Lions/Getty
4. Marthe Cnockaert: *I Was a Spy!*; Louise de Bettignies: GRANGER – Historical Picture Archive/Alamy Stock Photo
5. *La Libre Belgique*: History and Art Collection/Alamy Stock Photo; Mme Rischard and her house: Janet Morgan, *The Secrets of Rue St Roch: Intelligence Operations Behind Enemy Lines in the First World War* (Allen Lane, 2004)
6. Saint-Gilles: Smith Collection/Gado/Getty; Edith Cavell: © Imperial War Museum (Q 15064)
7. Cavell's cell: Chronicle/Alamy Stock Photo; Louise Thuliez and Countess de Belleville: Louise Thuliez, *Condemned to Death* (Methuen, 1934)
8. Petit memorial: Chronicle/Alamy Stock Photo; Cavell memorial: Wellcome Collection

Source Notes

Prologue

1   On the evening of 31 March 1916 a 23-year-old woman ...: De
Schaepdrijver, Sophie, *Gabrielle Petit: The Death and Life of a Female
Spy in the First World War* (Bloomsbury Academic, 2015), 111
1   One of the guards reported that the young woman walked ...: ibid., 114
1   'I am not afraid of looking into the rifles': ibid., 115
2   The young woman began to recite the rosary ...: ibid.

1. Death Comes to Sarajevo

7   On Sunday, 28 June 1914 ...: Stone, Norman, *World War One: A Short
History* (Basic Books, 2010), Kindle edition
8   Every day at 8am her father led them in prayer to a God that demanded
sacrifice, devotion and service to the poor: Souhami, Diana, *Edith
Cavell* (Quercus, 2010), 15
9   In Devon, the 39-year-old Princess Marie de Croÿ was also on holiday ...:
De Croÿ, Princess Marie, *War Memories* (Macmillan and Co., 1932), 1
10   'someday, somehow, I am going to do something useful ...': Souhami,
op. cit., 33
10   ... Gabrielle Petit, wrote to her fiancé, the cavalry sergeant
Maurice Gobert, who she knew would soon be sent to the front: De
Schaepdrijver, op. cit., 111
11   Her mother had died when in her early thirties and her father was a
ne'er-do-well spendthrift who had abandoned his family: ibid., 19
13   Eventually Camille and his wife returned to their large, comfortable
villa ...: Morgan, Janet, *The Secrets of Rue St Roch: Intelligence
Operations Behind Enemy Lines in the First World War* (Allen Lane,
2004), 199. The description of the villa is taken from the text and

photographs of the house at No. 20 boulevard Royale in Janet Morgan's book.

13   Davignon was known to be imperturbable; people liked him and found him charmingly optimistic: Lipkes, Jeff, *Rehearsals: The German Army in Belgium, August 1914* (Leuven University Press, 2007), 23, quoting A. Klobukowski, *Souvenirs de Belgique*

13   The door opened and the count staggered in, a tall, distinguished German aristocrat, elegant with a waxed black moustache: Whitlock, Brand, *Belgium: A Personal Narrative* (University of Pennsylvania, 1919). Also Lipkes, op. cit., 21

15   He felt crushed by what he knew and wondered if he was in the grip of a nightmare that he might suddenly wake up from: Bassompierre quoted in Lipkes, op. cit., 28

15   Louise knew what the pealing bells were saying – they were ringing the tocsin, the alarm that war was about to break out: Thuliez, Louise, trans. Marie Poett-Velitchko, *Condemned to Death* (Methuen, 1934), x (Author's preface)

15   Then he looked up at Whitlock and said, 'Oh those poor Belgians! Why don't they get out of the way?': Bassompierre, quoted in Lipkes, op. cit., 15

16   'The sooner you will achieve victory! Spare only the railway stations – they will be more useful to us than the cathedrals!': Somville, Gustave, trans. Bernard Miall, *The Road to Liège: The Path of Crime* (Hodder and Stoughton, 1916), 10

2. The Germans Invade

18   The officer finished reading: Lipkes, op. cit., 39

18   The party over, Mrs Cnockaert was ironing when her husband burst into the room: McKenna, Marthe, *I Was a Spy!* (Pool of London Press, 2015), 11

19   He was immediately arrested and shot: Somville, op. cit., 179

19   The streets were crowded with people talking about the war and wondering if it would soon be over: Souhami, op. cit., 135

19   Sigismund Payne Best spent it in the Café Royal in Piccadilly, London, sitting with his friends drinking 'endless cups of coffee': Andrew, Christopher, *Secret Service: The Making of the British Intelligence Community* (Heinemann, 1985), 128

20   He had already earmarked some men and was looking for officers who could speak French and German: ibid., 127

20   In her hospital . . .: *Nursing Mirror*, 22 August 1914. Cavell contributed an article called 'Nursing in War Time'.

21   People appeared offering rooms and beds, or to help rolling bandages,

anything, even motor cars to transport the wounded when they arrived: Souhami, op. cit., 136

21 Soon the makeshift medical station was lined with narrow beds, each 'with white linen sheets and blankets neatly tucked in': ibid., 137

21 ... led by officers who, days before, had been asked to settle their mess bills and get their swords sharpened: Terraine, John, *Mons: The Retreat to Victory* (B. T. Batsford, 1960), 28

21 In the village of Fécher, German troops began to smash open the doors of houses, dragging out the owners and force-marching them to a new, half-built church, driving them along with their rifle butts: Somville, op. cit., 114

22 In the nearby town of Verviers ...: Somville, op. cit., 97

3. The British Army Arrives

28 With Jourdain was a younger man, Eugène van Doren, a relation by marriage: Millard, Oscar E., *Uncensored: The True Story of the Clandestine Newspaper 'La Libre Belgique' Published in Brussels During the German Occupation* (Robert Hale and Co., 1937), 106

30 In the darkness of the night of 20 August ...: Thuliez, op. cit., 86

30 In the afternoon sun Harry Beaumont was crossing a stubble field when German machine guns opened up: Beaumont, Harry, *Old Contemptible: A Personal Narrative* (Hutchinson, 1967), 38

32 ... 'feeling like a character out of Alice' ...: De Croÿ, op. cit., 12

32 The wounded lay on carts ...: Holmes, Richard, *Riding the Retreat: Mons to the Marne 1914 Revisited* (Jonathan Cape, 1995), 168

33 Two days later Louise Thuliez watched as Scottish and Irish troops retreating from Mons passed through her village, Saint-Waast-la-Vallée: Thuliez, op. cit., 1

33 One of the women with her whispered, 'What does it matter? We will not be conquered until we are all dead': De Croÿ, op. cit., 17

36 At the top of the village the Germans berated the mayor, demanding that he provide bread for them: Thuliez, op. cit., 8

37 '... I will begin by sending your brother as a prisoner of war to Germany': De Croÿ, op. cit., 25

39 In spite of this, her nurses were exhausted and many spent their off-duty time lying weeping on their beds: Souhami, op. cit., 150

4. Defeat

40 On 2 September the princess de Croÿ ...: De Croÿ, op. cit., 39

41 The people of Bellignies ...:: Stone, op. cit.

42 In the Belgian village of Westrozebeke rumours of what was

happening reached Marthe Cnockaert and her family: McKenna, op. cit., 14

43 Then the first shell landed: McKenna, op. cit., 46

46 ... blood and, above all, the stench of the dead – men and animals, shattered, torn apart, too many to bury, bloating and putrefying in the sun: Tuchman, Barbara W., *The Guns of August* (Folio Society, 1995), Kindle edition

46 Their commander, General Moltke, had a nervous breakdown ...: Afflerbach, Holger, trans. Anne Buckley and Caroline Summers, *On a Knife Edge: How Germany Lost the First World War* (Cambridge University Press, 2022), 51

47 Reginald immediately offered a refuge at Bellignies if he could get there: De Croÿ, op. cit., 71

47 Then he put his cap on the pillow, hoping that in the gloom it would look as though he were still in the bed: ibid., 73

5. Occupation

50 'For all acts of hostility the following principles will be applied: all punishments will be executed without mercy, the whole ...': Tuchman, op. cit.

51 At Saint-Waast the six men in the care of Henriette Moriamé and Louise Thuliez were recovering and the problem of feeding them was getting worse: Thuliez, op. cit., 1

51 They arrived to find the princess and her brother walking on the lawn: De Croÿ, op. cit., 68

52 Reginald learned that there were other men in the forest and, on the pretext of visiting his sick employees, he again took the two women ...: Thuliez, op. cit., 17

52 The gamekeeper led them deep into the forest ...: Thuliez, op. cit., 6; De Croÿ, op. cit., 80. Both accounts have been used to describe the trip into the forest.

53 She set off in a broken-down cart pulled by a scruffy donkey ...: De Croÿ, op. cit., 79

54 The men were having a good day away from the war and, thinking the women were simple peasants, waved them on their way: ibid., 88

56 Marie Birckel and her neighbours knew the French army was not far away and prayed for the day they would once again see the familiar red trousers worn by the soldiers: Durand, Paul, *Agents secrets: l'affaire Fauquenot–Birckel* (Payot, 1937), 17

56 Another woman on the run was ...: Reider, Antoine, trans. Olive Hall, *The Story of Louise de Bettignies* (Hutchinson, 1926), 4

6. The First Fugitives

61   Eventually satisfied that the men were British, she took them through the night to where the other men were hiding: Thuliez, op. cit., 22

62   At just after two in the morning the two groups arrived at Bellignies: ibid., 28

63   'Think of us all, for if you are caught we shall all be shot and the village burned to the ground': De Croÿ, op. cit., 90

64   Brand Whitlock described him as 'a man whose name is destined to stand forth in the world as a symbol of one of the darkest, cruellest and most sinister pages of its miserable history': Souhami, op. cit., 181, quoting Brand Whitlock, *Belgium Under the German Occupation*

65   In one issue the governor general was shown sitting at his desk reading the paper; the caption said that 'His Excellency the Governor' was looking for the truth in his 'dear friend *La Libre Belgique*': Souhami, op. cit., 175, 181

66   On 28 December 1914, a message was sent to Louise Thuliez ...: Thuliez, op. cit., 32

66   Later, at Enghien all the passengers were made to get off the tram and wait while their passports were examined: De Croÿ, op. cit., 101

67   The routine after that was to take them via a series of safe houses to the Dutch border: Thuliez, op. cit., 43

68   Another incident occurred when two soldiers whom they were trying to help, one of them a Canadian, disappeared, leaving a note saying they did not trust the women: ibid., 53

69   As darkness fell people dropped into the hospital ...: Souhami, op. cit., 196

7. Resistance Begins

74   ... the Cereal Company: Landau, Capt., *Secrets of the White Lady* (Putnam's Sons, 1935), 274

76   For his part, the commander of the British Expeditionary Force ...: Andrew, op. cit., 133

77   Sigismund went on alone: ibid., 135

77   From then on, whenever he saw an opportunity he took it ...: De Schaepdrijver, op. cit., 49, quoting Best at the end of his life

78   She had been granted a pass that allowed her to move around the town during the curfew in case there was an emergency: McKenna, op. cit., 33

80   Come to the second farm on the right-hand side of the road to Zwevezele. Ask for Lisette, who is expecting to see you at nine o'clock tonight: ibid., 39

81   Mrs Cameron was released early while Aylmer served the full term, gaining his freedom in 1914: Andrew, op. cit., 140

81   Spying was not a question of large discoveries ...: De Schaepdrijver, op. cit., 57

82   A key element in this was the observation of movements of men and materiel by rail: ibid.

85   One soldier later described the ordeal: Ryder, Roland, *Edith Cavell* (Book Club Edition, 1975), 146

86   Edith kept meticulous records of all the men who stayed with her: Souhami, op. cit., 201

87   ... 'like dead fish': Girard, Professor Marion Leslie, *A Strange and Formidable Weapon: British Responses to World War I Poison Gas* (University of Nebraska Press, 2008), 13, quoting Sgt Cotton

8. The Wire of Death

89   At the beginning of April 1915 ...: Abbenhuis, Maartje M., *The Art of Staying Neutral: The Netherlands in the First World War, 1914–1918* (Amsterdam University Press, 2006), 164–9

92   She was, they said, the ideal person to establish a surveillance network, but the problem was: how were they going to insert her?: Durand, op. cit., 23

92   This was tried but the Germans turned the application down: ibid., 60

92   A 27-year-old woman, Louise Derache, was regularly crossing the border from Holland into Belgium: *La Résistance en France et en Belgique occupées (1914–1918)* (Publications de l'Institut de recherches historiques du Septentrion, 2018), 217–32

94   Edith was now having difficulty with the soldiers who passed through her hospital: Ryder, op. cit., 139

96   Among the bodies it picked up was that of Marie Depage: Souhami, op. cit., 221

97   Ide was very impressed with her dedication, finding her intelligent and with a keen desire to learn: De Schaepdrijver, op. cit., 50

97   ... methods to assess the strength of units travelling by train: ibid., 58

9. Civil Disobedience and the Police

99   Brussels was described as 'a beautiful, impulsive, edgy, hate-filled capital' ...: The German poet and Nobel Prize-winner Gottfried Benn, quoted in De Schaepdrijver, op. cit., 47

102 He stayed in the hospital for two days and, on the day he left, three strange men were seen talking to employees working in the kitchen garden: Souhami, op. cit., 226

105 That way, said Edith, anyone following her would be thrown off guard. The princess did exactly as she was told: ibid., 229; also De Croÿ, op. cit., 128

106   A few days later, on 31 July, Louise Thuliez arranged to meet six
      metalworkers in a café near the Gare du Midi in Brussels: Thuliez, op.
      cit., 109

107   In the attic Baucq's 13-year-old niece had forced open a window and
      was trying to hide copies of *La Libre Belgique* on the window ledge:
      Souhami, op. cit., 234

107   He told them that, in Louise Thuliez's handbag, they had found a receipt
      for sixty-six francs for the 'lodging of six men for four days': Ryder, op.
      cit., 175

108   Sister Wilkins watched Cavell walking ahead of her, her slight body
      erect, her demeanour calm: Souhami, op. cit., 238

10. Interrogation

110   In the quiet of the garden at Bellignies the princess and her brother were
      walking with their grandmother: De Croÿ, op. cit., 134

112   In the morning she was told that the governor general had refused to
      accept her letter: ibid., 159

114   Gabrielle Petit was on her way back to Belgium . . .: De Schaepdrijver,
      op. cit., 58

114   The girl who had once been so poor . . .: ibid., 59

115   This time Gabrielle shrugged, laughed and said, 'You only die once':
      ibid., 59

116   Meanwhile, the network set up by Louise de Bettignies . . .: Reider, op.
      cit.; also the Walter Kirk diaries held by the Imperial War Museum,
      quoted in Andrew, op. cit., 144

120   'From what I can ascertain some of the division did actually reach the
      enemy trenches, for their bodies can now be seen on the barbed wire':
      Holmes, Richard, *The Little Field Marshal, Sir John French* (Jonathan
      Cape, 1981), 302–5

121   The next day Gabrielle Petit was again in Tournai: ibid., 62

121   Every night trains full of troops arrived, officers stumbled out of their
      quarters . . .: ibid.

123   Later she was visited by three officers from the military police:
      McKenna, op. cit., 52

125   A recent edict demanded that owners of carrier pigeons must shoot them
      or themselves be shot: 'Occupied Bruges and the *Marinegebiet* (Marine
      Area), 1914–1918'

126   He told her that he was a member of the German secret service:
      McKenna, op. cit., 145

127   Before the plan could be put into operation he was discovered by the
      German secret service and killed trying to escape: ibid.

11. Success and Failure

129   In the solitude of her cell ...: The quotations from *The Imitation* are taken from the facsimile edition of Cavell's: Kempis, Thomas à, *The Imitation of Christ: The 'Edith Cavell' Edition* (M. Milford, 1920). For Cavell's annotated edition online see also: https://onlinebooks.library. upenn.edu/webbin/book/lookupid?key=olbp41475

131   When Louise Thuliez was questioned by the same men, she claimed that she had worked alone. She signed her deposition ...: Thuliez, op. cit., 128

133   Louise Thuliez thought the same thing as she was led from the court ...: ibid., 134

137   She hoped that if this was to be her cross, then like her Lord Jesus she would find the courage to bear it: Thuliez, op. cit., 143

137   One man in the room wanted to applaud her and regretted to the end of his days that his courage failed him: Souhami, op. cit., 298

138   The Countess de Belleville wondered how she would face her maker and hoped that her imperfections would be balanced by the sacrifice she had made for her country: ibid., 145

143   A small group of women ...: ibid., 317

143   There was talk of telephoning the Kaiser: Gibson, Hugh, *A Journal from our Legation in Belgium: A Diplomatic Diary* (Doubleday, 1917)

145   Two days after Edith's execution, Elizabeth Wilkins, who was also the accountant for the hospital and Edith's executor, made an inventory of her effects: Ryder, op. cit., 150

145   The news of Edith's death reached the War Office in London and an official was told to ring her mother with the news of her execution: ibid.

146   One of the few lawyers who had been allowed to defend those brought before the German military tribunals was Sadi Kirschen: Gheude, Charles, *Nos années terribles, 1914–1918*, Vol. 1, 167–8, quoted in De Schaepdrijver, op. cit., 75

146   'How they testify to the valour of a country that is determined not to die, that mobilises all its resources and bravely resists the boot that wants to crush it': ibid.

12. Living with the Invader

147   On 5 November 1915 the Princess de Croÿ ...: De Croÿ, op. cit., 202

150   Louise Thuliez sat in the prison of Saint-Gilles ...: Thuliez, op. cit., 172

152   By Christmas 1915 food shortages were severe in Roulers ...: McKenna, op. cit., 166

152   Three young girls, all under twelve, were sentenced to ten weeks for picking up bits of coke lying along the railway leading into Roulers station: ibid., 166

153 As the year progressed they had become lazy and they too were hungry. In the end it became possible to bribe the two men with food and get them to turn a blind eye: ibid.

13. The Police Close In

159 As the winter set in Gabrielle Petit was evicted from her rooms . . .: De Schaepdrijver, op. cit., 68

160 But she added, 'I will shut up from now . . .': ibid., 70

160 She wrote that the controllers in Holland 'are safe behind the border and betray us and steal from us': ibid.

161 Police Bureau A had a genius for penetrating the amateur Belgian resistance networks that had formed soon after the invasion: Andrew, op. cit., 150

162 The man standing next to Goldschmidt stepped forward and punched Gabrielle hard in the stomach . . .: De Schaepdrijver, op. cit., 85

163 A day after her cell door had first slammed shut she was visited by an official who, with great punctiliousness, handed her one hundred francs: ibid., 87

164 Each cell had a radiator bolted to the wall . . .: Reider, op. cit., 168

165 Earlier in the month, on the same day that Gabrielle Petit was arrested, 2 February . . .: Durand, op. cit., 26

165 The weather was bitter; it snowed and the wind howled: ibid., 29

14. Judgement

167 One said, 'We must take action and bring the war to its conclusion. To this end I believe we must attack and take Verdun': Afflerbach, op. cit., 154

167 He told one general that if his plan worked the war could be decided in fourteen days: ibid., 155

168 At 7:15am on 21 February, in the bitter cold . . .: ibid., 158

168 The thundering could be heard: Mason, David, *Verdun* (The Windrush Press, 2000), 49–51

169 On 31 March 1916, while the battle of Verdun raged, British GHQ moved to Montreuil-sur-Mer: Fox, Sir Frank, 'G.S.O.', *G.H.Q. Montreuil-Sur-Mer* (Beaumont Fox, 2015), 22

170 The adjutant of his regiment had given him the address . . .: Landau, op. cit., 91

170 This was the legendary 'C', Captain Mansfield Smith-Cumming . . .: Andrew, op. cit., 169

172 Her prosecutor was Eduard Stoeber . . .: De Schaepdrijver, op. cit., 90

174 The next day, at eight o'clock . . .: ibid., 96

180 The next morning, 1 April . . .: De Schaepdrijver, ibid., 115

15. More Arrests

182   ... another agent sat in a cell waiting ...: Landau, op. cit., 22

184   The next day Lambrecht's cousin Walthère Dewé ...: ibid., 26

186   The German defensive positions formed a lethal band nearly 30 miles
long and up to 5 miles deep: Afflerbach, op. cit., 177

187   Meanwhile, Marie Birckel had arrived in Holland ...: Durand, op. cit.,
45

188   When they set off the next night ...: ibid., 51

193   One was a Belgian nun, Sister Mélanie, who was allowed to provide
spiritual comfort to the female inmates: Landau, op. cit.,107

194   Meanwhile, in Luxembourg, Mme Lise Rischard ...: Morgan, Janet,
*The Secrets of Rue St Roch: Intelligence Operations Behind Enemy
Lines in the First World War* (Allen Lane, 2004), 50

16. The War Drags On

210   If the Allies declined, then the Germans and her allies were prepared ...:
Afflerbach, op. cit., 227

211   Using the singing to hide their voices they whispered to each other: De
Croÿ, op. cit., 244

212   'No man who falls into enemy hands can reckon with a pardon': Ernst
Junger, quoted in Afflerbach, op. cit., 174

212   Humanity is mad ...: Horne, Alistair, *The Price of Glory: Verdun 1916*
(Penguin, 1993), 236

17. The Road to Luxembourg

215   On 23 February 1917, International Women's Day ...: Stone, op. cit.

215   The Princess de Croÿ ...: De Croÿ, op. cit., 245

216   Meanwhile, the work of espionage went on ...: Morgan, op. cit., 51

219   The second option ran the risk of arrest ...: ibid., 74

220   She assured him that, in spite of everything, he could rely on her
complete loyalty: ibid., 80

18. La Dame Blanche Arrives

222   Lemaire had been sent to ask the Allies for money and for help getting
information out of Belgium: Landau, op. cit., 50

224   After making her oath of allegiance she was ...: ibid., 122

227   Mme Rischard spent the next week alone and wrote four letters:
Morgan, op. cit., 103

228   Later, she learned that her request for a visa had been refused: ibid., 28

19. Young Women Spies

236 At the end of November Mme Rischard received a letter ...: Morgan, op. cit., 149

239 I have fallen once more into the deepest despair: ibid., 156

239 A91 contacted his father, an old soldier ...: Landau, op. cit., 72

242 He asserted that if his plan succeeded ...: Keegan, John, *The First World War* (Hutchinson, 1998), 230

242 He gave the operation the codename 'Michael': Middlebrook, Martin, *The Kaiser's Battle, 21 March 1918* (Allen Lane, 1978), 30

20. Home Run for Mme Rischard

245 The grand duchess's string-pulling had worked. Mme Rischard could leave in two or three weeks: Morgan, op. cit., 165

248 By now Mme Rischard and her husband Camille had recruited some senior railway officials ...: ibid., 222

248 Field Marshal Haig wrote in his diaries of exciting documents ...: Andrew, op. cit., 170

251 The Collard brothers were in solitary confinement and could not be contacted: Landau, op. cit., 146

21. Battles and Balloons

253 By chance Ludendorff had chosen to attack in the weakest sector of the British front ...: Keegan, op. cit.

254 'The safety of our homes and the freedom of mankind alike depend on the conduct of each one of us at this critical moment': Commander-in-Chief's Order of the Day, 11 April 1918, ibid.

254 The two men crept along the corridor ...: Durand, op. cit., 156

256 When the balloon was fully inflated and straining against the ropes tying it down ...: Morgan, op. cit., 286

22. The Long Day's Dying

258 After further cross-examination the judge called the proceedings to a halt, saying he would sentence her in a few days: Durand, op. cit., 198

260 On the other side of the front, the British were about to send in hundreds of tanks at Amiens ...: Afflerbach, op. cit., 375

260 Food was short in Germany ...: Durand, op. cit., 205

262 As he spoke in his high-pitched, strained voice several of his officers broke down and most men present had tears running down their faces: Afflerbach, op. cit., 389

263   In Siegburg prison Louise Thuliez saw ...: Thuliez, op. cit., 235
265   In Cologne, Marie de Croÿ saw banners on which was written the legend: 'Welcome to our unconquered armies': De Croÿ, op. cit., 229

Epilogue

267   Louise de Bettignies' body was repatriated on 21 February 1920: https://www.westernfrontassociation.com: 'On This Day, 27 September 1918', David O'Mara
267   The year before, on 17 March 1919, Edith Cavell's had been disinterred: Souhami, op. cit., 355
268   In the early morning of 27 May 1919 ...: De Schaepdrijver, op. cit., 11

When All Was Said and Done: 1919–1968

271   At the end of the war ...: Morgan, op. cit., 331
271   It was May 1940 and they were three months too late ...: ibid., 341
271   Once more she joined the resistance movement ...: Amalric, Hélène, *Princesse et combattante* (Bibliomnibus, 2015)
272   By the outbreak of the Second World War ...: Van Seters, Deborah E., *Oxford Dictionary of National Biography* (Oxford University Press, 2004)
272   In 1928 a fictional version of Edith Cavell's life, *Dawn* ...: Low, Rachael, *History of the British Film, 1918–1929* (George Allen & Unwin, 1971)
273   'Dear old Jack', Edith Cavell's dog ...: https://www.thehistorypress.co.uk/articles/edith-cavell-and-her-furry-four-legged-friends/

BIBLIOGRAPHY

Abbenhuis, Maartje M., *The Art of Staying Neutral: The Netherlands in the First World War, 1914–1918*, Amsterdam University Press, 2006

Afflerbach, Holger, *On a Knife Edge: How Germany Lost the First World War*, trans. Anne Buckley and Caroline Summers, Cambridge University Press, 2022

Amalric, Hélène, *Princesse et combattante*, Bibliomnibus, 2015

Andrew, Christopher, *Secret Service: The Making of the British Intelligence Community*, Heinemann, 1985

Baker, Kenneth M., *The Obscure Heroes of Liberty: The Belgian People who Aided Escaped Allied Soldiers During the Great War, 1914–1918*, Kenneth M. Baker, 2018

Beach, Jim, *Haig's Intelligence: GHQ and the German Army, 1916–1918*, Cambridge University Press, 2013

Beaumont, Harry, *Old Contemptible: A Personal Narrative*, ed. A. E. Clark-Kennedy, Hutchinson, 1967

Brown, Gordon, *Courage: Eight Portraits*, Bloomsbury, 2007

Clarke, I. F., *Voices Prophesying War, 1763–1984*, Oxford University Press, 1966

Clayton, Anthony, *Paths of Glory: The French Army, 1914–1918*, Cassell, 2003

Coulson, Major Thomas, *The Queen of Spies: Louise de Bettignies*, Constable, 1935

Datta, Venetia, *Heroes and Legends of Fin-de-Siècle France: Gender, Politics, and the Nation*, Cambridge University Press, 2011

Decock, Pierre, *La Dame blanche: un réseau de renseignements de la Grande Guerre, 1916–1918*, Université Libre de Bruxelles, 1981

De Croÿ, Princess Marie, *War Memories*, Macmillan and Co., 1932

De Schaepdrijver, Sophie, *Gabrielle Petit: The Death and Life of a Female Spy in the First World War*, Bloomsbury Academic, 2015

Durand, Paul, *Agents secrets: l'affaire Fauquenot–Birckel*, Payot, 1937

Falkenhayn, General Erich von, *General Headquarters, 1914–1916, and its Critical Decisions*, Hutchinson and Co., 1919

Ferris, J., *The British Army and Signals Intelligence During the First World War* (Army Records Society), Alan Sutton, 1992

Fox, Sir Frank, *'G.S.O.', G.H.Q. Montreuil-Sur-Mer*, Beaumont Fox, 2015

——*The Agony of Belgium: The Invasion, August–December 1914*, Beaumont Fox, 2014

Gibson, Hugh, *A Journal from our Legation in Belgium: A Diplomatic Diary*, Doubleday, 1917

Girard, Professor Marion Leslie, *A Strange and Formidable Weapon: British Responses to World War 1 Poison Gas*, University of Nebraska Press, 2008

Gullace, Nicoletta F., *'The Blood of our Sons': Men, Women, and the Renegotiation of British Citizenship During the Great War*, Palgrave Macmillan, 2002

Haste, Katie, *Keep the Home Fires Burning: Propaganda in the First World War*, Allen Lane, 1977.

Haswell, Jock, *Spies and Spymasters: A Concise History of Intelligence*, Thames and Hudson, 1977

Hoehling, A. A., *Edith Cavell*, Cassell and Company Ltd, 1958

Holmes, Richard, *Riding the Retreat: Mons to the Marne 1914 Revisited*, Jonathan Cape, 1995

——*The Little Field Marshal, Sir John French*, Jonathan Cape, 1981

Horne, Alistair, *The Price of Glory: Verdun 1916*, Penguin, 1993

Horne, John and Kramer, Alan, *German Atrocities, 1914: A History of Denial*, Yale University Press, 2001

Hostelet, Georges, 'Nurse Cavell: The Story of her Trial by One of the Condemned', *The Nineteenth Century and After*, 35 (January–June 1919), 523–547

Judd, Alan, *The Quest for C: Sir Mansfield Cumming and the Founding of the British Secret Service*, HarperCollins, 1999

Keegan, John, *The First World War*, Hutchinson, 1998

Kempis, Thomas à, *The Imitation of Christ*, M. Milford, 1920 (facsimile of Cavell's edition). For Cavell's annotated copy see also: https:/onlinebooks.library.upenn.edu/webbin/book/lookupid?key=olbp41475

Knightly, Phillip, *The Second Oldest Profession: Spies and Spying in the Twentieth Century*, W. W. Norton, 1987

Kramer, Ann, *Women Wartime Spies*, Pen and Sword, 2011

Landau, Captain, *All's Fair: The Story of the Secret Service Behind Enemy Lines*, Putnam's Sons, 1934

——*Secrets of the White Lady*, Putnam's Sons, 1935

Lipkes, Jeff, *Rehearsals: The German Army in Belgium, August 1914*, Leuven University Press, 2007

Low, Rachael, *History of the British Film, 1918–1929*, George Allen & Unwin, 1971

Mason, David, *Verdun,* The Windrush Press, 2000

Mathews, Shailer, *The Imitation of Christ: The Biblical World*, University of Chicago Press, 1905

Mayhew, Emily, *Wounded: The Long Journey Home from the Great War*, Vintage, 2014

McKenna, Marthe, *I Was a Spy!*, Pool of London Press, 2015

Middlebrook, Martin, *The Kaiser's Battle, 21 March 1918: The First Day of the German Spring Offensive*, Allen Lane, 1978

Millard, Oscar E., *Uncensored: The True Story of the Clandestine Newspaper 'La Libre Belgique' Published in Brussels During the German Occupation*, Robert Hale and Co., 1937

Morgan, Janet, *The Secrets of Rue St Roch: Intelligence Operations Behind Enemy Lines in the First World War*, Allen Lane, 2004

Moriaud, Gem, *Louise de Bettignies: une héroïne française*, Jules Tallendier, 1928

Mosse, George L., *Fallen Soldiers: Reshaping the Memory of the World Wars*, Oxford University Press, 1990

Nabulsi, Karma, *Traditions of War: Occupation, Resistance and the Law*, Oxford University Press, 1999

Nevins, Allan, ed., *The Letters and Journal of Brand Whitlock*, Appleton, 1936

Occleshaw, Michael, *Armour Against Fate: British Military Intelligence in the First World War*, Omnibus Books, 1989

Osborne Humphries, Mark and Maker, John, eds., *Germany's Western Front: Translations from the German Official History of the Great War, Part 2*, Wilfrid Laurier University Press, 2010

Proctor, Tammy, *Female Intelligence: Women and Espionage in the First World War*, New York University Press, 2003

Rathbone, Irene, *We that Were Young*, Virago Press, 1988

Reider, Antoine, trans. Olive Hall, *The Story of Louise de Bettignies (La Guerre des femmes)*, Hutchinson, 1926

Ruiss, Edwin, *Spynest: British and German Espionage from Neutral Holland, 1914–1918*, The History Press, 2016

Ryder, Roland, *Edith Cavell*, Book Club Edition, 1975

Somville, Gustave, trans. Bernard Miall, *The Road to Liège: The Path of Crime*, Hodder and Stoughton, 1916

Souhami, Diana, *Edith Cavell*, Quercus, 2010

Stone, Norman, *World War One: A Short History*, Basic Books, 2010 (Kindle edition)

Strachan, Hew, *The First World War, Vol. 1*, Oxford University Press, 2001

Terraine, John, *Mons: The Retreat to Victory*, B. T. Batsford, 1960

Thuliez, Louise, trans. Marie Poett-Velitchko, *Condemned to Death*, Methuen, 1934

Tuchman, Barbara, *The Guns of August*, Folio Society, 1995
    (Kindle edition)
Tuohy, Captain Ferdinand, *The Secret Corps: A Tale of
    'Intelligence' on All Fronts*, John Murray, 1920
Van Seters, Deborah E., *Oxford Dictionary of National
    Biography*, Oxford University Press, 2004
Wharton, Edith, *Fighting France: From Dunkerque to Belfort*,
    Edinburgh University Press, 2015
Wheelwright, Julie, *The Fatal Lover: Mata Hari and the Myth of
    Women in Espionage*, Collins and Brown, 1992
Whitlock, Brand, *Belgium: A Personal Narrative*, University of
    Pennsylvania, 1919
——*Belgium Under the German Occupation*, 2 vols, William
    Heinemann Ltd, 1919

Additional sources

La Résistance en France et en Belgique occupées (1914–1918),
Publications de l'Institut de recherches historiques du Septentrion,
coll. «Histoire et littérature du Septentrion (IRHiS)», 27 novembre
2018 (ISBN 978-2-490296-23-1, lire en ligne [archive]), 217–232

'Occupied Bruges and the *Marinegebiet* (Marine Area), 1914–
1918', *Cahiers Bruxellois – Brusselse Cahiers* 2014/1E (XLVI),
93–104, Éditions Musées et Archives de la Ville de Bruxelles
(ISSN 1784-5157, ISBN 978-2-87488-015-5)
DOI 10.3917/brux.046e.0093. De Schaepdrijver

INDEX